Lecture Notes of the Institute for Computer Sciences, Social Informatics and Telecommunications Engineering   **448**

More information about this series at https://link.springer.com/bookseries/8197

Jingqiang Lin · Qiang Tang (Eds.)

Applied Cryptography in Computer and Communications

Second EAI International Conference, AC3 2022
Virtual Event, May 14–15, 2022
Proceedings

Editors
Jingqiang Lin 🆔
University of Science and Technology
of China
Hefei, Anhui, China

Qiang Tang
The University of Sydney
Sydney, NSW, Australia

ISSN 1867-8211   ISSN 1867-822X (electronic)
Lecture Notes of the Institute for Computer Sciences, Social Informatics
and Telecommunications Engineering
ISBN 978-3-031-17080-5   ISBN 978-3-031-17081-2 (eBook)
https://doi.org/10.1007/978-3-031-17081-2

This Springer imprint is published by the registered company Springer Nature Switzerland AG
The registered company address is: Gewerbestrasse 11, 6330 Cham, Switzerland

Preface

We are delighted to introduce the proceedings of the 2022 European Alliance for Innovation (EAI) International Conference on Applied Cryptography in Computer and Communications (AC3 2022). This conference brought together researchers, developers, and practitioners around the world who focus on all technical aspects of applied cryptography including, but not limited to, cryptographic algorithms, protocols, implementations, standards and practices, and applications of cryptography in computer, information, and system security. Some of the works presented at AC3 2022 also applied cryptographic technologies to solve security problems in real-world systems, including cloud services, the Internet of Things, cyber-physical systems, distributed systems, edge computing, information-centric networks, databases, data centers, etc.

The technical program of AC3 2022 consisted of 14 papers in oral presentation sessions at six main conference tracks: Track 1 – Quantum-Safe Cryptographic Solution; Track 2 – Applied Cryptography for IoT; Track 3 – Authentication Protocol; Track 4 – Real-World Applied Cryptography; Track 5 – Network Attack and Defense; and Track 6 – Security Application. Aside from the high-quality technical paper presentations, the technical program also featured two keynote speeches delivered by Juan A. Garay from Texas A&M University, USA, and Meiqin Wang from Shandong University, China.

Coordination with the steering committee, including Imrich Chlamtac (chair), Bo Chen, and Bo Luo, was essential for the success of the conference. We sincerely appreciate their constant support and guidance. It was also a great pleasure to work with such an excellent organizing committee team for their hard work in organizing and supporting the conference. In particular, we are grateful to the Technical Program Committee, who completed the peer-review process for the technical papers and helped to put together a high-quality technical program. We are also grateful to Conference Managers Martin Vojtek and Lucia Sedlarova for their support and all the authors who submitted their papers to the AC3 2022 conference.

We strongly believe that the AC3 conference provides a good forum for all researchers, developers, and practitioners to discuss all science and technology aspects that are relevant to applied cryptography. We also expect that the future AC3 conferences will be as successful and stimulating as this year's, as indicated by the contributions presented in this volume.

May 2021

Jingqiang Lin
Qiang Tang

Organization

Steering Committee

Imrich Chlamtac	University of Trento, Italy
Bo Chen	Michigan Technological University, USA
Jingqiang Lin	University of Science and Technology of China, China
Bo Luo	University of Kansas, USA

Organizing Committee

Honorary Chair

Yongbiao Liu	Jinling Institute of Technology, China

General Chairs

Bo Luo	University of Kansas, USA
Zheng Zhang	Jinling Institute of Technology, China

Technical Program Committee Chairs

Jingqiang Lin	University of Science and Technology of China, China
Qiang Tang	University of Sydney, Australia

Sponsorship and Exhibit Chair

Huimin You	Jiangsu Computer Society, China

Local Chair

Aiyan Qu	Jinling Institute of Technology, China

Workshops Chair

Le Guan	University of Georgia, USA

Publicity and Social Media Chairs

Jun Dai	California State University, USA
Jun Shao	Zhejiang Gongshang University, China
Chenglu Jin	CWI Amsterdam, The Netherlands

Publications Chairs

Yuan Hong	Illinois Institute of Technology, USA
Shucheng Yu	Stevens Institute of Technology, USA

Web Chair

Zeyan Liu	University of Kansas, USA

Posters and PhD Track Chairs

Alex Bardas	University of Kansas, USA
Drew Davidson	University of Kansas, USA

Demos Chair

Shuhui Yang	Purdue University Northwest, USA

Technical Program Committee

Anjia Yang	Jinan University, China
Bernardo David	IT University of Copenhagen, Denmark
Bingyu Li	Beihang University, China
Debiao He	Wuhan University, China
Ding Wang	Nankai University, China
Fei Gao	Beijing University of Posts and Communications, China
Guangquan Xu	Tianjin University, China
Haixin Duan	Tsinghua University, China
Jiageng Chen	Central China Normal University, China
Jian Shen	Nanjing University of Information Science and Technology, China
Jing Chen	Wuhan University, China
Josef Pieprzyk	CSIRO Data61, Australia
Jun Shao	Zhejiang Gongshang University, China
Khoa Nguyen	University of Wollongong, Australia
Le Guan	University of Georgia, USA

Li Yang	Xidian University, China
Long Chen	Institute of Software, Chinese Academy of Sciences, China
Ping Chen	Fudan University, China
Qiongxiao Wang	Institute of Information Engineering, Chinese Academy of Sciences, China
Sherman S. M. Chow	The Chinese University of Hong Kong, Hong Kong
Shijie Jia	Institute of Information Engineering, Chinese Academy of Sciences, China
Tianqi Zhou	Nanjing University of Information Science and Technology, China
Ximeng Liu	Fuzhou University, China
Xiuhua Wang	Huazhong University of Science and Technology, China
Xuyun Nie	University of Electronic Science and Technology of China, China
Yongjun Zhao	Nanyang Technological University, Singapore
Yueqiang Cheng	NIO Security Research, USA

Contents

Quantum-Safe Cryptographic Solution

DU-QS22: A Dataset for Analyzing QC-MDPC-Based Quantum-Safe Cryptosystems

Mohammad Reza Nosouhi[1,2]([✉]), Syed W. Shah[1,2], Lei Pan[1,2], and Robin Doss[1,2]

[1] Centre for Cyber Security Research and Innovation, Deakin University, Geelong, Australia
{m.nosouhi,syed.shah,l.pan,robin.doss}@deakin.edu.au
[2] Cyber Security Cooperative Research Centre (CSCRC), Joondalup, Australia

Abstract. Cryptographically Relevant Quantum Computers (CRQC) will likely compromise the security of current Public-Key Encryption (PKE) mechanisms and make them unusable in the near future. In view of this, the National Institute of Standards and Technology (NIST) is currently undertaking the standardization of post-quantum Key Encapsulation Mechanisms (KEM) such that they can withstand quantum-capable attackers. One potential standardization candidate (i.e., BIKE) is based upon Quasi-Cyclic Moderate Density (QC-MDPC) codes and offers benefits in terms of security and key-size compared with other candidates. Since this candidate is highly dependent upon the performance of the decoder employed in the decapsulation subroutine, we in this paper, present a dataset for benchmarking the performance of various instantiations of decoders that may be proposed by the wider research community in future. To the best of our knowledge, no other dataset exists for researchers to benchmark their decoders for QC-MDPC-based cryptosystems.

Keywords: PKE · KEMs · Quantum-safe · QC-MDPC-based cryptosystem

1 Introduction

KEMs play a critical role in ensuring the security of today's communication systems. However, their reliance on public-key infrastructure (e.g., RSA [1]) will make them vulnerable in the future if CRQCs are ever built. In view of these anticipated problems, NIST is currently undergoing a standardization process to propose alternate KEMs such that they are deployable on contemporary devices and will be quantum-safe – i.e., they will not be compromised if an attacker is leveraging a CRQC (such as nation state actors) to launch the attacks.

In the previous round of the NIST standardization process (i.e., Round 3), various schemes for encryptions were shortlisted either as finalists or alternate candidates. These schemes are largely code-based, lattice-based, or isogeny-based mechanisms proposed for the post-quantum era [2]. Of these candidates, code-based schemes are receiving a lot of interest from the wider research community. One attractive code-based KEM

J. Lin and Q. Tang (Eds.): AC3 2022, LNICST 448, pp. 3–10, 2022.
https://doi.org/10.1007/978-3-031-17081-2_1

included in NIST's Round 3 is referred to as Bit Flipping Key Encapsulation (BIKE [9]) that is based upon the QC-MDPC variant of the original code-based cryptosystem proposed by McEliece in 1978 [3]. This variant is interesting because of its smaller key-sizes compared with other proposal. The security of QC-MDPC-based quantum-safe cryptosystems (e.g., BIKE) depends on the Decoder Failure Rate (DFR) of the decoder employed in decapsulation subroutine of the receiver can facilitate some attacks. For example, prior research has indicated the potential of a particular side-channel attack in compromising private-keys by leveraging the DFR [4].

Keeping in view the importance of decoder and decoder failures in the facilitation of side-channel attacks, the research community has proposed various decoders for code-based cryptosystems. For example, different instantiations of decoders are proposed in [5–7], all based on the Bit-Flipping decoder proposed in [8]. However, the horizon scan of related literature identifies no dataset that can be used to benchmark different instantiations of decoders (i.e., both previously proposed and any future modifications). Specifically, in decoder DFR evaluations, the decoder needs to be tested with a large number of ciphertexts.

Therefore, in this paper, we present a brief overview of our software implementation of QC-MDPC-based cryptosystem (i.e., in MATLAB) and release the resultant dataset that may help in benchmarking the decoders. Precisely, we release randomly generated private keys, the corresponding public keys, and ciphertexts generated using the public keys and random message vectors. The generated keys and ciphertexts have been saved in '*.txt' files for benchmarking purposes. We believe that this dataset will help the wider research community to analyze and benchmark the decoders instead of doing an end-to-end implementation of a cryptosystem that can be both time consuming and inadequate for comparison purposes. In other words, using our dataset, researchers can focus on the decryption (or decoder) subroutine without implementing the key generation and encryption subroutines.

The rest of the paper is organized as follows: Sect. 2 presents a brief overview of the QC-MDPC-based cryptosystem. Section 3 contains an elaboration on the importance of decoders. Sections 4 and 5 contain an overview of our implementation and a description of our dataset, respectively. Finally, our concluding remarks appear in Sect. 6.

2   QC-MDPC-Based Cryptosystem

This section presents a brief overview of the QC-MDPC-based cryptosystem originally proposed by Misoczki et al. in [10]. The block diagram of the original QC-MDPC-based cryptosystem is shown in Fig. 1.

As is evident from Fig. 1, the QC-MDPC-based cryptosystem is comprised of two subroutines – i.e., Encryption and Decryption. However, both subroutines are facilitated by a third subroutine that generates the private and public keys (i.e., Key-Generation Subroutine). In a QC-MDPC-based cryptosystem, a public key is a combination of 'Generator Matrix (G)' of the underlying QC-MDPC code and 'a Number (t)' representing the number of errors that need to be inserted in the valid codeword (i.e., the Hamming weight of the error vector e). On the other hand, a private key is the 'Parity-Check Matrix (H)' of the QC-MDPC code.

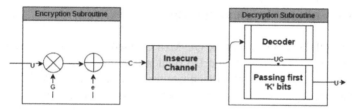

Fig. 1. Block diagram of the original QC-MDPC cryptosystem

In a nutshell, the plaintext 'U' is multiplied by 'Generator Matrix (**G**)' to get a codeword, in which 't' errors (**e**) are inserted by the sender. This constitutes the ciphertext that is sent to the receiver. The receiver's job is to find the error bits (**e**) and remove them to obtain the valid codeword (**UG**) by leveraging the private key (**H**). It is noteworthy that this constitutes a syndrome decoding problem proven to be NP-complete for a randomly chosen parity check matrix (**H**) [11]. Due to the aforementioned reason, these code-based cryptosystems are envisaged to be quantum-safe.

3 Importance of Decoder

Note that, the decryption process (see in Fig. 1) is mainly reliant upon the decoder (that utilizes the private key). The relevant decoders (such as those proposed in [5–7]) are generally based upon the Bit-Flipping algorithm [8]. The performance of the decoder is highly important in determining the security-level of the QC-MDPC-based cryptosystem (see details in [12]). For example, the GJS attack presented in [4] demonstrated the possibility of a particular side-channel attack on QC-MDPC-based cryptosystems that utilizes the decoder failure rates to fully recover the private key. In addition, a lower decoder failure rate that is needed for the higher security levels generally leads to a larger size of circulant blocks that define the size of private key (see details in [10]). Therefore, in pursuit of low decoder failure rates with relatively smaller key size, researchers continue to propose various instantiations of the Bit-Flipping algorithm.

Typically, the performance of these decoder(s) is analyzed by computing the decoder failures for smaller sizes of circulant blocks and then performing the linear extrapolation to the failures that correspond to the needed level of security (failures of $2^{-\lambda}$ for $\lambda - bit$ security, see further details in [5]). However, no benchmarking dataset exists that can facilitate the analysis of such decoders at the smaller sizes of circulant blocks and their comparison with other proposals for establishing their efficacy in achieving the required level of security. To fill this gap, we perform an end-to-end implementation of the QC-MDPC-based cryptosystem in MATLAB and provide a dataset that will help analyze the decoders and compute the decoder failure rate needed for the target security level (i.e., by performing linear extrapolation).

Next, we present a brief overview of our implementation that facilitates our data generation.

4 Overview of Our Implementation

We implement all three modules of the QC-MDPC-based cryptosystem in MATLAB –
i.e., Key-Generation, Encryption, and Decryption modules. The first two modules –
i.e., Key-Generation and Encryption facilitate the data generation that are needed for
analyzing the decoders and are released as a part of this work. The final module – i.e.,
the Decryption module is used to present a sample analysis to demonstrate how readers
can leverage this dataset. For this demonstration, we present the results obtained through
the Black-Grey Flip decoder implemented in MATLAB (the identical decoder is used
in BIKE [9]).

4.1 Key-Generation Module

The Key-Generation module generates both public and private keys that are used for
codewords generation and decoding, respectively. As pointed out in [13], the generation of public key from a private key needs polynomial inversion that can be
computationally laborious for the default method for inversion available in MAT-
LAB. To make this process computationally feasible, we implement the Itoh-Tsuji
Algorithm to facilitate efficient inversion through simple cyclic shifts (see details
in [14]). In addition, the public-key generation also involves multiplication operations. For the efficient implementation of multiplication, we perform multiplication in a polynomial domain with each coefficient of the product obtained as $c_i =
\sum_{j=0}^{r-1} a_j b_{(i-j+r) \bmod r} \bmod 2$ for $i = 1, 2, \ldots, r - 1$; where '$\mathbf{a}$' and '$\mathbf{b}$' represents two
polynomial and 'r' represents the size of the circulant block in the private key.

4.2 Encryption Module

The Encryption module generates the ciphertexts by utilizing the public-key generated
through 'Key-Generation' modules. This is accomplished by multiplying plaintext mes-
sage '$\mathbf{U}$' with '$\mathbf{G}$' (again the multiplication operation described above is utilized), that
leads to a codeword. The codeword is transformed into ciphertexts by adding random
errors '$\mathbf{e}$' with weight 't'. The addition is simply done by performing 'XOR' between
the codeword and the randomly chosen error vector.

4.3 Decryption Modules

The Decryption module leverages a decoder (i.e., any instantiation of the Bit-Flipping
algorithm) that uses a private key ($\mathbf{H}$) to eliminate the errors inserted in the codeword by
the sender. The Decoder provides the position of bits that are erroneous which are then
filliped to obtain the codeword. Once the codeword is obtained, it can be transformed
into plaintext by leveraging the systematic form of the public key – i.e., by just passing
the first 'K' bits to output ('K' is the size of plaintext).

5 DU-QS22 Dataset

For analyzing the performance of any instantiation of Bit-Flipping decoder, we need ciphertexts and associated private-keys (corresponding to the public-keys) with varying values of sizes of circulant blocks (that define the size of keys, alluded to as 'r' hereafter). In lines with prior works (e.g., [7]), we select the following values of 'r': 9461, 9539, 9643, 9817, and 10009 bits, for dataset generation, with parameters 't' and 'w' both fixed 134 and 142, respectively (- i.e., same as proposed in BIKE, see the details of parameters in [10]). Our analysis suggests that these values of 'r' are sufficient to capture the overall trend of decoder failure and apply linear extrapolation to the point that corresponds to the needed level of security. For each r value, we compute the number of ciphertexts that suffices for obtaining at least 1000 failures before the confidence in decoder failures is established (see the rationale for this threshold in [5]). Note that, the number of generated ciphers is increased since failures are much more difficult to obtain for larger values of 'r' (recall our target is to have 1000 failures as in prior works). Overall, our presented dataset is comprised of public-keys, private-keys, and ciphertext, as listed in Table 1.

Table 1. Size of dataset

'r'	Private-keys	Public-keys	No. of ciphers/key	Total ciphers
9461	20	20	500	10,000
9539	50	50	500	25,000
9643	50	50	1,000	50,000
9817	60	60	5,000	300,000
10009	75	75	10,000	750,000

Our dataset is made publicly available[1,2]. Note that, although only private keys and ciphertexts are needed for analyzing the decoders, we make public-keys publicly available as well (this can help generate additional ciphertexts if needed). All this data is contained in separate *.txt files and can be used to perform analysis irrespective of the platform used for decoding (such as MATLAB that we used for implementing the BGF decoder).

In addition to the keys and ciphertexts shown in Table 1, we also generated 900,000 ciphertexts using 90 keys for $r = 12323$, which is the value of 'r' recommended in the BIKE scheme with the 128-bit security level (see [9] for detail). We also include this data in our repository as these ciphertexts can be used for other purposes such as performance evaluation of decoders (e.g., modifying number of iterations to improve the efficiency) and security evaluations (e.g., analysis of different attack models) at the value of 'r' (i.e., 12323 as reported in BIKE [9]) appropriate for the 128-bit security (i.e., minimum requirement of NIST for standardization).

---

[1] Dataset is alluded to as DU-QS22 (i.e., Deakin University-Quantum Safe 2022).

[2] Dataset is available https://figshare.com/s/2df4edbbb2eb057e4e30.

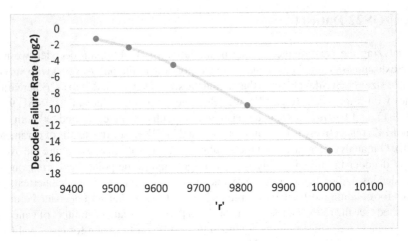

Fig. 2. A sample analysis of a decoder (BGF) with our dataset

How to use these data files? For performing the analysis of decoder, one can simply read the ciphertext files and used the corresponding private keys for decoding. For example, for $r = 10009$, we have 0.75 million ciphers generated through 75 keys. This means that for each key we have 10,000 ciphers. Therefore, for analysis, one can divide the total number of ciphertexts by the number of keys and decode the i_{th} chunk of ciphertexts with i_{th} private key. Note that, for private keys, we only saved the indices of non-zero bits (and thus must be considered accordingly while re-generating the private keys). We have also provided a detailed 'description' with a dataset belonging to different sizes of circulant blocks in our data repository (see the link provided above).

A Sample Analysis with BGF Decoder – To perform a sample analysis with the dataset (described in the previous section), we implemented (in MATLAB) the BGF decoder with the same parameters proposed in BIKE [9]. This decoder is a modification of the Bit-Flipping decoder proposed in [8]. It basically works by transforming a private key into a Tanner graph and computing syndrome vector that helps in determining the number of unsatisfied checks. These unsatisfied checks are then compared with a threshold to find the error bits (see detailed description in [8]). It is noteworthy that, for a constant time implementation the number of iterations is fixed which makes finding the error bits difficult (note that additional masking operations are performed in the BGF decoder – see details in [9]).

For each 'r' value in Table 1, we computed the average decoder failures (with a target of at least 1000 failures) and the resultant curve is shown below in Fig. 2. It is evident from Fig. 2 that the curve is concave (i.e., decaying) thereby making the application of linear extrapolation justified to find the value of 'r' corresponding to a needed level of security (e.g., 128 or 192-bits security that translates to decoder failure rates of 2^{-128} or 2^{-192}, , which is difficult to achieve even on powerful computing platforms, thus extrapolation is the only option). Similarly, one can use this synthetic dataset for analyzing different decoders and the impact of different parameters such as threshold and masking operation as used in the BGF decoder (see details in [9]) and weighting operations (such as those used in [7]).

6 Conclusion

This paper presents a dataset for benchmarking and cross-comparing different instantiation of Bit-Flipping decoders whose optimal performance is crucial for ensuring the needed level of security (e.g., minimum of 128-bits security required for NIST standardization). We also present an overview of our implementation of the QC-MDPC-based cryptosystem in MATLAB and details on how this dataset can be utilized. Finally, we present a sample analysis with the BGF decoder proposed for BIKE using the dataset generated in this work to guide the reader on how to analyze any decoder and apply linear extrapolation on the obtained curve. We maintain that this dataset can help the wider research community in benchmarking and comparing their proposed instantiations of decoders with other proposals and establish their efficacy.

Acknowledgment. This work was partially funded by the Cyber Security Cooperative Research Centre (CSCRC).

References

1. Rivest, R.L., Shamir, A., Adleman, L.: A method for obtaining digital signatures and public-key cryptosystems. Commun. ACM **21**(2), 120–126 (1978)
2. Beullens, W., et al.: Post-quantum cryptography. Technical report. European Union Agency for Cryptography (2021)
3. McEliece, R.J.: A public-key cryptosystem based on algebraic. Coding Thv. **4244**, 114–116 (1978)
4. Guo, Q., Johansson, T., Stankovski, P.: A key recovery attack on MDPC with CCA security using decoding errors. In: Cheon, J.H., Takagi, T. (eds.) ASIACRYPT 2016. LNCS, vol. 10031, pp. 789–815. Springer, Heidelberg (2016). https://doi.org/10.1007/978-3-662-53887-6_29
5. Sendrier, N., Vasseur, V.: About low DFR for QC-MDPC decoding. In: Ding, J., Tillich, J.-P. (eds.) PQCrypto 2020. LNCS, vol. 12100, pp. 20–34. Springer, Cham (2020). https://doi.org/10.1007/978-3-030-44223-1_2
6. Drucker, N., Gueron, S., Kostic, D.: On constant-time QC-MDPC decoding with negligible failure rate. IACR Cryptol. ePrint Arch. **2019**, 1289 (2019)
7. Nilsson, A., Bocharova, I., Kudryashov, B., Johansson, T.: A weighted bit flipping decoder for QC-MDPC-based cryptosystems. In: Proceedings of the 2021 IEEE International Symposium on Information Theory (2021)
8. Gallager, R.: Low-density parity-check codes. IRE Trans. Inf. Theory **8**(1), 21–28 (1962)
9. BIKE. https://bikesuite.org. Accessed 10 Jan 2022
10. Misoczki, R., Tillich, J.-P., Sendrier, N., Barreto, P.S.: MDPC-McEliece: new McEliece variants from moderate density parity-check codes. In: Proceedings of the 2013 IEEE International Symposium on Information Theory, pp. 2069–2073. IEEE (2013)
11. Berlekamp, E., McEliece, R., van Tilborg, H.: On the inherent intractability of certain coding problems. IEEE Trans. Inform. Theory **24**(3), 384–386 (1978)
12. Hofheinz, D., Hövelmanns, K., Kiltz, E.: A modular analysis of the Fujisaki-Okamoto transformation. In: Kalai, Y., Reyzin, L. (eds.) TCC 2017. LNCS, vol. 10677, pp. 341–371. Springer, Cham (2017). https://doi.org/10.1007/978-3-319-70500-2_12

13. Baldi, M.: QC-LDPC code-based cryptosystems. In: QC-LDPC Code-Based Cryptography. SpringerBriefs in Electrical and Computer Engineering, pp. 91–117. Springer, Cham (2014). https://doi.org/10.1007/978-3-319-02556-8_6
14. Drucker, N., Gueron, S., Kostic, D.: Fast polynomial inversion for post quantum QC-MDPC cryptography. In: Dolev, S., Kolesnikov, V., Lodha, S., Weiss, G. (eds.) CSCML 2020. LNCS, vol. 12161, pp. 110–127. Springer, Cham (2020). https://doi.org/10.1007/978-3-030-49785-9_8

Quantum-Safe Signing of Notification Messages in Intelligent Transport Systems

Sara Nikula[1]([✉]) [ID], Kimmo Halunen[2,3] [ID], and Visa Vallivaara[1] [ID]

[1] VTT Technical Research Centre of Finland, Oulu, Finland
{sara.nikula,visa.vallivaara}@vtt.fi
[2] Faculty of Information Technology and Electrical Engineering, University of Oulu, Oulu, Finland
kimmo.halunen@oulu.fi
[3] Department of Military Technology, National Defence University, Helsinki, Finland

Abstract. In this work, we integrated three quantum-safe digital signature algorithms, CRYSTALS-Dilithium, FALCON and Rainbow, into notification messages used in intelligent transport systems. We evaluated the performance of the algorithms by measuring the time required to sign and verify messages, as well as the size of the signed messages, and compared the quantum-safe options to the elliptic curves currently accepted by the standards. Our results show that quantum-safe digital signature algorithms could be used for signing notification messages in intelligent transport systems, with only moderate changes to performance. The results also provide an evaluation of three quantum-safe digital signature algorithms' suitability for this purpose, thus helping to choose suitable algorithms when migrating intelligent transport systems towards quantum resistance.

Keywords: Post-quantum cryptography · Digital signature · Intelligent transport systems

1 Introduction

Intelligent transport systems utilize wireless communication in order to improve fluency and safety in traffic. In these systems, notification messages require digital signatures, which assure the origin and the authenticity of the message. According to current European standards, the messages are signed using elliptic curve cryptography [19].

Elliptic curves, defined as a set of x- and y-coordinates on a plane, can be used in public key cryptography, digital signatures and key exchange. The mathematical problem underlying these operations is elliptic curve discrete logarithm problem, which is known to be a hard problem for modern computers [5]. However, Shor's algorithm allows to solve this problem efficiently with a quantum computer [40]. Thus, signatures based on elliptic curves are not quantum-safe as they

J. Lin and Q. Tang (Eds.): AC3 2022, LNICST 448, pp. 11–25, 2022.
https://doi.org/10.1007/978-3-031-17081-2_2

could be forged with a powerful enough quantum computer. Even though this kind of quantum computers do not exist at the moment, they are being developed and quantum technology has taken some significant advances in the last decades [3]. To address this threat, the National Institute of Standards and Technology (NIST) initiated a call for proposals for quantum-safe cryptographic algorithms to be standardized in late 2016. The competition was divided into two classes, one for digital signature algorithms and the other for key encapsulation mechanism (KEM) algorithms [1]. In 2020, three digital signature algorithms were chosen for the third and final round of the competition: CRYSTALS-Dilithium and FALCON, based on lattice problems, and Rainbow, based on multivariate public key cryptography [29].

Cooperative Intelligent Transport Systems (C-ITS) refers to vehicles and road infrastructure automatically generating and sharing information, thus making traffic more fluent and safe [10]. For example, this can mean a vehicle notifying geographically nearby other vehicles about poor road conditions, or an emergency vehicle warning other road users as it is approaching [16]. As these messages can be sent either by vehicles or road infrastructure, we refer to the parties of this communication as C-ITS stations. In practice, On-Board Unit (OBU), a particular device manufactured for communication purposes, carries out this communication [39]. Several commercial producers manufacture and sell OBU devices, which often are based on ARM architecture [6,11,15].

Communication between several parties requires diverse specifications in order to operate. European standardization organizations prepare and publish standards and technical specifications regarding communication between C-ITS stations. Safety and reliability of this communication is ensured by technical specifications developed by ETSI (European Telecommunications Standards Institute). These documents specify digital signing of specific message types, as well as a public key infrastructure for maintaining certificates and verifying signatures [10,19,20].

CAM (Cooperative Awareness Message) and DENM (Decentralized Environmental Notification Message) are special message types defined in standards ETSI EN 302 637-2 [18] and ETSI EN 302 637-3 [16]. CAM messages are relevant for co-operation, communicating information such as direction and speed of the sending vehicle. DENM messages notify geographically nearby vehicles about unusual situations, such as road works, poor road conditions or wild animals detected on the road. Both of these message types are sent in a digitally signed form [16,18]. In the current standards, elliptic curves are the only accepted digital signature type. The standards accept three different elliptic curves: NIST P-256, brainpoolP256r1 and brainpoolP384r1 [19,26]. Alongside the signed message, the sender sends their certificate, which is digitally signed by the certificate authorities. The certificate contains information about the public key which is used to verify the signature [19].

In this work, these notification messages are combined with quantum-safe digital signatures. Replacing elliptic curve digital signatures with quantum-safe alternatives makes the communication more robust towards attacks of quantum computers, thus mitigating the risk of forged signatures. The results section includes performance tests of CRYSTALS-Dilithium, FALCON and Rainbow, when used to sign notification messages of intelligent transport systems. This gives insights into the usability of quantum-safe digital signatures on this domain.

2 Previous Work

The field of post-quantum cryptography (PQC) that considers quantum-safe digital signature algorithms among other cryptographic primitives has been under active research since the threat against public-key cryptography by quantum computers has been known. There have been several proposals over the years, and covering the results of this field is out of scope of this paper. An interested reader can find more information about post-quantum cryptography in [8]. In this paper, we present relevant background and previous work related to the *implementation* of such algorithms, especially in the context of the ongoing standardisation effort.

Different applications of quantum-safe digital signature algorithms have been covered in previously published papers. In [41], the authors tested the suitability of quantum-safe digital signature algorithms with TLS 1.3 (Transport Layer Security). The results indicate that CRYSTALS-Dilithium and FALCON are suitable alternatives for this use. [28] showed that quantum-safe digital signature algorithms can be used to secure embedded devices. In [35], lattice-based quantum-safe digital signatures were used in industrial devices together with a X.509 certificate. These papers show that quantum-safe digital signatures are applicable in many different domains, but there are also some challenges that need to be addressed.

Intelligent transport is also a vast field of study with many results and research directions. In this section, we present some relevant previous work on the cybersecurity of intelligent transport systems and threats that it poses, which motivate also our research in this topic. There exist several ways for a malicious actor to cause disorder and potentially dangerous situations in traffic. A denial of service (DoS) attack could block the communication by sending numerous false messages, thus preventing the vehicles from processing authentic messages. Even a smaller amount of messages could cause disorder and slow down the traffic if, for example, a malicious vehicle pretended to be an emergency vehicle in an urgent duty [22]. Intentionally tampering safety-related messages can lead to dangerous situations by causing confusion about the real location and direction of nearly-operating vehicles. A malicious actor could also record and re-send messages sent by other vehicles [24].

The current technical specifications of ETSI mitigate the risk of tampered messages by digital signatures [19]. These are an efficient way to recognize forged messages as they can be used to verify the authenticity and the integrity of the message. However, as the current specification only accepts elliptic curve digital signatures, the era of quantum computers poses a risk to this communication.

This paper combines post-quantum digital signatures and cooperative intelligent transport systems, thus enhancing their security towards attacks of quantum computers.

A characteristic feature of communication between C-ITS stations is time-sensitivity. Critical messages must be delivered in a short enough time in order to be effective. Requirement for speed and security can lead to a contradiction: because of performance issues, excessive amounts of overhead bytes and processing should be avoided, but at the same time, some overhead is required to ensure the security of the communication [24]. This work aims to inspect the potential trade-off between security and efficiency when migrating to quantum-safe digital signatures.

ETSI is starting to migrate its standards towards quantum-resistancy and has its own technical committee for this purpose, CYBER QSC (Quantum Safe Cryptography) [14]. In 2021, CYBER QSC published two technical reports concerning digital signature and KEM algorithms in the NIST post-quantum cryptography standardization process [13]. Furthermore, CYBER QSC is preparing a report regarding migration of C-ITS use cases towards quantum-safety [14]. When conducting the performance tests presented in this paper, ETSI had not yet published these reports. Thus we have designed the tests and chosen the compared algorithms independently from these reports.

3 Test Program

In this work, we integrated three quantum-safe digital signature algorithms, CRYSTALS-Dilithium, FALCON and Rainbow, into the DENM message structures specified by ETSI, and used them to sign DENM messages quantum-safely. We evaluated the suitability of these algorithms by three different aspects: the time required to sign a message, the time required to verify a message, and the size of the signed message. On the grounds of these aspects, we assessed the suitability of these quantum-safe digital signature algorithms for this purpose. For comparison, we implemented the same functionalities with two different elliptic curves accepted by the current standard, NIST P-256 and brainpoolP256r1, and measured the same aspects when applying these. In this way we were able to assess how the migration to quantum-safe signatures would affect the fluency of the communication. According to the standards, CAM and DENM messages are sent using a similar signed message structure [16,18], and thus the achieved results can be generalized to concern CAM messages too.

3.1 Implementing the Digital Signature Algorithms

In its call for quantum-safe cryptography, NIST has defined five security levels for the cryptographic algorithms. The lowest level, security level 1, corresponds to 128 bits of security. The highest level corresponds to 256 bits of security, and the other levels lie somewhere in between. NIST recommended that the submissions would mainly concentrate on security levels 1–3 [30]. An elliptic curve using 256 bits long parameters offers a security level of 128 bits [5], thus corresponding to the security level 1 in this competition. All three quantum-safe digital signature algorithms included in this comparison offer reference implementations meeting several different security levels. In this work, we have utilized an implementation on security level 1 or the closest available level. With FALCON and Rainbow, this meant security level 1, and with CRYSTALS-Dilithium, security level 2. In this way, we compared the elliptic curve digital signature algorithms using 256-bit parameters with quantum-safe algorithms at the same security level. The third elliptic curve accepted by the current standard, brainpoolP384r1, was not included in the comparisons, because it meets a higher security level without offering security against quantum computers.

ETSI offers the message structures needed for a signed DENM message and the related structures in ASN.1 notation language in the attachments of the standardisation documents [16,19]. These structures do not include implementations of elliptic curve cryptography. In this work, we utilized elliptic curve digital signature algorithms from OpenSSL [32]. We chose OpenSSL because it is a widely known, well-documented and freely available cryptography library [33] and thus provides a good reference point for our quantum-safe implementations.

The three quantum-safe digital signature algorithms included in this comparison offer a reference implementation in C on their websites [12,21,38]. These implementations include functions for key generation, signing and verification. All three algorithms also offer an AVX2 optimized version, which improves performance by utilizing parallel processing [27]. However, some processors used in OBUs may not support this optimization. Processors based on ARM architecture use a different instruction set [2] and thus cannot benefit from AVX2 optimization. Thus, we compared only the standard reference implementations in C. While this might not give a fully truthful image of the performance of these algorithms, these results are hopefully better comparable across different processor architectures.

3.2   Performance Tests

In order to utilize quantum-safe digital signature algorithms, we adjusted the structures defined in ETSI's documents. In the current technical specifications, the signature structure allows a choice between three different elliptic curves [19,26]. We removed brainpoolP384r1 from the alternatives list, and added three quantum-safe alternatives: CRYSTALS-Dilithium, FALCON, and Rainbow. We modified the public key structure in the same way.

As stated in [24], real-time communication between C-ITS stations needs to be secure and efficient at the same time. In this work, we measured efficiency by three factors: how long it takes to sign a message, how long it takes to verify the signature and how many additional bytes need to be added to a message, contrasted to a situation where no digital signature is sent. These additional bytes consist of a digital signature and a certificate, which is needed to authenticate the message and verify the signature.

We implemented the tests described in this section in the C programming language. We used asn1c compiler [4] to obtain the needed message structures, defined in the documents [16,19], in C. Five different versions of the program included the same functionality, but using a different digital signature algorithm: CRYSTALS-Dilithium, FALCON, Rainbow, elliptic curve NIST P-256 or elliptic curve brainpoolP256r1. We conducted the tests with operating system Ubuntu 16.04 LTS and processor Intel Core i7-8665U, with base frequency of 1.90 GHz, and compiled the test programs with GCC 5.4.0. GCC offers several options for optimizing the code. In these tests, we used the optimization mentioned in the reference implementation files. With OpenSSL, CRYSTALS-Dilithium and Rainbow, this meant optimization -O3, and with FALCON, optimization -O2.

We decided that the implementation of a full certificate chain was out of scope for this research and thus we did not use the issuer and signature fields in the certificate. This somewhat shortens the certificate, but does not affect the comparison between algorithms.

In order to measure the speed of signing and verifying, we created a test program that created, signed and verified DENM messages. First, the program created a new pair of keys, and copied the public part of these keys in a certificate. Then, the program created a new DENM message, signed it and packaged it into a signed data structure together with the certificate. Now the program moved to the second part, opening and verifying the message. The program fetched the signature and the public key from the signed message and checked if it could successfully verify the signature with the public key. If not, the program notified the user about this and exited. If yes, it opened the DENM message and presented it to the user. When signing and verifying with elliptic curves, we called OpenSSL functions ECDSA_sign and ECDSA_verify. When using quantum-safe algorithms, we called functions crypto_sign and crypto_sign_open, defined in the reference implementations.

Fields of a DENM message have no significant impact on the signing speed as the message is hashed before signing it, as stated in the technical specification [19]. However, for the sake of credibility, we also filled in the necessary fields in the DENM message. A DENM message should include two mandatory fields including information about the message, such as the protocol version, information of the sending C-ITS station, location and generation time of the notification message. On top of these, the message can contain additional information about the observed situation [16]. We filled the protocol version field as specified in the standard, and the rest of the fields with imaginary information. In our imaginary DENM message, the identification number of the sending ITS-station was 123, the detection time was the current time obtained from the clock of the computer, the geographical coordinates were (66.5, 25.7) and the cause code for the observed event was 11, meaning "Animals on the road" [16]. As station type, depicting the type of the sending vehicle, we filled 5, which means a passenger car [17].

We carried out the performance measurements by executing the test program 5000 times in a row, each time collecting information about the time required to sign and verify the message, and finally counting averages of these times. In the time measurements, we used the C command `clock`, which measures the elapsed time in microseconds. The program outputted no text when executing the performance tests, so that this would not affect the time measurements. In addition to this, we modified one version of the program to output information about the size of the message in bytes. The program divided the message into three parts: the signature, the certificate, and other data, and outputted the size of all three parts separately. This allowed us to compare the internal structures of the messages signed with the different algorithms. The size of the certificate is dependent on the size of the public key, which is copied into the certificate. Other data refers to all other data except the certificate and the signature, and in this setting, this portion was always 160 bytes long.

The functions provided by OpenSSL and the quantum-safe reference implementations were designed differently with regard to hashing the message. The quantum-safe signature functions included hashing the message; multivariate-based Rainbow uses OpenSSL implementation of SHA256 hash algorithm [37], whereas lattice-based CRYSTALS-Dilithium and FALCON require a specific type of extendable-output hash function [7,23] for conducting the mathematical operations included in the signing procedure. The OpenSSL functions contained no hashing but presumed that the input to the function would be the hash of the message. Thus, we needed to apply a hash function once before using the OpenSSL sign function. OpenSSL offers SHA256 hash function [34], which the standard approves [19,25], and we used this function when signing with OpenSSL functions. While conducting performance measurements, we counted the time required to hash the message into the signing times of elliptic curves.

4   Results

Results of the performance measurements are depicted in Figs. 1 and 2. The fastest algorithm in signing was elliptic curve NIST P-256 (0,06 ms), and the second fastest was Rainbow (0,16 ms). CRYSTALS-Dilithium (0,46 ms) was slightly faster than elliptic curve brainpoolP256r1 (0,55 ms). Evidently the slowest signer was FALCON (4,89 ms).

In verification, the fastest algorithm was Rainbow (0,029 ms), and the second fastest was FALCON (0,042 ms). NIST P-256 (0,078 ms) and CRYSTALS-Dilithium (0,113 ms) performed a bit slower. The slowest verifier was brainpoolP256r1 (0,39 ms). These results show that the times required to verify a message are not as diverse as those in signing; the difference between the slowest and the fastest verifier is 13-fold (Rainbow and brainpoolP256r1), whereas the difference between the slowest and the fastest signer is 81-fold (NIST P-256 and FALCON).

Figure 3 depicts the sizes of the signed messages in bytes. Elliptic curves yielded the smallest signed messages, both resulting to 343 bytes, whereas Rainbow yielded the largest message, 161938 bytes. Messages yielded by the lattice-based alternatives lie somewhere in between; a message signed with CRYSTALS-

Signing time, milliseconds

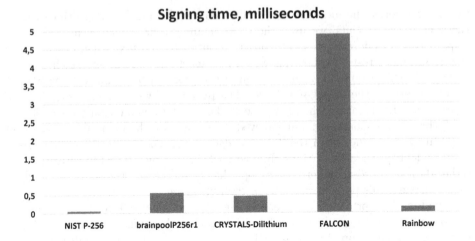

Fig. 1. Signing times of the compared digital signature algorithms.

Verification time, milliseconds

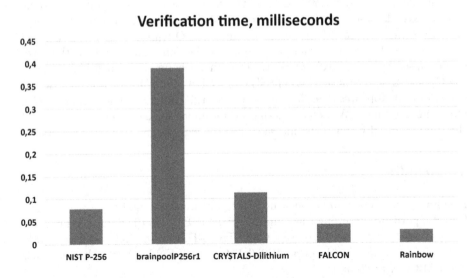

Fig. 2. Verification times of the compared digital signature algorithms.

Dilithium was 4004 bytes long and a message signed with FALCON was 1825 bytes long.

Figure 4 depicts the structures of the signed messages. Messages signed with elliptic curves had certificates (112 bytes) and signatures (71 bytes) of the same size, and these together took a bit over half of the whole message. CRYSTALS-Dilithium's signature was 2484 bytes and the certificate 1360 bytes. FALCON's signature was 720 bytes and the certificate 945 bytes long. Rainbow's signature took 130 bytes and the certificate 161648 bytes. In this setting, the fields for certificate issuer and signature of the certificate authority were removed, but as

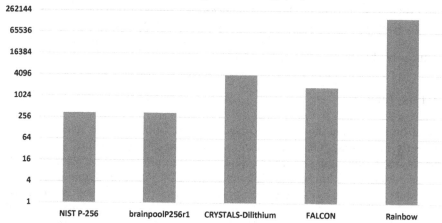

Fig. 3. Sizes of the signed messages yielded by the compared digital signature algorithms. Note that the scale is logarithmic.

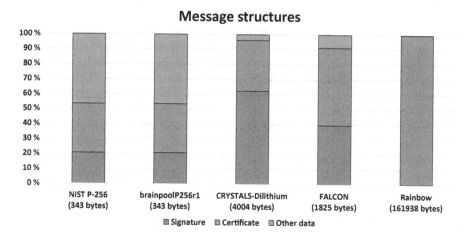

Fig. 4. Structures of the signed messages yielded by the compared digital signature algorithms.

mentioned, this has no significant effect on the comparison between the algorithms.

An important note regarding the message sizes is that the quantum-safe reference implementations were designed to make a copy of the original message alongside with signing. This was unnecessary with regard to the technical specifications, which supposed the original message to be elsewhere in the signed message structure. In this case, this message was 64 bytes long (two consecutive 32-byte outputs of SHA256 hash, as defined in the standard [19,25]), and thus

64 bytes can be reduced from the presented quantum-safely signed messages to obtain their length without excessive copies of the hashes. When taking this into account, Rainbow's signature would actually be shorter than that yielded with elliptic curves, only 66 bytes. Other proportions between the messages are not significantly changed by this extra 64 bytes.

5 Discussion

As can be seen from the signing times, the two elliptic curves perform quite differently in signing. Thus, migration to quantum-safe algorithms will have a different effect depending on if the original curve in use is NIST P-256, in which case any other algorithm in this comparison will slow down the signing, or brainpoolP256r1, in which case the quantum-safe alternatives can either speed up or slow down the signing. A noteworthy aspect in the verification times is that all quantum-safe algorithms are faster than brainpoolP256r1, and only CRYSTALS-Dilithium is slightly slower than NIST P-256. This implies that migration to the quantum-safe algorithms in C-ITS use will not be a problem with regard to verification performance. The results also show that the fastest algorithm in signing is not necessarily the fastest in verification. Rainbow was the fastest quantum-safe algorithm in both signing and verification. CRYSTALS-Dilithium seems to lie somewhere in between in both signing and verification, whereas FALCON performs notably better in verification than in signing. These factors need to be considered, when choosing the best alternative for C-ITS use. This requires more real world data on how the signatures are used by different participants in the C-ITS framework.

CRYSTALS-Dilithium and FALCON offer a possibility to reduce their key sizes by compression [7,21]. When using compression, only a seed value is stored in memory, and when needed, the actual key is calculated on the grounds of this value. CRYSTALS-Dilithium offers this possibility for its public key and FALCON for its private key. This would save memory space, or with regard to public keys, reduce the size of the certificate. However, compression means more real-time computing, which may not be desirable in real time applications such as many C-ITS use cases.

Of the lattice-based alternatives, FALCON produced shorter signed messages. CRYSTALS-Dilithium was notably faster than FALCON in signing, but slower in verification. Thus, which one of these alternatives would better suit this use, depends on which aspects one chooses emphasize: signing time, verification time or size of the signed message. A single C-ITS station probably executes verification more often than signing, because it can receive messages from several senders around it. On the other hand, the public key infrastructure defined by ETSI includes also certificate authorities, which sign certificates of other users on a regular basis. In this context, also signing time is a considerable feature. As proposed in [41], one possible option is to implement different parts of the public key infrastructure by combining different digital signature algorithms, in this way utilizing the most efficient algorithm for each part of the infrastructure.

FALCON's signing algorithm utilizes complex numbers, which the processor handles as floating-point numbers [23]. In case there is no floating-point unit (FPU) available, FALCON can perform notably slower in signing [35,36]. This effect did not apply in this work, as the processor used in the comparisons included a FPU. However, as also noted in [28,41], this may be a concern with regard to FALCON's portability to different processor architectures. With regard to varying architectures of the commercially available OBU devices, an ideal digital signature algorithm for C-ITS use would suit as many processor architectures as possible. This would refer to CRYSTALS-Dilithium being a safer option in this application domain. In our performance tests, FALCON was compiled with different optimization (-O2) than the other algorithms (-O3). According to our tests, running FALCON with optimization -O3 would not have significantly improved its performance in signing.

Multivariate-based Rainbow performed well in the performance tests, being faster than the lattice-based alternatives. However, because of a large public key, it produced very large messages. In addition, new cryptanalysis results [9] found during the third round in NIST PQC competition have revealed some security issues regarding Rainbow. Because of the questionable security of the multivariate-based schemes, NIST opened a possibility to send new general-purpose digital signature schemes which are not based on structured lattices to the competition [31]. Because of these issues, we do not believe that Rainbow would be an ideal alternative for C-ITS applications in its current form.

The submitters offered also two alternative implementations of Rainbow, Cyclic Rainbow and Compressed Rainbow. Cyclic-version would have decreased the size of the public key by over 50% [38], although it would still have been significantly larger than that of any other algorithm in this comparison. However, if Rainbow would otherwise turn out to be suitable for C-ITS use cases, using Cyclic-version would probably be beneficial.

The main contribution achieved by these results is increased knowledge of how suitable the different quantum-safe digital signature algorithms are for signing notification messages sent in intelligent transport systems. It is important to note that the message structures specified by ETSI are not restricted to notification messages, but also other message types are needed in communication between vehicles. Some of these messages need to be encrypted [19] and in these cases, creating and verifying digital signatures is not enough. Quantum-safe key exchange protocols for implementing these message types need to be evaluated against different criteria. These were out of the scope for this work and are left for future research. However, signed DENM and CAM messages are an important message type in C-ITS communication and thus we think that our performance tests provide relevant information about quantum-safe communication in C-ITS, even though all message types are not covered.

6 Future Research

NIST will choose one or more quantum-safe digital signature algorithms to be standardized in a few years. After that, it will be useful to test the winner algorithm with the commercial OBUs available on the market, and possibly optimize the algorithm for this use. For some message types in C-ITS, ETSI's documents define symmetric encryption and encrypting the symmetric keys using elliptic curves [20]. It would be interesting to discover how the quantum-safe KEM algorithms in the NIST standardization contest perform in this use, how often these operations need to be performed and which KEM algorithm would be the best alternative for this purpose.

ETSI's technical specifications also define a complete certificate chain [20], which this work did not. Implementing the certificate chain quantum-safely is also an interesting object for further research. Empirically gathered statistics about how often signatures are created and verified would be beneficial in assessing the suitability of these quantum-safe digital signature algorithms. This statistics should also include signing and verification done by certificate authorities, which behave differently from common vehicles. These data would serve as a basis for choosing one or more optimal algorithms for the different stages of the certificate chain.

7   Summary

In the future, communication between vehicles will need to be secured against attacks of quantum computers. Thus, it is beneficial to have information about performance and potential usability issues of different quantum-safe digital signature alternatives with regard to this specific usage.

This paper presents an evaluation of the quantum-safe digital signature algorithms' suitability to be used by intelligent transport systems. We conducted tests based on ETSI's documents, defining a public key infrastructure and digital signing of messages. The current standard accepts elliptic curves for digital signing. However, quantum computers could potentially break these signatures. The test program implemented creating, signing and verification of a notification message, using either elliptic curves or one of the three quantum-safe digital signature algorithms: CRYSTALS-Dilithium, FALCON or Rainbow. We measured the performance of these algorithms in signing and verification, and measured the size of the message signed with the different algorithms.

The results show that the quantum-safe algorithms produce larger signed messages than elliptic curves, but their signing and verification speed is quite competitive. Based on these results, intelligent transport systems could use quantum-safe digital signature algorithms in their communication. Implementing a full certificate chain is one object for future research. To be able to better justify the choice of the digital signature algorithms, gathering statistics about how often messages are signed and verified in traffic would be beneficial. Furthermore, the C-ITS standards specify also other message types requiring different cryptographic operations. The suitable quantum-safe algorithms used with these message types need to be evaluated against different criteria.

Acknowledgment. This research was supported by PQC Finland project funded by Business Finland's Digital Trust program.

References

1. Alagic, G., et al.: Status report on the first round of the NIST post-quantum cryptography standardization process. NIST Interagency/Internal Report (NISTIR), National Institute of Standards and Technology, Gaithersburg, MD (2019). https://doi.org/10.6028/NIST.IR.8240
2. Arm Architecture: A Foundation for Computing Everywhere. https://www.arm.com/why-arm/architecture/cpu. Accessed 19 Aug 2021
3. Arute, F., et al.: Quantum supremacy using a programmable superconducting processor. Nature **574**, 505–510 (2019)
4. asn1c - ASN.1 Compiler. https://manpages.ubuntu.com/manpages/trusty/man1/asn1c.1.html. Accessed 27 July 2021
5. Aumasson, J.P.: Serious Cryptography: A Practical Introduction to Modern Encryption. No Starch Press, San Fransisco (2018)
6. OBU-301E Specification. https://www.unex.com.tw/sheet/OBU-301E.pdf. Accessed 10 Nov 2021
7. Bai, S., et al.: CRYSTALS-Dilithium Algorithm Specifications and Supporting Documentation (Version 3.1) (2021). https://pq-crystals.org/dilithium/data/dilithium-specification-round3-20210208.pdf. Accessed 30 July 2021
8. Bernstein, D.J., Buchmann, J., Dahmen, E. (eds.): Post-Quantum Cryptography. Springer, Heidelberg (2009). https://doi.org/10.1007/978-3-540-88702-7d
9. Beullens, W.: Improved cryptanalysis of UOV and Rainbow. In: Canteaut, A., Standaert, F.-X. (eds.) EUROCRYPT 2021. LNCS, vol. 12696, pp. 348–373. Springer, Cham (2021). https://doi.org/10.1007/978-3-030-77870-5_13
10. C-ITS Secure Communications. https://www.itsstandards.eu/highlighted-projects/c-its-secure-communications/. Accessed 28 July 2021
11. Powerful V2X Onboard Unit. https://www.commsignia.com/products/obu/. Accessed 10 Nov 2021
12. Dilithium. https://pq-crystals.org/dilithium/index.shtml. Accessed 19 July 2021
13. ETSI releases two Technical Reports to support US NIST standards for post-quantum cryptography. https://www.etsi.org/newsroom/news/1981-2021-10-etsi-releases-two-technical-reports-to-support-us-nist-standards-for-post-quantum-cryptography. Accessed 8 Nov 2021
14. Technical Committee (TC) CYBER (Cybersecurity) Activity Report 2020. https://www.etsi.org/committee-activity/activity-report-cyber. Accessed 29 Mar 2022
15. Ettifos On-Board Unit (OBU). https://www.ettifos.com/platforms. Accessed 10 Nov 2021
16. European Telecommunications Standards Institute: ETSI EN 302 637-3 V1.2.2 (2014). https://www.etsi.org/deliver/etsi_en/302600_302699/30263703/01.02.02_60/en_30263703v010202p.pdf
17. European Telecommunications Standards Institute: ETSI TS 102 894-2 V1.3.1 (2018). URL: https://www.etsi.org/deliver/etsi_ts/102800_102899/10289402/01.03.01_60/ts_10289402v010301p.pdfD
18. European Telecommunications Standards Institute: ETSI EN 302 637-2 V1.4.1 (2019). https://www.etsi.org/deliver/etsi_en/302600_302699/30263702/01.04.01_60/en_30263702v010401p.pdf
19. European Telecommunications Standards Institute: ETSI TS 103 097 V1.4.1 (2020). https://www.etsi.org/deliver/etsi_ts/103000_103099/103097/01.04.01_60/ts_103097v010401p.pdf

20. European Telecommunications Standards Institute: ETSI TS 102 941 V1.4.1 (2021). https://www.etsi.org/deliver/etsi_ts/102900_102999/102941/01.04.01_60/ts_102941v010401p.pdf

21. FALCON - Fast-Fourier Lattice-based Compact Signatures over NTRU. https://falcon-sign.info/. Accessed 19 July 2021

22. Fernandes, B., Rufino, J., Alam, M., Ferreira, J.: Implementation and analysis of IEEE and ETSI security standards for vehicular communications. Mob. Netw. Appl. **23**(3), 469–478 (2018). https://doi.org/10.1007/s11036-018-1019-x

23. Fouque, P.A., et al.: FALCON: Fast-Fourier Lattice-based Compact Signatures over NTRU - Specification v1.2 (2020). https://falcon-sign.info/falcon.pdf. Accessed 19 July 2021

24. Hamida, E.B., Noura, H.N., Znaidi, W.: Security of cooperative intelligent transport systems: standards, threats analysis and cryptographic countermeasures. Electronics **4**, 380–423 (2015)

25. IEEE Vehicular Technology Society: IEEE Standard for Wireless Access in Vehicular Environments—Security Services for Applications and Management Messages (2016). https://doi.org/10.1109/IEEESTD.2016.7426684

26. IEEE Vehicular Technology Society: IEEE Standard for Wireless Access in Vehicular Environments—Security Services for Applications and Management Messages: Amendment 1 (2017). https://doi.org/10.1109/IEEESTD.2017.8065169

27. Overview: Intrinsics for Intel®Advanced Vector Extensions 2 (Intel®AVX2) Instructions. https://software.intel.com/content/www/us/en/develop/documentation/cpp-compiler-developer-guide-and-reference/top/compiler-reference/intrinsics/intrinsics-for-intel-advanced-vector-extensions-2/overview-intrinsics-for-intel-advanced-vector-extensions-2-intel-avx2-instructions.html. Accessed 28 July 2021

28. Marzougui, S., Krämer, J.: Post-quantum cryptography in embedded systems. In: ARES 2019: Proceedings of the 14th International Conference on Availability, Reliability and Security, pp. 1–7. Association for Computing Machinery (2019). https://doi.org/10.1145/3339252.3341475

29. PQC Standardization Process: Third Round Candidate Announcement. https://csrc.nist.gov/News/2020/pqc-third-round-candidate-announcement. Accessed 28 July 2021

30. Security (Evaluation Criteria). https://csrc.nist.gov/projects/post-quantum-cryptography/post-quantum-cryptography-standardization/evaluation-criteria/security-(evaluation-criteria). Accessed 28 July 2021

31. Status Update on the 3rd Round. https://csrc.nist.gov/Presentations/2021/status-update-on-the-3rd-round. Accessed 10 Aug 2021

32. ECDSA_SIG_new. https://www.openssl.org/docs/man1.1.1/man3/ECDSA_SIG_get0_r.html. Accessed 6 Aug 2021

33. OpenSSL. https://www.openssl.org/. Accessed 27 July 2021

34. SHA256_Init. https://www.openssl.org/docs/man1.1.1/man3/SHA1.html. Accessed 2 Aug 2021

35. Paul, S., Scheible, P.: Towards post-quantum security for cyber-physical systems: integrating PQC into industrial M2M communication. In: Chen, L., Li, N., Liang, K., Schneider, S. (eds.) ESORICS 2020. LNCS, vol. 12309, pp. 295–316. Springer, Cham (2020). https://doi.org/10.1007/978-3-030-59013-0_15

36. Pornin, T.: New Efficient, Constant-Time Implementations of Falcon. Cryptology ePrint Archive, Report 2019/893 (2019). https://ia.cr/2019/893

37. GitHub - fast-crypto-lab/rainbow-submission-round2: Rainbow signature system for Round THREE submission. https://github.com/fast-crypto-lab/rainbow-submission-round2. Accessed 30 July 2021
38. Rainbow Signature. https://www.pqcrainbow.org/. Accessed 19 July 2021
39. Sedar, R., et al.: Standards-compliant multi-protocol on-board unit for the evaluation of connected and automated mobility services in multi-vendor environments. Sensors **21**(6), 2090 (2021). https://doi.org/10.3390/s21062090
40. Shor, P.W.: Polynomial-time algorithms for prime factorization and discrete logarithms on a quantum computer. SIAM J. Comput. **26**(5), 1484–1509 (1997)
41. Sikeridis, D., Kampanakis, P., Devetsikiotis, M.: Post-Quantum Authentication in TLS 1.3: A Performance Study. International Association for Cryptologic Research (IACR) Cryptology ePrint Archive 2020 (2020)

Applied Cryptography for IoT

WB-GWS: An IoT-Oriented Lightweight Gateway System Based on White-Box Cryptography

Jinfu Hao[1], Yongbao Wang[2], Weijie Deng[1], Nanjiang Xie[1], and Zheng Gong[1(✉)]

[1] School of Computer Science, South China Normal University, Guangzhou, China
cis.gong@gmail.com
[2] AISINO CO.LTD, Beijing, China

Abstract. The Internet of Things (IoTs) has been widely applied for convenient data gathering. Therefore, the security and privacy issues related to IoT applications attract more and more attentions. Secure data transmission plays pivotal role of the security of IoT applications. However, there are still many IoT devices do not support cryptographic functions due to their constrained resources. Moreover, cryptographic key storage also becomes a practical security context problem in resource-constrained devices. In this paper, an IoT-oriented lightweight gateway system, which is named WB-GWS, is proposed by using white-box cryptography. WB-GWS is designed for the secure data transmission in typical IoT applications, and reduces the risk of key leakage in the white-box security context. The performance of WB-GWS is analyzed amongst different platforms. The experiment results support that WB-GWS can meet the security requirements of IoT applications with low-rate data transmission.

Keywords: Iot security · Secure data transmission · Virtual tunneling · White-box cryptography

1 Introduction

With the rapid development of IoT applications, people are aware of the vital security and privacy issues of data gathering and transmission [1,19,27,34]. Atzori *et al.* described the IoT system as a three-layer architectural model which consists of a perception layer, a network layer, and a layer of services [3]. The security architecture of the IoT can also be divided into these three layers. Due to its constrained resources, there are still many IoT systems that cannot support secure data transmission. The transport layer security can use public key cryptography and symmetric cryptography to ensure its security. Researchers use SSL/TLS (combination of public key cryptography and symmetric cryptography) in combination with HTTP or MQTT to ensure the secure transmission of

© ICST Institute for Computer Sciences, Social Informatics and Telecommunications Engineering 2022
Published by Springer Nature Switzerland AG 2022. All Rights Reserved
J. Lin and Q. Tang (Eds.): AC3 2022, LNICST 448, pp. 29–45, 2022.
https://doi.org/10.1007/978-3-031-17081-2_3

data [22]. Mazen *et al.* developed a Hybrid End-to-End VPN security approach by combining the IPSec/IPv6 and OpenSSL security approaches for secure data transfer for the IoT [18]. However, many IoT devices with constrained resources are not suitable for using public key cryptography. On the other hand , it is still challenging that public key cryptography to work with IoT devices [17].

IoT devices are commonly implemented in open access environment, or the environment cannot to be trusted [17]. Therefore, it could be feasible for hacking the cryptographic key from the devices. For mitigating key exposure and code-lifting problems in untrusted environments, many white-box cryptography (WBC) schemes have been proposed [12,24,25,33]. In 2019, Saha *et al.* used WBC to increase the security of IoT systems [31]. To the best of our knowledge, there is little research on WBC in secure data transmission of gateway based IoT system.

Our Contribution. In this paper, the design and implementation of an IoT-oriented lightweight gateway system based on white-box cryptography (WB-GWS) is proposed. WB-GWS is a secure data transmission system designed for gateway based IoT system. Firstly, a secure data transfer capabilities is provided for IoT systems that do not support secure data transformation. Secondly, the problem of insecure key storage on the IoT client is solved by using white-box cryptographic services. Finally, the performance of WB-GWS is analyzed amongst different platforms for convincing the practicality of the WB-GWS in the IoT environment.

Organization. The remainder of this paper is organized as follows. In Sect. 2, notions and notation that related to WB-GWS are described. Section 3 presents the design of WB-GWS and its protocols. Section 4 and 5 describe how to manage nodes in WB-GWS. The security analysis and performance results are given in Sect. 6 and 7, respectively. Section 8 concludes this paper.

2   Preliminaries

In this section, first the IoT protocols that are related to WB-GWS are briefly introduced. And then white-box cryptography is recalled. Table 1 summarizes the symbols and acronyms used in this paper.

IoT Transport Layer Protocol. IoT communication protocol can use the traditional TCP/IP protocol. MQTT, CoAP [4,30], and other protocols designed for the IoT can also be used [22]. A security layer is added to these protocols to secure the transmission of data. The Transport Layer Security (TLS) protocol and its datagram-oriented variant Datagram TLS (DTLS) protocol are the actual protocols for communication security in IoT applications [2,26]. However, the current authentication approaches of TLS are confronted with the heavy overhead and security issues in the resource-constrained IoT scenario. Although the standardized Internet security protocols have many advantages, typical deployment scenarios of IoT limit the feasibility of TLS because of highly constrained devices in low-power and lossy networks [26,29]. The standard TLS protocol not

Table 1. List of symbols and acronyms.

$WBEnc\{\cdot\}$	White-box encryption
$WBDec\{\cdot\}$	White-box decryption
$LUT\_Gen\{\cdot\}$	Generate a LUT
$Token\_Gen\{\cdot\}$	Generate download LUT credential
$Virtual\_IP\_Gen\{\cdot\}$	Generate virtual IP address
$Tag\_Gen\{\cdot\}$	Generate GCM message authentication code
$Auth\{Tag\}$	Data integrity check
$Check\{v\}$	Check that the current LUT of v is up to date
$Verify\{v\}$	Verify the validity of the IoTS-GW v
$Free\{r\}$	Release resource r
$Add\_To\_Reg\{v\}$	Add a GN v to the registry
$Remove\_From\_Reg\{v\}$	Remove GN v from the registry
$Send\_To\_AS\{m\}$	Send message m to the application server
$Shutdown\{s\}$	Stop the service s
	A sends the following type of message m to B
	REGISTER: a request for registration
$A \rightarrow B : [type]\|m$	REQUEST: a common request
	RESPONSE: return information
	DOWNLOAD: download the LUT
$\|$	Concatenation operator
$IoTD_i$	The IoT device i
$IoTS-GW$	The IoT-side gateway
$SS-GW$	The server-side gateway
GN	The gateway node IoTS-GW or SS-GW
V_*	Set of GN
$WBCS$	The white-box cryptography service
AS	The application service
IV	The initialization vector
N_v	Nonce sent by v
$Flag$	The flag of IoTS-GW or SS-GW
LUT	The white-box look-up table
$token$	The credential used to download the LUT
$Virtual\_IP$	The virtual IP address
Ver	Version of the LUT
Tag	GCM certification mark
Ret	The result of validating or establishing a connection
$PMsg$	The plaintext message
$CMsg$	The ciphertext message
ID_v	The identity of v
$rand$	The random number
$release\ the\ connection$	The release connection message
$acknowledgement\ character$	The confirmation message
APP_A	Common application of host A
VPN_A	Application layer VPN implementation of host A
$Stack_A$	Kernel network protocol stack of host A
$eth0_A$	Physical network interface card (NIC) of host A
$tun0_A$	Virtual NIC of host A

will be implemented in WB-GWS. Instead, WBC is used at the transport layer for the confidentiality and integrity of the data.

White-Box Cryptography. WBC was first proposed by Chow *et al.* in SAC 2002 [12], which is also called CEJO framework hereafter. The core idea of CEJO framework is to transform the round functions into a series of look-up tables (LUTs). And secret invertible encodings are used to protect the intermediate values. Let T denote a LUT, f and g be random bijective mappings. Then the encoded LUT T' is defined as $T' = g \circ T \circ f^{-1}$, where f^{-1} and g are called the input and output encodings, respectively. To maintain the functionality of AES [14], the input and output encodings of consecutive rounds should be constructed as pairwise invertible mappings. Let an encoded LUT R' be defined as $R' = h \circ R \circ g^{-1}$ such that a networked encoding can be depicted as $R' \circ T' = (h \circ R \circ g^{-1}) \circ (g \circ T \circ f^{-1}) = h \circ (R \circ T) \circ f^{-1}$.

The intermediate state of AES can be represented by a byte array such that the index is ranked from 0 to 15. For each round of AES, AddRoundKey and SubBytes can be combined into LUT operations called T-box. For a byte x input, it is computed as follows.

$$T_i^r(x) = S(x \bigoplus \hat{k}_{r-1}[i]), \qquad i = 0 \cdots 15, r = 1 \cdots 9,$$

$$T_i^{10}(x) = S(x \bigoplus \hat{k}_9[i]) \bigoplus \hat{k}_{10}[i], \qquad i = 0 \cdots 15,$$

where S denotes the Sbox and $\hat{k}_r$ represents the result of applying ShiftRows to the byte array of round key. For more details on the implementation of WBC, please refer to Muir's tutorial on white-box AES [24].

Although there are many attacks against WBC, such as DCA [11,21], DFA [15,20], and adaptive side-channel analysis [32], researchers are also designing new WBC proposals [7,9,10] to resist these attacks. Without losing of generality, we note that it is assumed that WB-GWS uses a secure WBC implementation.

Virtual Tunnel Technology. Tunneling is a virtual link between networks that uses the Internet infrastructure to transmit data [35]. The tunneling technology can be used to transmit protocol data unit (PDU) of different protocols. And it can also facilitate the transformation of data in the channel, such as encryption and integrity check. Tunnel protocols include L2TP, IPsec, and SSL VPN [6,35] *etc.* The reason why mentioned above tunneling protocols are not used is that it is difficult to apply WBC to the modification of those protocols. In this paper, Linux virtual network technology TUN/TAP is used to implement the tunnel protocol. Whilst a white-box block cipher is used to encrypt and decrypt data in tunnels.

Without tunneling, the process of sending data from host A to host B is illustrated by the dotted arrow in Fig. 1.

1. APP_A constructs the packet and sends it to kernel $Stack_A$.
2. The packet is sent to $eth0_A$ after $Stack_A$ adds the TCP header, IP header and other processing.

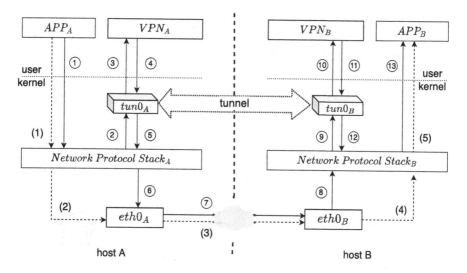

Fig. 1. The principle of virtual tunnel technology.

3. $eth0_A$ sends packet to $eth0_B$ over the Internet.
4. $eth0_B$ sends the received packet to $Stack_B$.
5. $Stack_B$ processes the packet and sends it to APP_B.

When data is transmitted over a virtual tunnel, the data flow of host A and host B is shown by the solid arrows in Fig. 1.

1. The APP_A constructs the packet and sends it to kernel $Stack_A$.
2. The data processed by $Stack_A$ is not directly sent to $eth0_A$, but forwarded to $tun0_A$.
3. The VPN_A listens to $tun0_A$ and reads the packets received by $tun0_A$.
4. The VPN_A can reprocess packet, such as data encryption and decryption, and integrity check. VPN_A then writes the processed data to $tun0_A$.
5. The $tun0_A$ receives the data and forwards it to $Stack_A$.
6. The packet is processed by $Stack_A$ and sent to $eth0_A$.
7. The $eth0_A$ sends packet to $eth0_B$ over the Internet.
8. The $eth0_B$ sends the received packet to $Stack_B$.
9. The $Stack_B$ writes data to $tun0_B$ after removing IP and TCP headers.
10. The VPN_B listens to $tun0_B$ and reads the packets received by $tun0_B$.
11. The VPN_B can reprocess packet, such as data encryption and decryption, and integrity check. VPN_B then writes the processed data to $tun0_B$.
12. The $tun0_B$ receives the packet and forwards it to $Stack_B$.
13. $Stack_B$ processes the packet and sends it to APP_B.

Although one can directly encrypt and decrypt data and verify the integrity in the application layer, we use a virtual tunnel that can encrypt and decrypt the data sent between APP_A and APP_B and verify the integrity without changing APP_A and APP_B. Therefore, data can be transparently and securely transmitted between A and B.

3   The Construction of WB-GWS

In this section, the framework of WB-GWS is illustrated and then the protocols of WB-GWS are demonstrated.

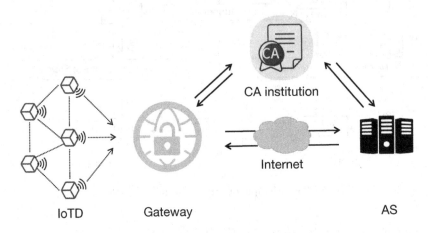

Fig. 2. The architecture of a gateway based IoT system.

3.1   The Framework of WB-GWS

According to the architecture of a gateway based IoT system, a gateway and a dedicated AS are illustrated in Fig. 2. IoT-side gateway (IoTS-GW) and server-side gateway (SS-GW) are added to the gateway and AS, respectively. Before the IoTS-GW and the SS-GW communicates, a virtual tunnel is established through Internet. The tunnel is located at the transport layer of the TCP/IP protocol family. Furthermore, when data is transmitted through the tunnel, WBC is used for confidentiality and integrity. This process is transparent to sender and receiver. Consequently, for managing the LUTs and virtual IP addresses, the white-box cryptography service (WBCS) was introduced into WB-GWS. WB-GWS adds IoTS-GW, SS-GW, and WBCS to the original gateway based IoT system, which is depicted in Fig. 3. Typically, WBCS and SS-GW are deployed in the same Intranet environment, so the channel between them is secure. Although WBCS and IoTS-GW use an insecure channel, the LUTs obtained by IoTS-GW can only be used for encryption and will be replaced periodically. Even if an attacker obtains a LUT from IoTS-GW, it cannot decrypt the transmitted message. The functionalities of each part of WB-GWS are summarized as follows.

- **IoTD:** IoT devices are the sender of data transmissions, such as temperature and humidity sensing.

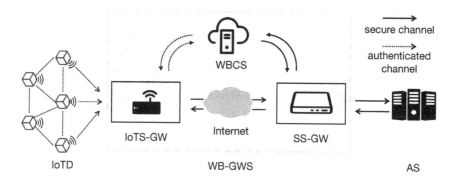

Fig. 3. The architecture of WB-GWS.

- **IoTS-GW:** Establishes a security tunnel with the SS-GW and encrypts the data. IoTS-GW is used to collect data generated by IoT devices and send them to SS-GW.
- **SS-GW:** Establishes a security tunnel with the IoTS-GW and decrypts the data from the IoTS-GW. SS-GW also transfers its received data to AS. A SS-GW can communicate with multiple IoTS-GWs simultaneously.
- **WBCS:** Managing LUTs and virtual IP addresses. WBCS is also responsible for message and client authentications.
- **AS:** The application server for the underlying IoT system.

3.2   The Protocols of WB-GWS

The main process of WB-GWS can be divided into four phases: bootstrap, WBCS establish, data transmission and release connection.

Bootstrap. This protocol occurs when WB-GWS is initialized or a new GN requests for registration. This process includes creating virtual IP addresses, generating LUTs, and downloading LUTs, which are described in Fig. 4. A formal definition can be represented in the following steps.

1. First a request of REGISTER is generated by a gateway node (denoted by v, and V_* represents the gateway nodes set).
2. WBCS generates a series of data including virtual IP address, LUTs, *token*, and version number, and responds to gateway node with IP address, *token*, and version number.
3. While the response is confirmed, the gateway node will make another request to WBCS based on the returned *token* to download the LUTs. We note that both IoTS-GW and SS-GW need to run the bootstrap protocol with WBCS.

Protocol 1.   Bootstrap protocol

$\forall v \in V_*$ (set of GN),

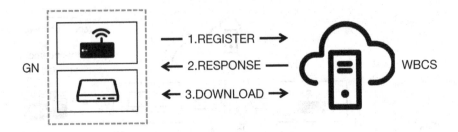

Fig. 4. The bootstrap phase.

$v \longrightarrow WBCS$ (White-box cryptography server):

$\qquad\qquad$ **REGISTER**$\| \ ID_v \ \| \ N_v$

$WBCS \qquad\quad : LUT = LUT\_Gen\{ \ rand \ \}$

$\qquad\qquad\qquad token = Token\_Gen\{ID_v \ \| \ rand\}$

$\qquad\qquad\qquad Virtual\_IP = Virtual\_IP\_Gen\{ID_v\}$

$\qquad\qquad\qquad Add\_To\_Reg\{v\}$

$WBCS \longrightarrow v : token \ \| \ Virtual\_IP \ \| \ Ver$

$v \qquad\qquad\quad : Check\{v\}$

$v \longrightarrow WBCS : $ **DOWNLOAD** $\| \ token$

WBCS Establish. Before data transmission, a virtual channel will be created between the IoTS-GW and SS-GW with a virtual IP assigned by WBCS. And then a connection is established over the virtual channel, which is described in Fig. 5. Device authentication will also be performed during connection establishment. The procedure is described in Protocol 2 and the steps can be described as follows.

1. IoTS-GW makes a request for WBCS to obtain the *Virtual_IP* of the server and the tag to establish the connection.
2. WBCS generates a tag and returns the tag and *Virtual_IP* of SS-GW to IoTS-GW.
3. IoTS-GW encrypts the tag by using the WBC and random IV, and then sends the ciphertext, IV, ID to SS-GW.
4. SS-GW uses WBC and IV to decrypt the ciphertext and sends the plaintext and ID to WBCS for verification.
5. WBCS checks whether the plaintext is the same as the authentication code sent to the IoTS-GW, and returns the verification result to SS-GW.
6. SS-GW determines the verification result returned by WBCS. And SS-GW returns the final result to IoTS-GW.

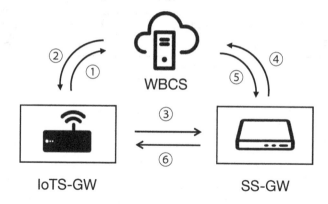

Fig. 5. The WBCS establish phase.

Protocol 2.   WBCS establish protocol

$\forall v \in V_*$ (IoTS-GW set),

$v \longrightarrow WBCS : \textbf{REQUEST} \parallel ID_v \parallel N_v$

$WBCS \qquad : Flag = Flag\_Gen\{\cdot\}$

$WBCS \longrightarrow v : \textbf{RESPONSE} \parallel Flag \parallel Virtual\_IP$

$v \qquad : CMsg = WBEnc\{PMsg \parallel IV\}$

$v \longrightarrow SS\text{--}GW : \textbf{REQUEST} \parallel ID_v \parallel CMsg \parallel IV$

$SS\text{--}GW \qquad : PMsg = WBDec\{CMsg \parallel IV\}$

$SS\text{--}GW \longrightarrow WBCS : \textbf{REQUEST} \parallel ID_v \parallel PMsg$

$WBCS \qquad : Ret = Verify\{v\}$

$WBCS \longrightarrow SS\text{--}GW : \textbf{RESPONSE} \parallel Ret$

$SS\text{--}GW \longrightarrow \qquad v : \textbf{RESPONSE} \parallel Ret$

Data Transmission. Data transmission between IoTS-GW and SS-GW takes place through a secure virtual tunnel that is created in WBCS establish. During communication between IoTS-GW and SS-GW, data will be encrypted and decrypted using WBC. Whilst message authentication codes are also necessary for verifying data integrity (Fig. 6).

Protocol 3.   Data transmission protocol

$IoTS\text{--}GW \qquad : CMsg = WBEnc\{PMsg\},$

$\qquad Tag = Tag\_Gen\{CMsg \parallel IV\}$

$IoTS\text{--}GW \longrightarrow SS\text{--}GW : \textbf{REQUEST} \parallel CMsg \parallel Tag \parallel Ver$

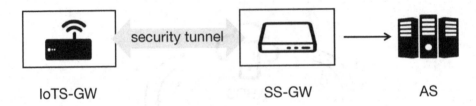

IoTS-GW   SS-GW   AS

Fig. 6. The data transmission phase.

$$SS\text{--}GW \qquad\qquad : Ret = Auth\{Tag\}$$
$$PMsg = WBDec\{CMsg\}$$
$$SS\text{--}GW \quad\longrightarrow\quad AS \;: Send\_To\_AS\{PMsg\}$$

Release Connection. This protocol will take effect under one of the following circumstances: 1) GN is out of service. 2) IoTS-GW sends a request to release the connection.

Protocol 4.   Release connection protocol

$\forall v \in V_*$ (set of GN),

Case 1: v is out of service.

WBCS   : Free{ LUT $\parallel$ *Virtual_IP* }

: Remove_From_Reg{ v }

Case 2: IoTS-GW sends a request to release the connection

$v \longrightarrow$ WBCS : **REQUEST** $\parallel$ *release the connection*

WBCS $\longrightarrow v$: **RESPONSE** $\parallel$ *acknowledgement character*

v : Shutdown$\{v\}$

WBCS   : Free{ LUT $\parallel$ *Virtual_IP* }

: Remove_From_Reg{ v }

4   Gateway Addition

WB-GWS supports multiple IoTS-GW nodes. For adding IoTS-GW nodes during system initialization, new nodes can also be added while the system is running. WB-GWS will dynamically assign *Virtual_IPs* to new nodes, create LUTs, and add new nodes to the registration list. After new nodes are added successfully, they can communicate with SS-GW in the system.

Among the three core parts of WB-GWS, only IoTS-GW supports multi-node deployment. The SS-GW node and WBCS can run only on a single node.

To add a new IoTS-GW node to WB-GWS, one should execute the following steps.

1. Bootstraps a new IoTS-GW node and sends a registration request to WBCS.
2. WBCS assigns virtual IP addresses to IoTS-GW and creates LUTs.
3. IoTS-GW, SS-GW, and WBCS establish connections.
4. The WBCS adds new IoTS-GW node to the registration list.

5   Gateway Removal

To reduce system overhead, one can remove an IoTS-GW node while it is out of service (Protocol 4). There are two conditions that can trigger a node removal operation: 1) The WB-GWS will remove IoTS-GW after it is out of service. 2) When an IoTS-GW node is unnecessary, IoTS-GW can actively send a request to remove it. When an IoTS-GW node is removed, the virtual IP address and LUTs of IoTS-GW will be released as well.

6   Security Analysis

IoTS-GW Access Authentication. Device access security is one of the important factors of IoT system security. Current IoT security solutions include standards-based proposals. Among them, the TLS and VPN are the de-facto protocols for communication security in the IoT. These two protocols support authentication using the symmetric pre-shared key (PSK) or public-key certificates. Although PSK based authentication consumes a small amount of computing resources. There exist key scalability and management issues when using the PSK. Additionally, the PSK established out of band is assailable to attacks due to restricted security features and uncontrolled deployment environment. Certificate-based authentication can resolve many problems where specifically PSK-based solutions fall short, so plenty of IoT systems choose certificates as the authentication method. However, it also has some problems such as cumbersome use and difficult certificate revocation. In IoTS-GW, we assign LUTs for device access authentication. Only IoTS-GW with a LUT can be successfully authenticated. The WB-GWS has the same authentication security as PSK in IoT systems. In addition, the problem of an attacker sending data through a forged IoTS-GW after acquiring a LUT can be solved by device binding or APP binding [5,8,28] technology, which is not implemented in this paper.

Security of Data Transmission. In IoT systems using TLS and VPN protocols, the security of data transmission is guaranteed by cryptographic Primitive. Data is encrypted and integrity checked during data transmission. After data is encrypted using an encryption algorithm, it is transmitted in ciphertext over the network. An attacker cannot obtain useful information even after listening to ciphertext messages, which ensures the confidentiality of data transmission. Because data is checked for integrity, attackers cannot tamper or manipulate it.

In other words, even if an attacker modifies to the data, they can be detected. The WB-GWS also encrypts and verifies the integrity of data. Because of the secure WBC algorithm used in WB-GWS, it is difficult for an attacker to recover plaintext from ciphertext. Therefore WB-GWS has the same security of data transmission as TLS and VPN. Meanwhile, WB-GWS is more flexible and secure than the traditional black-box mode when the LUT is lost.

Forward Security After GN Remove or Release. There are forward security issues with the pre-sharing key (PSK) mode. After an attacker obtains pre-sharing key, all the secret messages transmitted using the key are broken. For IoT systems that use public-key cryptography, a new session key is created for each session. The attacker obtains the current session key at a certain moment. Because the key is changed, the attacker cannot decrypt the previous session information with this key. Therefore, there is no forward security problem in IoT systems using public-key. WB-GWS takes the following three measures to ensure forward security. 1) Regularly WB-GWS will update the distributed LUTs. 2) For GNs that are removed or released, their LUTs become invalid. 3) The LUTs of each GN can only be used for encryption or decryption, *i.e.*, just like public-key algorithm.

7   Experiment

In order to verify the performance of WB-GWS, two experiments are implemented separately. The first is the experiment based on temperature and humidity (T/H) sensor system. The other is a performance comparison experiment. Nevertheless, the data transmission and encryption speeds of WB-GWS are tested on different platforms.

Table 2. The testbenches of WB-GWS modules.

Module	CPU	software
IoTD	T/H sensor DHT11 [16]	–
IoTS-GW	ARMv7 Processor rev @1.20 GHz	Linux Raspberry Pi 5.10.17-v7+
SS-GW	Intel (R) Xeon (R) Platinum 8255C CPU @2.50 GHz	Linux VM-0-13-centos 3.10.0-1127.19.1.e17.x86_64
WBCS	Intel (R) Xeon (R) Platinum 8255C CPU @2.50 GHz	Linux VM-0-13-centos 3.10.0-1127.19.1.e17.x86_64
AS	Intel (R) Xeon (R) Platinum 8255C CPU @2.50 GHz	Linux VM-0-13-centos 3.10.0-1127.19.1.e17.x86_64

7.1 The Experiment Base on Temperature and Humidity Sensor System

In this experiment, the T/H sensor is used as an IoT device. IoTS-GW and SS-GW are deployed on Raspberry Pi and VM-0–13-centos respectively. The Table 2 describes the CPU and software of WB-GWS modules. We let the T/H sensor send T/H data to the AS every 10 s. Wireshark [13] was used to capture the data transmitted between the IoTS-GW and the SS-GW, but the plaintext of the data could not be seen. Moreover, we kept the WB-GWS running for 30 days and counted the receipts received in the database, and none of the data was lost.

JMeter [23] is a performance testing tool originally designed primarily for testing web applications. But it can also be extended to test in other areas. In this experiment, JMeter is used to test the pressure of the system. System loads of 50, 100, 200, and 300 requests per second were tested. The test results are shown in Table 3 (Fig. 7).

Table 3. System pressure test results.

Requests per second	Expected receive	Actual receive	Lost
50	50	50	0
100	100	100	0
150	150	120	30
200	200	120	80
300	300	120	180

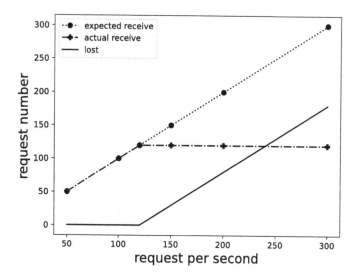

Fig. 7. System pressure test result.

According to the performance test results, data loss occurs when the number of concurrent requests exceeds 100, and the maximum number of concurrent requests is 120. Due to the limitations of the experimental environment, we did not conduct experiments in more IoT scenarios. However, through this experiment, we found that WB-GWS can be successfully run in the IoT environment with low data transfer.

7.2 The Performance Comparison

Transmission rate is one of the most critical evaluation metrics used to measure the performance of the data transferring in the IoT networks. Firstly, the benchmark test of WBC in each platform is done. Secondly, we tested the transfer rate on different platforms by transferring files from the IoTS-GW to the SS-GW. The file transfer monitors the average transfer rate for 1000 experiments by using tools such as Netperf, Iperf. In our experiments, we use Raspberry Pi 3 B (ARMv7 Processor rev @1.20 GHz) as IoTS-GW, use different platforms as SS-GW. The configurations and performance of different platforms are demonstrated as shown in Table 4. In practice, SS-GW will not be deployed on the Raspberry Pi due to its lack of performance. Therefore the transmission speed on Raspberry Pi is not given. The result indicates that the bottleneck of transmission speed for WB-GWS is the hardware limitations of Raspberry Pi.

Table 4. The performance of WB-GWS on different platforms.

Platform	Configuration		Transmission speed (Mbit/s)	Encryption speed (Mbit/s)
	CPU	software		
Raspberry Pi	ARMv7 Processor rev @1.20 GHz	Linux Raspberry Pi 5.10.17-v7+	–	2.48
mac OS	Intel Core i5 @1.6 GHz	macOS Big Sur 11.5.2	0.97	20.82
Linux	Intel (R) Xeon (R) Platinum 8255 C CPU @2.50 GHz	Linux VM-0-13- centos 3.10.0–11 27.19.1.e17.x86_64	1.32	22.24
Windows	Intel (R) Core (TM) i7-11800 H @2.30 GHz	Windows 10 20 H2	1.58	52.83

This paper does not provide a comparative analysis of efficiency with existing schemes, due to the following reasons. 1) There are few studies on the application of white-box cryptography to secure data transmission in the IoT, and there is no mature solutions for the time being. 2) Compared with solutions such as SSL VPN, this research scheme has too many variables to make an effective comparison.

8　Conclusions

Device authentication and secure data transmission play a vital role in secure communication between smart IoT objects. WB-GWS provides a solution for secure data transmission in IoT systems by using WBC in combination with tunneling technology. The proposed solution of WB-GWS can compatible with legacy IoT systems which have lack of cryptographic function support. Also, it can manage keys efficiently with the help of WBC. The disadvantage of WB-GWS is that it is currently only applicable to gateway-based IoT architectures, not to the architectures where devices can directly connect to cloud services. In future work, it is challenging to improve the performance of WB-GWS and to provide a secure WBC instance for the implementation of WB-GWS.

Acknowledgments. We are grateful to the anonymous reviewers for their insightful comments. This work was supported in part by National Natural Science Foundation of China (62072192) and National Defense Technology 173 Basic Improvement Project (2121-JCJQ-JJ-0931).

References

1. Aboubakar, M., Kellil, M., Roux, P.: A review of IoT network management: current status and perspectives. Elsevier (2021)
2. Ammar, M., Russello, G., Crispo, B.: Internet of things: a survey on the security of IoT frameworks. **38** (2018). https://doi.org/10.1016/j.jisa.2017.11.002
3. Atzori, L., Iera, A., Morabito, G.: The internet of things: a survey. **54** (2010)
4. Aziz, B.: A formal model and analysis of an IoT protocol. Ad Hoc Netw. **36**, 49–57 (2016). https://doi.org/10.1016/j.adhoc.2015.05.013
5. Balfanz, D., Smetters, D.K., Stewart, P., Wong, H.C.: Talking to strangers: authentication in ad-hoc wireless networks. In: NDSS. Citeseer (2002)
6. Berger, T.: Analysis of current VPN technologies. In: Proceedings of the The First International Conference on Availability, Reliability and Security, ARES 2006, The International Dependability Conference - Bridging Theory and Practice, 20–22 April 2006, Vienna University of Technology, Austria. IEEE Computer Society (2006). https://doi.org/10.1109/ARES.2006.30
7. Biryukov, A., Bouillaguet, C., Khovratovich, D.: Cryptographic schemes based on the ASASA structure: black-box, white-box, and public-key (extended abstract). In: Sarkar, P., Iwata, T. (eds.) ASIACRYPT 2014, Part I. LNCS, vol. 8873, pp. 63–84. Springer, Heidelberg (2014). https://doi.org/10.1007/978-3-662-45611-8_4
8. Bock, E.A., Amadori, A., Brzuska, C., Michiels, W.: On the security goals of white-box cryptography. IACR Trans. Crypt. Hardware Embed. Syst. **2020**, 327–357 (2020)
9. Bogdanov, A., Isobe, T.: White-box cryptography revisited: space-hard ciphers. In: Ray, I., Li, N., Kruegel, C. (eds.) Proceedings of the 22nd ACM SIGSAC Conference on Computer and Communications Security, Denver, CO, USA, 12–16 October 2015, pp. 1058–1069. ACM (2015). https://doi.org/10.1145/2810103.2813699
10. Bogdanov, A., Isobe, T., Tischhauser, E.: Towards practical whitebox cryptography: optimizing efficiency and space hardness. In: Cheon, J.H., Takagi, T. (eds.) ASIACRYPT 2016, Part I. LNCS, vol. 10031, pp. 126–158. Springer, Heidelberg (2016). https://doi.org/10.1007/978-3-662-53887-6_5

11. Bos, J.W., Hubain, C., Michiels, W., Teuwen, P.: Differential computation analysis: hiding your white-box designs is not enough. In: Gierlichs, B., Poschmann, A.Y. (eds.) CHES 2016. LNCS, vol. 9813, pp. 215–236. Springer, Heidelberg (2016). https://doi.org/10.1007/978-3-662-53140-2_11

12. Chow, S., Eisen, P., Johnson, H., Van Oorschot, P.C.: White-box cryptography and an AES implementation. In: Nyberg, K., Heys, H. (eds.) SAC 2002. LNCS, vol. 2595, pp. 250–270. Springer, Heidelberg (2003). https://doi.org/10.1007/3-540-36492-7_17

13. Combs, G.: Wireshark: go deep. https://www.wireshark.org/. Accessed 14 Nov 2021

14. Daemen, J., Rijmen, V.: The Design of Rijndael: AES - The Advanced Encryption Standard. Information Security and Cryptography, Springer, Heidelberg (2002). https://doi.org/10.1007/978-3-662-04722-4

15. Dusart, P., Letourneux, G., Vivolo, O.: Differential fault analysis on A.E.S. In: Zhou, J., Yung, M., Han, Y. (eds.) ACNS 2003. LNCS, vol. 2846, pp. 293–306. Springer, Heidelberg (2003). https://doi.org/10.1007/978-3-540-45203-4_23

16. elink: Wifi temperature and humidity sensor DHT11 version (support MQTT, Baidu Cloud IoT, etc.). https://item.taobao.com/item.htm?spm=a1z09.2.0.0.3ce72e8d8radF8&id=622084892800&_u=fvrdd9137b5. Accessed 14 Nov 2021

17. Granjal, J., Monteiro, E., Silva, J.S.: Security for the internet of things: A survey of existing protocols and open research issues. **17** (2015). https://doi.org/10.1109/COMST.2015.2388550

18. Juma, M., Monem, A.A., Shaalan, K.: Hybrid end-to-end VPN security approach for smart IoT objects. **158** (2020). https://doi.org/10.1016/j.jnca.2020.102598

19. Kouicem, D.E., Bouabdallah, A., Lakhlef, H.: Internet of things security: a top-down survey. **141** (2018). https://doi.org/10.1016/j.comnet.2018.03.012

20. Lee, S., Jho, N., Kim, M.: Table redundancy method for protecting against fault attacks. **9** (2021). https://doi.org/10.1109/ACCESS.2021.3092314

21. Lee, S., Kim, M.: Improvement on a masked white-box cryptographic implementation. **8** (2020). https://doi.org/10.1109/ACCESS.2020.2993651

22. Li, P., Su, J., Wang, X.: ITLS: lightweight transport-layer security protocol for IOT with minimal latency and perfect forward secrecy. IEEE Internet Things J. **7**(8), 6828–6841 (2020). https://doi.org/10.1109/JIOT.2020.2988126

23. Mazzocchi, S.: Apache JMeter. https://github.com/apache/jmeter. Accessed 22 Feb. 2022

24. Muir, J.A.: A tutorial on white-box AES (2013). http://eprint.iacr.org/2013/104

25. De Mulder, Y., Roelse, P., Preneel, B.: Cryptanalysis of the Xiao – Lai white-box AES implementation. In: Knudsen, L.R., Wu, H. (eds.) SAC 2012. LNCS, vol. 7707, pp. 34–49. Springer, Heidelberg (2013). https://doi.org/10.1007/978-3-642-35999-6_3

26. Nguyen, K.T., Laurent, M., Oualha, N.: Survey on secure communication protocols for the internet of things. Ad Hoc Netw. **32**, 17–31 (2015). https://doi.org/10.1016/j.adhoc.2015.01.006

27. Noor, M.B.M., Hassan, W.H.: Current research on Internet of Things (IoT) security: a survey. **148** (2019). https://doi.org/10.1016/j.comnet.2018.11.025

28. Pan, S., et al.: Universense: IoT device pairing through heterogeneous sensing signals. In: Proceedings of the 19th International Workshop on Mobile Computing Systems & Applications, pp. 55–60 (2018)

29. Radoglou-Grammatikis, P.I., Sarigiannidis, P.G., Moscholios, I.D.: Securing the internet of things: challenges, threats and solutions. Internet Things **5**, 41–70 (2019). https://doi.org/10.1016/j.iot.2018.11.003

30. Rahman, R.A., Shah, B.: Security analysis of IoT protocols: a focus in CoAP. In: 2016 3rd MEC International Conference on Big Data and Smart City (ICBDSC). IEEE (2016)
31. Saha, A., Srinivasan, C.: White-box cryptography based data encryption-decryption scheme for IoT environment. In: 2019 5th International Conference on Advanced Computing & Communication Systems (ICACCS). IEEE (2019)
32. Tang, Y., Gong, Z., Sun, T., Chen, J., Zhang, F.: Adaptive side-channel analysis model and its applications to White-box block cipher implementations. In: Yu, Yu., Yung, M. (eds.) Inscrypt 2021. LNCS, vol. 13007, pp. 399–417. Springer, Cham (2021). https://doi.org/10.1007/978-3-030-88323-2_22
33. Xiao, Y., Lai, X.: A secure implementation of white-box AES. In: 2009 2nd International Conference on Computer Science and its Applications, pp. 1–6. IEEE (2009)
34. Yang, G., Xu, J., Chen, W., Qi, Z.H., Wang, H.Y.: Security characteristic and technology in the internet of things, vol. 30. Nanjing University of Posts and Telecommunication (2010)
35. Yuan, R., Strayer, W.T.: Virtual Private Networks: Technologies and Solutions. Addison-Wesley Longman Publishing Co., Inc. (2001)

Symmetric Key Based Scheme for Verification Token Generation in Internet of Things Communication Environment

Keyan Abdul-Aziz Mutlaq[1,2], Vincent Omollo Nyangaresi[3], Mohd Adib Omar[1(✉)], and Zaid Ameen Abduljabbar[4]

[1] School of Computer Sciences, Universiti Sains Malaysia, USM, 11800 Gelugor, Penang, Malaysia
keyan.alsibahi@student.usm.my, keyan.alsibahi@uobasrah.edu.iq, adib@usm.my
[2] IT and Communications Center, University of Basrah, Basrah 61004, Iraq
[3] Faculty of Biological and Physical Sciences, Tom Mboya University College, Homabay, Kenya
vnyangaresi@tmuc.ac.ke
[4] Department of Computer Science, College of Education for Pure Sciences, University of Basrah, Basrah 61004, Iraq
zaid.ameen@uobasrah.edu.iq

Abstract. The traditional power grid systems are being replaced with smart grids so as to offer the required levels of flexibility, reliability, efficiency and dynamic power adjustments. However, security and privacy challenges are serious issues in smart grid environment due to a myriad of heterogeneous appliances that interconnect with the grid system. Consequently, many security and privacy preservation schemes have been developed based on techniques such as elliptic curve cryptography, blockchains, homomorphic encryption, public key certificates and bilinear pairing operations among others. However, these schemes have numerous performance and security constraints. In addition, some of these protocols require tamper proof devices which ride on unrealistic security assumptions. In this paper, a symmetric key based scheme for verification token generation is developed for internet of things communication environment. Extensive performance evaluation is executed in terms of computation, communication and space complexities. The results show that the proposed scheme has relatively low storage complexity, and the least computation and communication complexities. This renders it applicable in smart grid communication environment. In terms of security and privacy, a number of hypotheses are formulated and proofed to show that this scheme is secure under both the Dolev-Yao (DY) and the Canetti-Krawczyk threat models.

Keywords: Authentication · IoT · Key agreement · Pseudonymity · Time-stamping

J. Lin and Q. Tang (Eds.): AC3 2022, LNICST 448, pp. 46–64, 2022.
https://doi.org/10.1007/978-3-031-17081-2_4

1 Introduction

The smart grid (SG) integrates information and communication technology to the traditional power grids to offer intelligent services such as real-time electricity data management and end-to-end connectivity between consumers and utility service providers (USPs). This integration also achieves some levels of enhanced efficiency, flexibility and dependability in grid data processing [1]. As pointed out in [2], smart grids improve the power supply quality, reduce power consumption, and facilitate the support of new technologies such as electric vehicles. A typical smart grid comprises of smart meters (SMs), wireless access channels, energy resources and smart appliances [3]. Compared with the traditional electric power systems, smart grids are efficient in addressing economic, social and industrial challenges of the conventional power systems [4]. Essentially, the smart grid executes continuous monitoring of the power consumption and provides the required adjustments [5, 6].

In smart grids, the smart meter has two interfaces, with one monitoring power consumption while the other one provides the communicating gateway. As such, the smart meter offers power measurement, monitoring as well as control [7]. All the consumption information collected at the consumer side are regularly forwarded to the neighboring node, which can be a gateway, data collector, another smart meter or control center. This neighboring node continuously aggregates data from diverse smart meters until all consumer data from a particular area are collected. Afterwards, these consumption reports are forwarded to the utility service provider. Here, the USP deploys the received reports to evaluate the power supply and demand, and provide dynamic price or power supply adjustments [1]. As such, it is possible for the USP to utilize the smart grid to estimate energy consumption and formulate a stochastic pricing strategy [8]. Further, the SMs can provide power theft detection, power quality monitoring and on-demand reading [9].

Despite all the benefits that come with the deployment of smart grids, numerous security and privacy issues lurk in these grids [10]. For instance, the smart grid components can be physically captured and the communication pathways can be eavesdropped. As pointed out in [3], security threats are some of the challenges facing the integration of the power grid with information and communication technology. According to [11], malevolent command injection, eavesdropping, false data injection, private data theft, Man-In-The-Middle (MITM) and Denial of Service (DoS) attacks are serious issues in smart grids. In addition, authors in [12] identify privacy leaks as one of the factors that impede smart grid deployments. For instance, adversaries can analyze consumer power consumption reports and hence infer about home occupancy, consumer daily activities and lifestyle [1, 13].

According to [14], the interconnection among many smart grids and appliances offers a large surface from which attacks may be launched. In addition, the IP-based communication in smart grids produces high volumes of control and sensitive data which can be targeted by adversaries. The continued incorporation of new technologies further exposes the smart grids to new security threats [15]. Consequently, security and privacy have become major challenges in these grids. In particular, the preservation of confidentiality, integrity and availability is crucial in these networks [16]. As pointed out in [17] and [18], mutual authentications as well as secure communication between the users and the USP are some of the key steps towards addressing cyber threats in this environment. In addition, encryption, network segmentation, firewalls, passwords and anti-malware programs may be deployed. However, all these techniques have their own challenges that limit their applicability in smart grids. For instance, the usage of low entropy passwords may be easily broken by polynomial time adversaries. As such, the design of ideal authentication and key agreement protocols for smart grids is challenging owing to the diverse security and privacy requirements among its components [7]. The specific contributions of this paper are as follows:

- A scheme that leverages on pseudonymity and time-stamping is developed to protect against replay and impersonation attacks.
- A session key is negotiated among the communicating entities to encipher the packets exchanged after successful authentication procedures.
- Extensive security analysis is carried out to show that the proposed scheme is secure under both the Dolev-Yao (DY) and the Canetti-Krawczyk threat models.
- Performance evaluation is executed to show that the proposed scheme has lower storage costs and the least computation and communication complexities.

The rest of this research article is structured as follows: Sect. 2 discusses related work while Sect. 3 elaborates the adopted system model for the proposed scheme. On the other hand, Sect. 4 executes security analysis and comparative evaluation of the proposed protocol. Finally, Sect. 5 concludes the paper and provides some future research directions.

2 Related Work

Many authentication and key agreement schemes have been presented in literature, although each of these schemes exhibits some security, privacy or performance weaknesses. For instance, the lightweight privacy protection scheme introduced in [19] incurs high communication and computation overheads. In addition, the transmission of secret credentials over the open wireless channels can lead to impersonation attacks. On the other hand, the scheme in [20] requires a fully trusted third party entity which is cumbersome to get in the real world [1]. A bilinear pairing based authentication and key agreement scheme has been developed in [21]. Although this protocol offers smart meter privacy and session key secrecy, it is susceptible to impersonation and traceability attacks [22]. In addition, the usage of pairing operations increases its computation costs [23]. Authors in [14] have presented a lightweight authorization protocol for smart grids. However, the identities of the communicating entities are sent in plain-text over insecure channels and hence they are susceptible to impersonation attacks [24]. In addition, it fails to offer user anonymity. An identity-based scheme is developed in [25], while Elliptic Curve Cryptography (ECC) based protocols are introduced in [24] and [26]. However, these protocols experience high computation overheads due to time consuming elliptic curve point multiplication operations [27]. An anonymous authentication protocol is developed in [28] for multi-granular energy management. However, this protocol has unrealistic requirement that the terminal device communicate directly with the control center [12]. Homomorphic encryption based schemes have been introduced in [8] and [29–31] for data privacy protection. However, homomorphic encryption techniques have high computation overheads hence not ideal for smart meters [1]. Based on ECC, a lightweight authentication protocol for smart grids is developed in [32]. Unfortunately, this scheme does not offer user anonymity [33]. Although the message authentication scheme in [34] offers session key establishment, user anonymity and mutual authentication, it is susceptible to privileged insider attacks [14]. Moreover, it incurs high storage costs and fails to offer perfect forward key secrecy.

Schemes for electricity theft detection are presented in [35–37], while an ECC based lightweight authentication protocol is introduced in [15]. However, the protocol in [15] is vulnerable to attacks such as known session specific temporary information (KSSTI), server masquerading, privileged insider and impersonation [38]. In addition, it does not offer user anonymity, private key protection and is susceptible to de-synchronization attacks [32]. Although the scheme in [39] offers user and smart meter anonymity, it is vulnerable to session key leakage attacks [21] and has high computation costs due to bilinear operations [40, 41]. Similarly, the bilinear pairing based authentication protocols in [9] and [42] have high computation overheads [19]. Although the scheme in [43] offers error detection in smart grids, it fails to offer session key negotiation [15].

To enhance trust in smart grids, a blockchain based framework is presented in [44] for distributed trust, availability, data anonymity and integrity. However, blockchain introduces some computation and storage burdens to the smart meters [45]. Although the user authentication scheme in [46] provides data integrity and user anonymity, it incurs high communication and computation overheads. In addition, the deployment of static keys implies the protocol cannot offer perfect forward key secrecy [34]. A scheme that offers anonymous smart meter authentication to the USP is presented in [47]. Unfortunately, this scheme has challenges with the revocation of malicious anonymous users [12]. On the other hand, the authenticated key agreement protocol in [48] cannot thwart ephemeral secret leakage attacks. To protect against side-channeling attacks, a Physical Unclonable Function (PUF) based scheme is presented in [49], while a distributed authentication scheme is introduced in [50]. However, the protocol in [50] incurs high communication overheads.

A lightweight key sharing protocol is presented in [40], but is susceptible to KSSTI leakage and smart meter private key disclosure attacks [51]. Although the group signature based scheme in [52] offers user privacy and thwarts both replay and spamming attacks, it cannot revoke malicious user anonymity. On the other hand, the public key certificate based protocol in [53] requires high computation costs for certificate management [34, 54]. To provide smart grid security, a password-based anonymous authentication protocol is developed in [55]. Unfortunately, password based schemes are susceptible to brute force as well as dictionary attacks. Although the user authentication scheme in [56] has low communication and computation costs, it is vulnerable to privileged insider attacks. On the other hand, the cryptographic hash function based scheme in [57] deploys timestamps and hence is susceptible to de-synchronization attacks [19, 58]. To offer session key security, an ECC based protocol is developed in [59], while a two-phase authentication protocol is presented in [60]. However, the protocol in [60] is insecure [51].

Based on the discussion above, it is evident that most of the current smart grid security and privacy preservation protocols have numerous challenges that render them unsuitable for deployment in this environment. In this paper, a scheme that addresses some of these security, performance and privacy issues is developed.

3   System Model

In order to offer the required levels of privacy and security protection in smart grids, an efficient and provably secure message verification scheme is required. All the communicating entities must be properly authenticated so as to thwart any adversarial modification of energy consumption reports, privacy leaks, erroneous billing or power adjustments. In the proposed scheme, the major components include the smart meters that are installed at the customer premises, the Trusted Control Server (TCS), data aggregator (DA) and the Utility Service Provider (USP) as shown in Fig. 1. In this environment, the smart meters and the USP have to register at the TCS upon which they are issued with the relevant security tokens to enable them communicate securely.

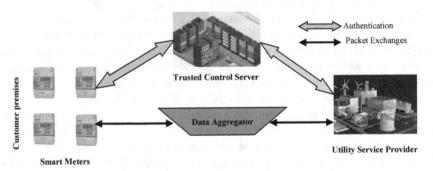

Fig.1. Network architecture

On the other hand, the data aggregator amalgamates energy consumption reports from various consumers before forwarding these reports to the USP. Table 1 presents the symbols deployed in this article, together with their brief descriptions.

The four major phases that make up the propose scheme include the system setup, registration, authentication and session key negotiation. The specifics of these phases are described in the sub-sections below.

3.1   System Setup Phase

During the system setup phase, the trusted control server generates its master key. In addition, other security parameters that will be utilized during message verification are also derived. This is a two-step procedure whose details are described below.

Step 1: To start off the system setup phase, the TCS randomly generates master key MK_T followed by the selection of SV_T as its secret value that is utilized in the derivation

Table 1. Symbols and their descriptions

Symbol	Description
MK_T	TCS master key
S_P	USP secret parameter
k	TCS public parameter
ID_S	Smart meter unique identity
$Rand_i$	Random number i
SV_T	TCS secret value
PN_U	USP pseudonym
PN_T	TCS pseudonym
PN_S	SM pseudonym
ID_T	TCS unique identity
T_{st_i}	Timestamp i
ΔT_{st}	Maximum allowed transmission delay
RM_i	Registration message i
AM_i	Authentication message i
SK_{SU}	Session key established between SM & USP
ID_U	USP unique identity
$h(.)$	Hashing operation
$\parallel$	Concatenation operation
$\oplus$	XOR operation

of other security parameters for the smart meter and the utility service provider. It also chooses k as its public security parameter.

Step 2: The TCS selects $h:\{0,1\}^* \rightarrow Z_k$ as the one-way hashing function that is used to encipher the exchanged security parameters during and after registration phase. Next, the TSC derives its unique identity ID_T that it utilizes to compute its pseudonym $PN_T = h(ID_T \parallel SV_T)$. Finally, it saves $\{MK_T, SV_T\}$ in its database before publishing parameter set $\{k, PN_T, h(.)\}$.

3.2 Registration Phase

Before the smart meter and the utility service provider can establish any communication session, they need to register with the trusted control center. In this arrangement, the TCS acts as an intermediately between the smart meter and the utility service provider. It offers some of the services of typical gateway node in addition to the control functionality. This phase serves to assign the smart meter and the utility service provider some secret security parameters required to establish a secure channel between them.

3.2.1 Utility Service Provider Registration

To register itself to the TCS, the USP executes the 3 critical steps. The exact cryptographic operations carried out are discussed below.

Step 1: The USP randomly chooses ID_U and S_P as its unique identity and secret parameter respectively. Next, it uses secure channels to transmit registration request U_{RR} to the TCS, accompanied by its identity ID_U.

Step 2: On receiving the USP's registration request, the TCS derives USP's pseudonym $PN_U = h(ID_U \| SV_T)$ and $H_1 = h(ID_U \| MK_T)$. It then securely stores parameter set $\{ID_U,$ $H_1, PN_U\}$ in its database before composing message $RM_1 = \{H_1, PN_U\}$ that is then sent over to the USP in registration response U_{RS} through some secure channels as shown in Fig. 2.

Step 3: After obtaining RM_1 from the TCS, the USP derives $H_2 = h(ID_U \| S_P) \oplus H_1$, $PN_U^* = h(ID_U \| S_P) \oplus PN_U$ and $PN_S = h(ID_U \| SV_T)$. Lastly, it stores parameters $\{H_2,$ $PN_U^*, PN_S\}$ in its database.

3.2.2 Smart Meter Registration

To usher in the smart meter registration, it first randomly chooses its identity that is then transmitted over to the TCS. In exchange, the TCS issues the smart meter with some secret key for use in the subsequent phase. This is a 3 step process as elaborated below.

Step 1: The smart meter chooses its unique identity ID_S that it then securely sends to the TCS in registration request S_{RR} over some trusted channels.

Step 2: Upon receiving this identity ID_S from the smart meter, the TCS computes PN_S^* $= h(ID_U \| SV_T)$ and $H_3 = h(ID_S \| MK_T)$. It then stores parameters $\{ID_S, H_3, PN_S^*\}$ in its database. Lastly, it composes message $RM_2 = \{H_3, PN_S^*\}$ that is transmitted in registration response S_{RS} to the smart meter over some trusted channels.

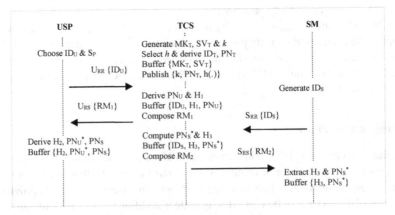

Fig. 2. System setup and registration

Step 3: After obtaining message RM_2, the smart meter extracts H_3 and $PN_S{}^*$ which it then stores securely in its memory.

3.3 Authentication and Session Key Negotiation Phase

After the successful registration of the smart meter and the utility service provider, these two entities need to negotiation a session key for secure communication between them. This phase is executed in 6 steps as discussed below.

Step 1: The USP initiates the authentication process by using its identity ID_U and secret parameter S_P to derive $PN_U = PN_U{}^* \oplus h(ID_U \| S_P)$, $H_1 = H_2 \oplus h(ID_U \| S_P)$. This is followed by the generation of random number $Rand_1 \in Z_k^*$ and the determination of the current timestamp, T_{st_1}. Using these values, the following parameters are computed:

$$Auth1 = h(PNT \| T_{st_1}) \oplus PNU$$
$$Auth_2 = h(PN_U \| PN_T \| H_1) \oplus Rand_1$$
$$Auth_3 = h(PNU \| PNT \| H1 \| Rand1) \oplus PNS$$
$$Auth_4 = h(PN_U \| PN_S \| PN_T \| H_1 \| Rand_1)$$

Lastly, the USP constructs message $AM_1 = \{Auth_1, Auth_2, Auth_3, Auth_4\}$ that is transmitted in authentication request U_{AR} to the TCS over public channels as shown in Fig. 3.

Step 2: Upon receiving AM_1 from the USP, the TCS establishes the current time T_{stc} and checks if $T_{stc} - T_{st_1} \leq \Delta T_{st}$. If this condition does not hold, the TCS rejects authentication message AM_1. However, if this condition holds, the TCS proceeds to compute $PN_U{}^{**} = Auth_1 \oplus h(PN_T \| T_{st_1})$. Afterwards, it retrieves $H_1{}^*$ from its database that it deploys to derive the following security parameters:

$$Rand_1{}^* = Auth_2 \oplus h(PN_U{}^{**} \| PN_T \| H_1{}^*)$$
$$PN_S{}^* = Auth_3 \oplus h(PN_U{}^{**} \| PN_T \| H_1{}^* \| Rand_1{}^*)$$
$$Auth_4{}^* = h(PN_U{}^{**} \| PN_S{}^* \| PN_T \| H_1{}^* \| Rand_1{}^*)$$

Step 3: The TCS then confirms whether $Auth_4{}^* \overset{?}{=} Auth_4$ such that the authentication request is rejected if these values are not identical. Otherwise, the TCS has authenticated the USP and hence proceeds to retrieve $H_3{}^*$ corresponding to $PN_S{}^*$ from its database. Next, the following parameters are computed:

$$Auth_5 = h(PN_S{}^* \| H_3{}^*) \oplus Rand_1{}^*$$
$$Auth_6 = h(PN_S * \| PN_T \| H_3 * \| Rand_1 *) \oplus PN_U **$$
$$Auth_7 = h(PN_U{}^{**} \| PN_S{}^* \| PN_T \| H_3{}^* \| Rand_1{}^*)$$

Finally, the TCS constructs message $AM_2 = \{Auth_5, Auth_6, Auth_7\}$ and sends it in authentication token S_{AT} to the smart meter over some public channels.

Step 4: On receiving message AM_2 from the TCS, the smart meter first derives the following parameters:

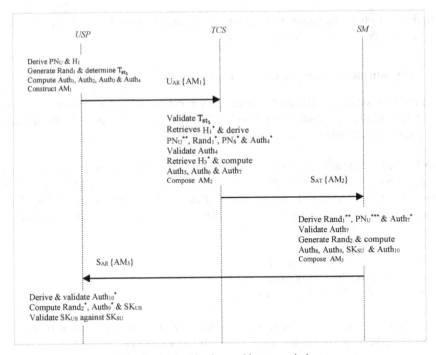

Fig. 3. Authentication and key negotiation

$$Rand_1^{**} = Auth_5 \oplus h(PN_S \| H_3)$$
$$PN_U^{***} = Auth_6 \oplus h(PN_S \| PN_T \| H_3 \| Rand_1^{**})$$
$$Auth_7^* = h(PN_U^{***} \| PN_S \| PN_T \| H_3 \| Rand_1^{**})$$

Step 5: The smart meter checks if $Auth_7^* \overset{?}{=} Auth_7$ such that the authentication request is reject when these two values are different. Otherwise, the smart meter has authenticated the TCS and proceeds to randomly select $Rand_2 \in Z_k^*$ that it utilizes to compute the following parameters:

$$Auth8 = h(PNS \| PNU^{***} \| Rand1^{**}) \oplus Rand2$$
$$Auth9 = h(Rand_1^{**} \| Rand_2)$$
$$SK_{SU} = h(PN_U^{***} \| PN_S \| PN_T \| Auth_9)$$
$$Auth_{10} = h(PN_U^{***} \| PN_S \| PN_T \| Rand_1^{**} \| Rand_2 \| Auth_9)$$

At the end, the smart meter composes message $AM_3 = \{Auth_8, Auth_{10}\}$ that is then sent in authentication response S_{AR} to the USP over public channels.

Step 6: Upon receiving AM_3 from the smart meter, the USP derives $Auth_{10}^* = h(PN_U \| PN_S \| PN_T \| Rand_1 \| Rand_2^*)$ before checking if $Auth_{10}^* \overset{?}{=} Auth_{10}$. Here, the authentication request is rejected when the two parameters are dissimilar. Otherwise, the smart meter is successfully authenticated. As such, the USP proceeds to derive the following parameters together with the session key SK_{US}:

$$Rand_2{}^* = Auth_8 \oplus h(PN_S \| PN_U \| Rand_1)$$
$$Auth_9{}^* = h(Rand_1 \| Rand_2{}^*)$$
$$SK_{US} = h(PN_U \| PN_S \| PN_T \| Auth_9{}^*)$$

This is followed by the verification of whether $SK_{US} \overset{?}{=} SK_{SU}$. Here, the authentication request is rejected when the two session keys are dissimilar. Otherwise, the smart meter, TCS and the USP have successfully authenticated each other.

4 Comparative Analysis and Evaluation

This section presents the security analysis of the proposed protocol, based on some most common threat models. This is followed by the performance evaluation, which is executed in terms of computation, storage and communication overheads.

4.1 Security Evaluation

In this sub-section, we show that the proposed protocol is secure under both the Dolev-Yao (DY) model and the Canetti-Krawczyk model. These two security models are the most popular in appraising authentication protocols, and their assumptions are detailed in [6]. To achieve this, the following 10 hypotheses are formulated and proofed.

Hypothesis 1: The proposed scheme is robust against forgery attacks.

Proof: Suppose that an attacker is interested in modifying messages such as $Auth_4$, $Auth_7$ and $Auth_{10}$ exchanged during the authentication phase. Here, $Auth_4 = h(PN_U \| PN_S \| PN_T \| H_1 \| Rand_1)$ and is sent from the USP towards the TCS, $Auth_7 = h(PN_U{}^{**} \| PN_S{}^* \| PN_T \| H_3{}^* \| Rand_1{}^*)$ and is sent from the TCS towards the SM while $Auth_{10} = h(PN_U{}^{***} \| PN_S \| PN_T \| Rand_1{}^{**} \| Rand_2 \| Auth_9)$ and is transmitted from the SM towards the USP. If this attack succeeds, then an adversary would have forged messages submitted by all the three communicating entities. However, message $Auth_4$ contains USP's secret key H_1 while $Auth_7$ contains the SM's secret key $H_3{}^*$. The validity of message $Auth_4$ and $Auth_7$ is confirmed through $Auth_4{}^* \overset{?}{=} Auth_4$ check at the TCS and $Auth_7{}^* \overset{?}{=} Auth_7$ check at the SM. As such, any forgery is easily detected. Regarding message $Auth_{10}$, it incorporates the USP's random number $Rand_1{}^{**}$ which is difficult to correctly guess. In addition, any forgery is easily detected at the USP by checking if $Auth_{10}{}^* \overset{?}{=} Auth_{10}$. Therefore, the proposed scheme is secure against forgery attacks.

Hypothesis 2: All the communicating entities are mutually authenticated in the proposed scheme.

Proof: Before the smart meter and the USP can exchange power consumption reports, they authenticate one another with the help of the TCS. This essentially serves to establish some trust levels between these communicating entities. In addition, the smart meter and the USP also authenticate the TCS. To start off, the USP derives $Auth_4 = h(PN_U \| PN_S \| PN_T \| H_1 \| Rand_1)$ which is authenticated by the TCS in step 3 using the re-computed $Auth_4^*$. Next, TCS computes $Auth_7 = h(PNU^{**}\|PN_S^*\|PN_T\|H_3^*\|Rand_1^*)$ that is authenticated at the smart meter in step 5 using the re-computed $Auth_7^*$. Similarly, the smart meter computes $Auth_{10} = h(PN_U^{***}\|PN_S\|PN_T\|Rand_1^{**}\|Rand_2\|Auth_9)$ that is authenticated at the USP using the re-computed $Auth_{10}^*$ in step 6. Evidently, the proposed scheme achieves mutual authentication among the USP, TCS and smart meter.

Hypothesis 3: The proposed scheme is resilient against known session key attacks.

Proof: Suppose that an attacker has captured the session keys such as $SK_{SU} = h(PN_U^{***}\|PN_S\|PN_T\|Auth_9)$ or $SK_{US} = h(PN_U\|PN_S\|PN_T\|Auth_9^*)$ that belong to a particular session. Here, $Auth_9 = h(Rand_1^{**}\|Rand_2)$ and $Auth_9^* = h(Rand_1\|Rand_2^*)$. The aim of the adversary is to utilize this current key to derive a valid session key for the next communication session. However, the session keys in this scheme are one-way hash values comprising of random numbers and the communicating entities' pseudonyms. Based on the collision-resistant property of the secure one-way hashing functions, an attacker is unable to parse these random numbers from the captured session keys. Consequently, an adversary cannot derive a valid session key devoid of these random numbers and pseudonyms PN_U, PN_S and PN_T. Therefore, this attack can never succeed against the proposed scheme.

Hypothesis 4: Anonymity of the communicating entities is upheld in this scheme.

Proof: In the proposed scheme, the identities of the smart meter, TCS and USP are ID_S, ID_T and ID_U respectively. All these unique identities are never transmitted in plain-text over public channels. For instance, the USP's identity is masked in pseudonym $PN_U = h(ID_U\|SV_T)$, which is in turn embedded in $Auth_1 = h(PN_T\|T_{st_1}) \oplus PN_U$. In addition, ID_S is masked in $H_3 = h(ID_S\|MK_T)$ while ID_T is encapsulated in $PN_T = h(ID_T\|SV_T)$. Since it is computationally difficult to guess with high accuracy the deployed random numbers, an attacker is unable to derive the entities' real identities devoid of master keys MK_T and SV_T.

Hypothesis 5: Man-in-the-middle attacks are effectively thwarted in the proposed scheme.

Proof: In our scheme, the USP is authenticated by the TCS by checking whether $Auth_4^* \stackrel{?}{=} Auth_4$, while the TCS is authenticated by the smart meter by confirming if $Auth_7^* \stackrel{?}{=} Auth_7$. On the other hand, the smart meter is identified by the USP through $Rand_1$. Similarly, the smart meter is authenticated by the USP by checking if $Auth_{10}^* \stackrel{?}{=} Auth_{10}$. As such, any MitM attacks using these authentication messages are effectively curbed.

Hypothesis 6: The proposed scheme is robust against replay attacks.

Proof: In this scheme, the USP chooses random number $Rand_1 \in Z_k^*$ while the smart meter selects $Rand_2 \in Z_k^*$. Here, the USP incorporates $Rand_1$ in message $Auth_4 = h(PN_U\|PN_S\|PN_T\|H_1\|Rand_1)$, while the smart meter incorporates $Rand_2$ in message $Auth_{10} = h(PN_U^{***}\|PN_S\|PN_T\|Rand_1^{**}\|Rand_2\|Auth_9)$. Since these random numbers are one-time, the TCS, USP and smart meters can detect bogus replayed messages. In addition, upon receiving $AM_1 = \{Auth_1, Auth_2, Auth_3, Auth_4)$ from the USP, the TCS validates the freshness of the timestamp T_{st_1} incorporated in $Auth_1 = h(PN_T \| T_{st_1})$ $\oplus PN_U$. As such, if AM_1 is replayed by an adversary, it will fail the freshness check $T_{stC} - T_{st_1} \leq \Delta T_{st}$ executed at the TCS.

Hypothesis 7: The smart meter and the USP negotiate a session key in the proposed scheme.

Proof: In the proposed scheme, the USP authenticates the smart meter by validating $Auth_{10}^* = h(PN_U \| PN_S \| PN_T \| Rand_1 \| Rand_2^*)$ against $Auth_{10}$ $= h(PN_U^{***} \| PN_S \| PN_T \| Rand_1^{**} \| Rand_2 \| Auth_9)$. On the other hand, the SM implicitly authenticates the USP by verifying $Auth_7^* = h(PN_U^{***} \| PN_S \| PN_T \| H_3 \| Rand_1^{**})$ against $Auth_7 = h(PN_U^{**} \| PN_S^* \| PN_T \| H_3^* \| Rand_1^*)$. By doing so, the two entities ensure that they possess valid random numbers $Rand_1$ and $Rand_2$ needed to derive the session key. After these checks, they derive session keys $SK_{SU} = h(PN_U^{***} \| PN_S \| PN_T \| Auth_9)$ and $SK_{US} = h(PN_U \| PN_S \| PN_T \| Auth_9^*)$. These session key must be similar and as such, the USP checks if $SK_{US} \overset{?}{=} SK_{SU}$. Provided that these session keys match, any traffic exchanged between the SM and USP is enciphered using this session key.

Hypothesis 8: The proposed scheme is robust against impersonation attacks.

Proof: Suppose that an attacker has successfully physically captured the smart meter and has deployed power analysis techniques to extract the security parameters stored in its memory. Next, the adversary makes attempts to impersonate the USP and SM. To successfully impersonate the USP, the attacker derives $Auth_1^{adv} = h(PN_T \| T_{st_1}) \oplus PN_U$ and $Auth_4^{adv} = h(PN_U \| PN_S \| PN_T \| H_1^{adv} \| Rand_1^{adv})$ and transmits them to the TCS. Here, H_1^{adv} and $Rand_1^{adv}$ have been randomly chosen by the attacker. Upon receiving these two messages, the TCS first parses PN_U from $Auth_1^{adv}$ and retrieves corresponding secret key H_1 from its database. Thereafter, the TCS derives $Auth_4^* =$ $h(PN_U^{**} \| PN_S^* \| PN_T \| H_1^* \| Rand_1^*)$ and checks if $Auth_4^* \overset{?}{=} Auth_4^{adv}$. Since an adversary does not know the actual H_1, this verification will fail at the TCS. Suppose that now the attacker wants to impersonate the SM. This requires that message $Auth_{10} =$ $h(PN_U^{***} \| PN_S \| PN_T \| Rand_1^{**} \| Rand_2 \| Auth_9)$ be derived and sent over to the USP. As such, the attacker randomly selects $Rand_1^{adv**}$ and $Rand_2^{adv}$ and computes $Auth_{10}^{adv}$ $= h(PN_U^{***} \| PN_S \| PN_T \| Rand_1^{adv**} \| Rand_2^{adv} \| Auth_9)$. Upon receiving $Auth_{10}^{adv}$, the USP computes $Auth_{10}^* = h(PN_U \| PN_S \| PN_T \| Rand_1 \| Rand_2^*)$ and checks if $Auth_{10}^*$ $\overset{?}{=} Auth_{10}$. Since the adversary does not know the actual values of random numbers $Rand_1^{**}$ and $Rand_2$, this verification will fail and hence the proposed scheme can distinguish legitimate and impersonated messages.

Hypothesis 9: Smart meter physical capture attacks are curbed in the proposed scheme.

Proof: The assumption made in these attacks is that an adversary has physically captured the smart meter and has extracted the stored security tokens such as $H_3 =$

$h(ID_S \| MK_T)$, $PN_S^* = h(ID_U \| SV_T)$ and $SK_{SU} = h(PN_U^{***} \| PN_S \| PN_T \| Auth_9)$. Here, $Auth_9 = h(Rand_1^{**} \| Rand_2)$. However, the master key MK_T and SV_T are both masked in one-way hashing function. As such, these two keys can never be derived from the captured parameters. In addition, the session key SK_{SU} incorporates pseudonyms and random numbers. Consequently, the session key for subsequent communication can never be derived using the captured tokens.

Hypothesis 10: The proposed scheme is robust against spoofing attacks.

Proof: Suppose that an attacker masquerades as the TCS and transmits message $Auth_7^{adv} = h(PN_U^{**} \| PN_S^* \| PN_T \| H_3^{adv*} \| Rand_1^*)$ to the smart meter. Here, H_3^{adv*} is the random parameter chosen by the attacker as the SM's secret key. Upon receiving message $Auth_7^{adv}$, the SM derives $Auth_7^* = h(PN_U^{***} \| PN_S \| PN_T \| H_3 \| Rand_1^{**})$ using the real H_3. Afterwards, the SM checks whether $Auth_7^* \overset{?}{=} Auth_7^{adv}$. Since $H_3^{adv*} \neq H_3$, this validation fails and hence malicious TCS is easily detected.

4.2 Performance Evaluation

In this sub-section, the proposed scheme is evaluated using computation, storage and communication complexities. These metrics are selected based on their prevalence during authentication protocol evaluations.

4.2.1 Computation Complexity

To evaluate the computation complexity of the propose scheme, the execution time of the various cryptographic primitives are considered. To achieve this, the authentication and key agreement phase is used and the obtained values are compared with other related schemes. In the proposed scheme, the utility service provider executes 10 one-way hashing operations (T_H) while the smart meter executes 7 one-way hashing operations. On its part, the trusted control server carries out 7 one-way hashing operations. As such, a total of $24T_H$ operations are executed in this scheme during the authentication and key agreement phase. Based on the values in [19] and [21], bilinear pairing operations T_{BP}, ECC point addition T_{ECA}, hashing operation T_H, ECC scalar multiplication T_{ECM}, symmetric encryption T_{SE} and symmetric decryption T_{SD} take 3160000 ns, 13670 ns, 1599 ns, 270016 ns, 3910 ns and 4367 ns respectively. As such, the total computation complexity of the proposed scheme is 38376 ns as shown in Table 2.

As shown in Table 2, the protocol in [39] has the highest computation complexity followed by the protocols in [15, 26] and [25] respectively. On the other hand, the proposed scheme has the lowest computation complexity. Since most of the components in the smart grid have limited computation power, the proposed scheme is the most suitable for deployment in this scenario.

4.2.2 Communication Complexity

During the authentication and key agreement phase the messages exchanged in the proposed scheme include the following:

Table 2. Computation complexities

Scheme	Overheads (ns)
[15]	1371745
[25]	1361273
[26]	1382624
[39]	8234379
Proposed	38376

$AM_1 = \{Auth_1, Auth_2, Auth_3, Auth_4\}$

$AM_2 = \{Auth_5, Auth_6, Auth_7\}$

$AM_3 = \{Auth_8, Auth_{10}\}$

Here, $Auth_1 = h(PN_T\|T_{st_1}) \oplus PN_U$, $Auth_2 = h(PN_U\|PN_T\|H_1) \oplus Rand_1$, $Auth_3 = h(PN_U\|PN_T\|H_1\|Rand_1) \oplus PN_S$, $Auth_4 = h(PN_U\|PN_S\|PN_T\|H_1\|Rand_1)$, $Auth_5 = h(PN_S{}^*\|H_3{}^*) \oplus Rand_1{}^*$, $Auth_6 = h(PN_S{}^*\|PN_T\|H_3{}^*\|Rand_1{}^*) \oplus PN_U{}^{**}$, $Auth_7 = h(PN_U{}^{**}\|PN_S{}^*\|PN_T\|H_3{}^*\|Rand_1{}^*)$, $Auth_8 = h(PN_S\|PN_U{}^{***}\|Rand_1{}^{**}) \oplus Rand_2$ and $Auth_{10} = h(PN_U{}^{***}\|PN_S\|PN_T\|Rand_1{}^{**}\|Rand_2\|Auth_9)$. Using the values in [19] and [21], Advanced Encryption Standard (AES) encryption, hash value, EC point, AES decryption, and timestamps are 128 bits, 160 bits, 320 bits, 128 bits and 32 bits long respectively. As such, the total communication complexity of the proposed scheme is 1440 bits, which is equivalent to 180 bytes as shown in Table 3.

Table 3. Communication complexities

Scheme	Overheads (bytes)
[15]	248
[25]	240
[26]	263
[39]	200
Proposed	180

As shown in Fig. 4, the protocol in [26] has the highest communication complexity followed by the protocols in [15, 25] and [39] respectively.

On the other hand, the proposed scheme has the lowest communication complexity. Consequently, the proposed scheme is the most appropriate for deployment in smart grid environment due to its lowest bandwidth requirements.

4.2.3 Storage Complexities

In the proposed scheme, the USP stores parameters $\{H_2, PN_U{}^*, PN_S\}$ in its database. On its part, the smart meter stores $\{H_3, PN_S{}^*\}$ in its memory. Here, $H_3 = H_2 = PN_S{}^*$

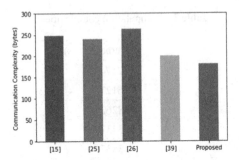

Fig. 4. Communication complexities

$= PN_U{}^* = PN_S = 160$ bits. Consequently, the overall storage cost of this scheme is 800 bits, which is equivalent to 100 bytes as shown in Table 4.

Table 4. Storage complexities

Scheme	Overheads (bytes)
[15]	60
[25]	100
[26]	160
[39]	160
Proposed	100

As shown in Fig. 5, the schemes in [26] and [39] have the highest space complexities followed by the proposed scheme and the protocol in [25] respectively. On the other hand, the protocol in [15] has the lowest space complexity.

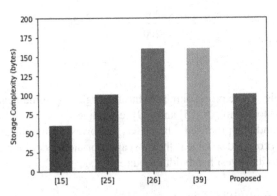

Fig. 5. Storage complexities

However, the scheme in [15] transmits identities of the communicating entities in plain-text over insecure channels, and hence it is susceptible to impersonation attacks. In addition, it fails to offer user anonymity. Consequently, the proposed scheme offers smart grid security and privacy at low computation, storage and communication costs.

5 Conclusion and Future Work

It is paramount that the signaling as well as energy consumption reports be protected from malicious modifications during their transmission over smart grid networks. In addition, eavesdropping of the smart meter collected data should be thwarted as it can potentially reveal the consumer lifestyle or home occupancy status. Although many protocols to address these issues have been presented over the recent past, a myriad of shortcomings are inherent in these schemes. Consequently, the attainment of perfect security and privacy protection at low computation, storage and communication complexities is still a mirage. The proposed scheme has been demonstrated to be secure under both the Dolev-Yao and the Canetti-Krawczyk threat models and hence potentially addresses majority of the security and privacy issues in the smart grids. In terms of performance, the proposed scheme has the least computation, and communication overheads. Since smart grid components such as smart meters are resource-constrained, the proposed scheme perfectly fits this application domain. Future work lies in the formal verification of the security features provided by the proposed scheme. There is also need for the deployment of the proposed scheme in a real smart grid environment so that its performance as well as security features can be validated.

References

1. Gai, N., Xue, K., Zhu, B., Yang, J., Liu, J., He, D.: An efficient data aggregation scheme with local differential privacy in smart grid. Digit. Commun. Netw. 1–10 (2022)
2. Desai, S., Alhadad, R., Chilamkurti, N., Mahmood, A.: A survey of privacy preserving schemes in IoE enabled smart grid advanced metering infrastructure. Clust. Comput. **22**(1), 43–69 (2019)
3. Tolba, A., Al-Makhadmeh, Z.: A cybersecurity user authentication approach for securing smart grid communications. Sustain. Energy Technol. Assess **46**, 101284 (2021)
4. Badra, M., Zeadally, S.: Lightweight and efficient privacy-preserving data aggregation approach for the Smart Grid. Ad Hoc Netw. **64**, 32–40 (2017)
5. Ferrag, M.A., Maglaras, L.A., Janicke, H., Jiang, J., Shu, L.: A systematic review of data protection and privacy preservation schemes for smart grid communications. Sustain. Cities Soc. **38**, 806–835 (2018)
6. Nyangaresi, V.O., Mohammad, Z.: Privacy preservation protocol for smart grid networks. In: 2021 International Telecommunications Conference (ITC-Egypt), pp. 1–4. IEEE (2021)
7. Luo, Y., Zheng, W.M., Chen, Y.C.: An anonymous authentication and key exchange protocol in smart grid. J. Netw. Intell. **6**(2), 206–215 (2021)
8. Liu, Y., Guo, W., Fan, C.I., Chang, L., Cheng, C.: A practical privacy-preserving data aggregation (3PDA) scheme for smart grid. IEEE Trans. Industr. Inf. **15**(3), 1767–1774 (2018)
9. Wu, T.Y., Lee, Y.Q., Chen, C.M., Tian, Y., Al-Nabhan, N.A.: An enhanced pairing-based authentication scheme for smart grid communications. J. Ambient Intell. Humaniz. Comput. 1–13 (2021)

10. Nyangaresi, V.O., Moundounga, A.R.A.: Secure data exchange scheme for smart grids. In: 2021 IEEE 6th International Forum on Research and Technology for Society and Industry (RTSI), pp. 312–316. IEEE (2021)

11. Ni, Z., Paul, S.: A multistage game in smart grid security: a reinforcement learning solution. IEEE Trans. Neural Netw. Learn. Syst. **30**(9), 2684–2695 (2019)

12. Kong, W., Shen, J., Vijayakumar, P., Cho, Y., Chang, V.: A practical group blind signature scheme for privacy protection in smart grid. J. Parallel Distrib. Comput. **136**, 29–39 (2020)

13. Nyangaresi, V.O., Alsamhi, S.H.: Towards secure traffic signaling in smart grids. In: 2021 3rd Global Power, Energy and Communication Conference (GPECOM), pp. 196–201. IEEE (2021)

14. Mahmood, K., Chaudhry, S.A., Naqvi, H., Shon, T., Ahmad, H.F.: A lightweight message authentication scheme for Smart Grid communications in power sector. Comput. Electr. Eng. **52**, 114–124 (2016)

15. Mahmood, K., Chaudhry, S.A., Naqvi, H., Kumari, S., Li, X., Sangaiah, A.K.: An elliptic curve cryptography based lightweight authentication scheme for smart grid communication. Futur. Gener. Comput. Syst. **81**, 557–565 (2018)

16. Hafizul Islam, S.K., Sabzinejad Farash, M., Biswas, G.P., Khurram Khan, M., Obaidat, M.S.: A pairing-free certificateless digital multisignature scheme using elliptic curve cryptography. Int. J. Comput. Math. **94**(1), 39–55 (2017)

17. Sadhukhan, D., Ray, S., Obaidat, M.S., Dasgupta, M.: A secure and privacy preserving lightweight authentication scheme for smart-grid communication using elliptic curve cryptography. J. Syst. Architect. **114**, 101938 (2021)

18. Nyangaresi, V.O., Rodrigues, A.J., Abeka, S.O.: ANN-FL secure handover protocol for 5G and beyond networks. In: Zitouni, R., Phokeer, A., Chavula, J., Elmokashfi, A., Gueye, A., Benamar, N. (eds.) AFRICOMM 2020. LNICSSITE, vol. 361, pp. 99–118. Springer, Cham (2021). https://doi.org/10.1007/978-3-030-70572-5_7

19. Zhang, L., Zhao, L., Yin, S., Chi, C.H., Liu, R., Zhang, Y.: A lightweight authentication scheme with privacy protection for smart grid communications. Futur. Gener. Comput. Syst. **100**, 770–778 (2019)

20. Jia, W., Zhu, H., Cao, Z., Dong, X., Xiao, C.: Human-factor aware privacy-preserving aggregation in smart grid. IEEE Syst. J. **8**(2), 598–607 (2013)

21. Odelu, V., Das, A.K., Wazid, M., Conti, M.: Provably secure authenticated key agreement scheme for smart grid. IEEE Trans. Smart Grid **9**(3), 1900–1910 (2016)

22. Chen, Y., Martínez, J.F., Castillejo, P., López, L.: An anonymous authentication and key establish scheme for smart grid: FAuth. Energies **10**(9), 1354 (2016)

23. Nyangaresi, V.O., Ogundoyin, S.O.: Certificate based authentication scheme for smart homes. In: 2021 3rd Global Power, Energy and Communication Conference (GPECOM), pp. 202–207. IEEE (2021)

24. Abbasinezhad-Mood, D., Nikooghadam, M.: An anonymous ECC-based self-certified key distribution scheme for the smart grid. IEEE Trans. Industr. Electron. **65**(10), 7996–8004 (2018)

25. Mohammadali, A., Haghighi, M.S., Tadayon, M.H., Mohammadi-Nodooshan, A.: A novel identity-based key establishment method for advanced metering infrastructure in smart grid. IEEE Trans. Smart Grid **9**(4), 2834–2842 (2016)

26. Kumar, N., Aujla, G.S., Das, A.K., Conti, M.: Eccauth: a secure authentication protocol for demand response management in a smart grid system. IEEE Trans. Industr. Inf. **15**(12), 6572–6582 (2019)

27. Zhang, L., Zhu, Y., Ren, W., Wang, Y., Choo, K.K.R., Xiong, N.N.: An energy-efficient authentication scheme based on Chebyshev chaotic map for smart grid environments. IEEE Internet Things J. **8**(23), 17120–17130 (2021)

28. Dimitriou, T., Karame, K.: Privacy-friendly tasking and trading of energy in smart grids. In: ACM Symposium on Applied Computing, vol. 21, no. 6, pp. 652–659 (2013)
29. Chen, L., Lu, R., Cao, Z.: PDAFT: A privacy-preserving data aggregation scheme with fault tolerance for smart grid communications. Peer-to-Peer Netw. Appl. **8**(6), 1122–1132 (2014). https://doi.org/10.1007/s12083-014-0255-5
30. Chim, T.W., Yiu, S.M., Li, V.O., Hui, L.C., Zhong, J.: PRGA: Privacy-preserving recording & gateway-assisted authentication of power usage information for smart grid. IEEE Trans. Dependable Secure Comput. **12**(1), 85–97 (2014)
31. Xue, K., et al.: PPSO: A privacy-preserving service outsourcing scheme for real-time pricing demand response in smart grid. IEEE Internet Things J. **6**(2), 2486–2496 (2018)
32. Abbasinezhad-Mood, D., Nikooghadam, M.: Design and hardware implementation of a security-enhanced elliptic curve cryptography based lightweight authentication scheme for smart grid communications. Futur. Gener. Comput. Syst. **84**, 47–57 (2018)
33. Wu, F., Xu, L., Li, X., Kumari, S., Karuppiah, M., Obaidat, M.S: A lightweight and provably secure key agreement system for a smart grid with elliptic curve cryptography. IEEE Syst. J. **13**(3), 2830–2838 (2018)
34. Zhang, L., Tang, S., Luo, H.: Elliptic curve cryptography-based authentication with identity protection for smart grids. PLoS One **11**(3), 151253 (2016)
35. Gao, Y., Foggo, B., Yu, N.: A physically inspired data-driven model for electricity theft detection with smart meter data. IEEE Trans. Industr. Inf. **15**(9), 5076–5088 (2019)
36. Yao, D., Wen, M., Liang, X., Fu, Z., Zhang, K., Yang, B.: Energy theft detection with energy privacy preservation in the smart grid. IEEE Internet Things J. **6**(5), 7659–7669 (2019)
37. Tao, J., Michailidis, G.: A statistical framework for detecting electricity theft activities in smart grid distribution networks. IEEE J. Sel. Areas Commun. **38**(1), 205–216 (2019)
38. Sadhukhan, D., Ray, S.: Cryptanalysis of an elliptic curve cryptography based lightweight authentication scheme for smart grid communication. In: 2018 4th International Conference on Recent Advances in Information Technology (RAIT), pp. 1–6. IEEE (2018)
39. Tsai, J.L., Lo, N.W.: Secure anonymous key distribution scheme for smart grid. IEEE Trans. Smart Grid **7**(2), 906–914 (2015)
40. He, D., Wang, H., Khan, M.K., Wang, L.: Lightweight anonymous key distribution scheme for smart grid using elliptic curve cryptography. IET Commun. **10**(14), 795–1802 (2016)
41. Nyangaresi, V.O.: Hardware assisted protocol for attacks prevention in ad hoc networks. In: Miraz, M.H., Southall, G., Ali, M., Ware, A., Soomro, S. (eds.) iCETiC 2021. LNICSSITE, vol. 395, pp. 3–20. Springer, Cham (2021). https://doi.org/10.1007/978-3-030-90016-8_1
42. Wan, Z., Wang, G., Yang, Y., Shi, S.: SKM: Scalable key management for advanced metering infrastructure in smart grids. IEEE Trans. Industr. Electron. **61**(12), 7055–7066 (2014)
43. Li, X., Wu, F., Kumari, S., Xu, L., Sangaiah, A.K., Choo, K.K.R.: A provably secure and anonymous message authentication scheme for smart grids. J. Parallel Distrib. Comput. **132**, 242–249 (2017)
44. Li, Y., Rahmani, R., Fouassier, N., Stenlund, P., Ouyang, K.: A blockchain-based architecture for stable and trustworthy smart grid. Proc. Comput. Sci. **155**, 410–416 (2019)
45. Nyangaresi, V.O.: Lightweight key agreement and authentication protocol for smart homes. In: 2021 IEEE AFRICON, pp. 1–6. IEEE (2021)
46. Li, H., Lin, X., Yang, H., Liang, X., Lu, R., Shen, X.: EPPDR: an efficient privacy-preserving demand response scheme with adaptive key evolution in smart grid. IEEE Trans. Parallel Distrib. Syst. **25**(8), 2053–2064 (2014)
47. Dimitriou, T., Karame, K.: Enabling anonymous authorization and rewarding in the smart grid. IEEE Trans. Dependable Secure Comput. **14**(5), 565–572 (2015)
48. Harishma, B., Patranabis, S., Chatterjee, U., Mukhopadhyay, D.: POSTER: authenticated key-exchange protocol for heterogeneous CPS. In: 2018 Asia Conference on Computer and Communications Security (ASIACCS), pp. 849–851, ACM, New York (2018)

49. Tahavori, M., Moazami, F.: Lightweight and secure PUF-based authenticated key agreement scheme for smart grid. Peer-to-Peer Netw. Appl. **13**(5), 1616–1628 (2020). https://doi.org/10.1007/s12083-020-00911-8

50. Gong, X., Hua, Q.S., Qian, L., Yu, D., Jin, H.: Communication efficient and privacy-preserving data aggregation without trusted authority. In: Proceedings of the 2018 IEEE Conference on Computer Communications (INFOCOM), pp. 1250–1258. IEEE (2018)

51. Abbasinezhad-Mood, D., Nikooghadam, M.: Efficient anonymous password-authenticated key exchange protocol to read isolated smart meters by utilization of extended Chebyshev chaotic maps. IEEE Trans. Industr. Inf. **14**(11), 4815–4828 (2018)

52. Jeske, T.: Privacy-preserving smart metering without a trusted-third party. In: Proceedings of the International Conference on Security and Cryptography, pp. 114–123. IEEE (2014)

53. Vaidya, B., Makrakis, D., Mouftah, H.T.: Efficient authentication mechanism for PEV charging infrastructure. In: 2011 IEEE International Conference on Communications (ICC), pp. 1–5. IEEE (2011)

54. Nyangaresi, V.O.: Provably secure protocol for 5G HetNets. In: 2021 IEEE International Conference on Microwaves, Antennas, Communications and Electronic Systems (COMCAS), pp. 17–22. IEEE (2021)

55. Khan, A.A., Kumar, V., Ahmad, M., Rana, S., Mishra, D.: PALK: password-based anonymous lightweight key agreement framework for smart grid. Int. J. Electr. Power Energy Syst. **121**, 106121 (2020)

56. Chen, Y., Martínez, J.F., Castillejo, P., López, L.: A privacy protection user authentication and key agreement scheme tailored for the internet of things environment: Priauth. Wirel. Commun. Mob. Comput. **5290579**, 1–17 (2017)

57. Kumar, P., Gurtov, A., Sain, M., Martin, A., Ha, P.H.: Lightweight authentication and key agreement for smart metering in smart energy networks. IEEE Trans. Smart Grid **10**(4), 4349–4359 (2018)

58. Nyangaresi, V.O., Rodrigues, A.J.: Efficient handover protocol for 5G and beyond networks. Comput. Secur. **113**, 102546 (2022)

59. Braeken, A., Kumar, P., Martin, A.: Efficient and provably secure key agreement for modern smart metering communications. Energies **11**(10), 2662 (2018)

60. Sha, K., Alatrash, N., Wang, Z.: A secure and efficient framework to read isolated smart grid devices. IEEE Trans. Smart Grid **8**(6), 2519–2531 (2017)

Resource Consumption Evaluation of C++ Cryptographic Libraries on Resource-Constrained Devices

Razvan Raducu$^{(\boxtimes)}$, Ricardo J. Rodríguez, and Pedro Álvarez

Dpto. de Informática e Ingeniería de Sistemas, Universidad de Zaragoza,
Zaragoza, Spain
{razvan,rjrodriguez,alvaper}@unizar.es

Abstract. With the constant growth of IoT devices, software performance and memory usage have become relevant aspects when choosing the most suitable and optimal configuration of these resource-constrained devices. Moreover, in certain scenarios security must be guaranteed to protect data confidentiality, which imposes another resource consumption overhead. In this work-in-progress we evaluate the resource consumption of two widely-used block ciphers (AES and 3DES) and stream ciphers (Salsa20 and Chacha20), implemented in two C++ libraries (Crypto++ and Botan), to find out which library and algorithms are the most efficient for such devices. In addition, we also evaluate whether the type of input data affects the resource consumption. Our results show that the memory consumption is similar across both libraries and algorithms. In terms of CPU, Crypto++ outperforms Botan, with ChaCha20 achieving the best performance rates. Regarding the type of input data, no major impact has been noticed.

Keywords: Performance evaluation · Memory usage · Cryptographic libraries · Resource-constrained devices

1 Introduction

The evaluation of a program's resource consumption helps engineering teams choose the system configuration in which their software programs can be optimally deployed. This kind of decision becomes especially critical when software programs are intended to be run on resource-constrained devices, such as Internet-of-Things devices or System-on-a-Chip boards [3].

In addition, these devices may require some sort of cryptography to guarantee data confidentiality. To incorporate this feature, software developers can make use of cryptographic libraries that provide cryptographic primitives implementing widely-known algorithms such as Advanced Encryption Standard (AES), Data Encryption Standard (DES), or Salsa20, to name a few.

© ICST Institute for Computer Sciences, Social Informatics and Telecommunications Engineering 2022
Published by Springer Nature Switzerland AG 2022. All Rights Reserved
J. Lin and Q. Tang (Eds.): AC3 2022, LNICST 448, pp. 65–75, 2022.
https://doi.org/10.1007/978-3-031-17081-2_5

However, the large number of cryptographic libraries available can make it difficult to choose which one is the best for a particular scenario. As the implementation of the cryptographic primitives varies, some of them will be inefficiently implemented, affecting the resource utilization and, consequently, execution time and energy consumption.

Modern cryptography is mainly divided into two types of encryption schemes: symmetric and asymmetric [14]. In the symmetric encryption scheme the key is used to both encrypt and decrypt data, whereas in the asymmetric scheme (also known as public-key encryption scheme) the key used for encryption and the one used for decryption are different but mathematically linked. For the sake of space, in this work-in-progress we only focus on symmetric encryption. We plan to extend this work to asymmetric encryption schemes as immediate future work. Symmetric encryption algorithms can be further divided into block or stream ciphers. Block ciphers split the data to be encrypted into fixed-size blocks and encrypt one block at a time. Stream ciphers, on the contrary, break the data down into bits and individually encrypt each one of them.

We evaluate the performance of cryptographic primitives in two cryptographic libraries written in C++, which are chosen because of their popularity and comprehensiveness. In particular, we evaluate two implementations of block ciphers and another two implementations of stream ciphers which are common across these libraries. These two kinds of symmetric ciphers were chosen as they are best suitable for different use cases: block ciphers are a good choice when the amount of data is known in advance, whereas stream ciphers are more appropriate when the amount of data is either unknown or continuous (such as in network streams). In addition, we evaluate whether the type of input data affects the performance of the cryptographic primitives.

In brief, the research questions (RQ) that we address in this work-in-progress are the following:

RQ1. Which cryptographic primitive is the most suitable for resource-constrained devices?

RQ1. Does the type of input data (i.e., random, video, audio, or text data type) affect the performance of the cryptographic algorithms?

The rest of this paper is organized as follows. Section 2 discusses the related work. Section 3 depicts the methodology we applied when performing the evaluation. Section 4 details the evaluation itself, describing the selected algorithms for comparison, the experimental setup, the discussion of the results, and the limitations of our work. Finally, Sect. 5 concludes our work and establishes future lines of work.

2   Related Work

The need of performance measurements dates several decades back [17]. One of the most common approaches when determining the performance of software in the discipline of software performance engineering is based on measurements during the actual program execution [30], as opposed to other approaches like model-based or performance prediction [4].

In any event, the evaluation of programs' resource consumption help developer teams choose the system in which their software can be optimally deployed. This kind of decision becomes critical especially when software programs are aimed to be executed in resource-constrained devices [3].

Performance of cryptographic primitives has been largely discussed in the literature. In what follows, we focus on the works most similar to ours.

In [28], Tamimi compared the performance of four of the most common cryptographic algorithms (DES, 3DES, Blowfish, and AES), using their own implementation in C# and compiled with Microsoft Visual C# .NET 2003. The results showed that Blowfish has the best performance while, on the other hand, AES has the worst. The authors in [20] also implemented widely used cryptographic algorithms (namely, DES, 3DES, AES, RSA, and Blowfish), but in Java language instead of C#. Regarding the type of input, only text and image data were used. Metrics such as performance or memory use, among others, were evaluated. An evaluation of symmetric (AES, DES, Blowfish) as well as asymmetric (RSA) cryptographic algorithms implemented in Java by taking different types of data like binary, text, and image is also provided in [19].

A comprehensive performance evaluation of popular symmetric and asymmetric key encryption algorithms is provided in [12]. The main purpose of the evaluation is selecting the best algorithm for resource-constraint devices. The authors tested symmetric key encryption (AES, RC4, Blowfish, CAST, 3DES, and Twofish) and asymmetric encryption (DSA and ElGamal) algorithms implemented in Python on various types of input files (text, audio, and video).

The seminal work of D. A. Menascé [18], presents a quantitative analysis to illustrate the effect of using a specific set of cryptographic algorithms on the performance of a computer system. In particular, the analysis is focused on the performance of digital signatures using MD5 and SHA-1 cryptographic hash functions and on the SSL protocol [11] using different combinations of symmetric key algorithms (RC4 and 3DES), two hash functions (MD5 and SHA-1 again), and three key lengths (512, 768, and 1,024 bits). Menascé concluded that there is a need to understand which level of security is required so as to be protected against possible threats while minimizing performance penalties as much as possible.

An extensive and complete analysis of eight open-source cryptography libraries is provided in [8], in which 15 different ciphers are examined and compiled using four different C++ compilers. However, unlike in this work, only electronic code-book (ECB) encryption mode is considered for the comparison.

Recently, the authors in [27] studied the performance of symmetric key algorithms (AES and DES) versus the RSA asymmetric key encryption algorithm, concluding that RSA takes the longest time for encryption while AES takes the shortest. Unlike ours, their work only considered text data for the evaluation.

The work most similar to ours is [1], in which the performance of ten block ciphers implemented in six C/C++ open source libraries under different data loads is assessed. Unlike us, they do not limit the experimental scenario to resource-constrained devices and only consider CBC mode for all block ciphers. However, no details are given on the type of input used for evaluation.

Our work differs in several ways from the works mentioned above. First, we focused on resource-constrained devices, carrying out the evaluation on a Raspberry Pi Model 4 B. Second, we evaluated four different cipher modes of operations, as well as two stream ciphers. Last, we considered four data types (random, video, audio, and textual data).

3   Methodology

The methodology we used to carry out the experiments is focused on finding out which algorithm of each type is the best in terms of performance and memory consumption, and then compare them.

We first evaluate and compare the block ciphers (AES and 3DES) with each other and the stream ciphers (Salsa20 and ChaCha20) in the same way. Regarding their configuration, we evaluate AES and 3DES with a key length of 192 bits in CBC, OFB, CTR, and CFB modes, and Salsa20 and ChaCha20 with key lengths of 128 and 256 bits. We use the same initialization vector and the same key for all algorithms. We then compare the best algorithm from each category using the same evaluation metrics.

For the input data of the assessment, we created a corpus comprising random data from /dev/urandom, audio data from a copyright-free version of *"Psychopathology of Everyday Life"*[1], video data from *"Night of the Living Dead"*[2] (also copyright-free), and textual data from *"El Quijote"*[3]. These inputs were divided into 128 KiB, 256 KiB, 512 KiB, 1 MiB, 4 MiB, and 8 MiB chunks.

Regarding execution, we launch one execution of each algorithm for each combination of input type, input size, key-length and operation mode, measuring the resource usage of each execution. Each execution consists of the encryption of the given input and the decryption of the result. In addition to the time measurement, we compute the MD5 of the decryption output to verify the correctness of the operations by comparing it to the MD5 of the original input file. This process was repeated 20 times to obtain the running average. The total execution time of these tests was almost 5780 min.

Furthermore, we developed a tool dubbed EvalMe to carry out all the experiments presented in this work-in-progress. It monitors the usage of two main resources: CPU and memory. We make use of Hyperfine [22], a cross-platform command-line benchmarking tool, to measure the CPU usage. Likewise, we use Psutil [24], a Python library for retrieving system resources utilization of running processes, to measure memory usage. EvalMe allows the user to specify

---

[1] Available in https://archive.org/details/psychopathology_everyday_life_ms_librivox, accessed on April 28, 2021.

[2] Available in https://archive.org/details/night_of_the_living_dead, accessed on April 28, 2021.

[3] Available in https://www.gutenberg.org/ebooks/2000, accessed on April 28, 2021.

how many executions of the program should be performed and monitored. By default, it performs 10 executions without a warm-up run. The results are the average resource consumption for all executions. EvalMe outputs results in either human-readable or JSON format, making it easy to integrate into pipelined analysis systems. EvalMe is open source and licensed under GNU/GPL v3, publicly available in our repository [23].

4   Evaluation

In this section we briefly present the tested algorithms, the settings we used in our experiments, the discussion of results, and the limitations of our work.

4.1   Selected Algorithms

Regarding the symmetric key algorithms selected for evaluation, we choose two block cipher algorithms and another two stream cipher algorithms. As block ciphers, we select 3DES and AES as they are the most secure block ciphers at the moment of this writing. As stream ciphers, we select Salsa20 and its evolution ChaCha20, which is becoming one of the most used stream ciphers [15]. We briefly explain them in the following.

Triple Data Encryption Standard (3DES). Developed in 1974, DES was the first encryption standard to be recommended by the National Institute of Standards and Technology (NIST). 3DES was proposed in 1998 as a replacement for DES due to advances in key searching [5]. 3DES applies the DES cipher algorithm three times to each data block. The block size is 64 bits and the key length varies between 168, 112, or 56 bits. 3DES supports different modes: ECB, Cipher Block Chaining (CBC), Cipher FeedBack (CFB), Output FeedBack (OFB), and Counter (CTR). Among these, ECB is generally not recommended as it is semantically insecure [2] (i.e., an adversary that merely observes an ECB-encrypted ciphertext can gain information about the corresponding plaintext).

Advanced Encryption Standard (AES). AES was also recommended by NIST as a replacement of DES in 1998, and standardized in 2001 [26]. The block size is 64-bit length and the key length varies between 128, 192, and 256 bits. As 3DES, it supports also different modes.

Salsa20. Salsa20 is a family of 256-bit stream ciphers designed in 2005 [7]. The block size is 64 bytes (512-bit) and the key length is either 128 bits or 256 bits. The encryption/decryption model used by Salsa20 is similar to the model followed by any block cipher in CFB, OFB, and OTR modes, among others modes (except CBC).

ChaCha20. ChaCha20 is an evolution of Salsa20, published in 2008 [6]. This stream cipher has been selected as a replacement for RC4 in the TLS protocol, used for Internet security. As in Salsa20, the block size is 64 bytes and the key length is either 128 bits or 256 bits. Regarding the encryption/decryption model, it is similar to the model used by Salsa20.

4.2 Experimental Setup

As experimental hardware, we use a Raspberry Pi 4 Model B rev 1.1 running a Raspbian GNU/Linux Debian 10 (buster) on top of a (32-bit little Endian architecture) ARM Cortex-A72 1.50 GHz CPU and 4 GiB of RAM. As software, we consider Crypto++ version 8.4 [9] and Botan version 2.17.3 [16]. These software libraries were compiled with GNU g++ version 8.3.0 (Raspbian 8.3.0-6+rpi1) and their default optimization flag (O3 in both cases). We use EvalMe to monitor resource consumption and automate the process as described in Sect. 3.

4.3 Discussion of Results

Figure 1 depicts the performance results of block ciphers in Crypto++ (top figures) and Botan (middle) and stream ciphers in Crypto++ (left-bottom) and in Botan (right-bottom). Regarding block ciphers, we evaluate 4 operation modes (CBC, OFB, CTR, and CFB) with 192-bit key length. AES always outperforms 3DES in every possible combination, regardless of the cryptographic library. No major differences are observed regarding the performance of modes in 3DES-Crypto++ (the best mode is CFB, with an average performance of 6.09 MiB/s, while OFB is the worst with 5.58 MiB/s). Regarding AES-Crypto++, the best performing mode is CBC (12.05 MiB/s) and the worst is CFB (10.92 MiB/s). On the contrary, the best 3DES-Botan mode is CBC with an average performance of 5.18 MiB/s, while the worst is CTR with 2.94 MiB/s. Regarding AES-Botan, the best operation mode is CBC (6.6 MiB/s) and the worst is CTR (3.29 MiB/s). Concerning stream ciphers, we evaluate both 128 and 256-bit key lengths. The difference of average performance is negligible in both libraries. In Crypto++, ChaCha20 with a 128-bit key length is the best cipher (13.12 MiB/s), while the worst is Salsa20 with a 128-bit key length (12.89 MiB/s). In Botan, the best cipher is Salsa20 with a 128-bit key length (4.16 MiB/s) and the worst is ChaCha20 with a 128-bit key length (3.93 MiB/s). As observed, Crypto++ always outperforms Botan.

Figure 2 shows the performance results of the best block cipher against the best stream cipher for each library with different input types and same key length. Regarding Crypto++ (top figures), ChaCha20 achieves better overall performance results than AES, regardless of the input type or its size. For AES, there are no noteworthy differences when encrypting and decrypting different input types with different sizes (except when working with textual data of 128 and 256 KiB and when dealing with video data of 128 KiB). The performance of ChaCha20 also tends to be similar, regardless of input type and sizes (except when dealing with textual and video data of 128 KiB). Regarding Botan, AES clearly outperforms Salsa20. There is also a clear tendency toward higher performance rates with larger files, regardless of the input type. This tendency has been previously documented [8]. We are currently conducting more detailed experiments in order to discover the reason for this behavior. There are also cases in which AES underperforms, such as audio data of 128 and 256 KiB, and

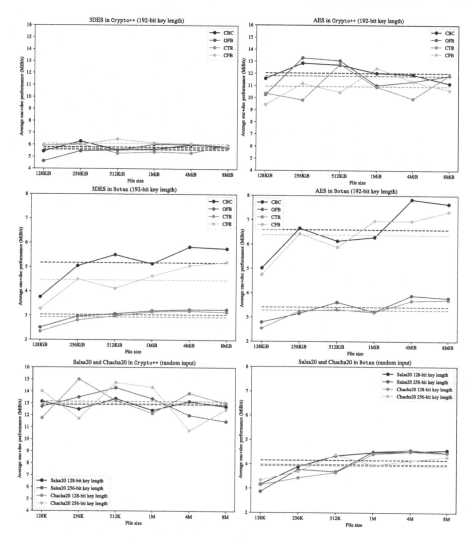

Fig. 1. Performance of block ciphers in `Crypto++` (top figures) and `Botan` (middle) and stream ciphers in `Crypto++` (left-bottom) and in `Botan` (right-bottom).

video data of 256 and 512 KiB. No major differences between input types are observed in Salsa20.

Regarding the memory consumption, we have observed no differences between executions. On average, 0.36 MiB of RAM were consumed, regardless of the library, algorithm, mode of operation, key length or input type. For the sake of space, we only show the memory consumption of AES in `Crypto++` (Fig. 3).

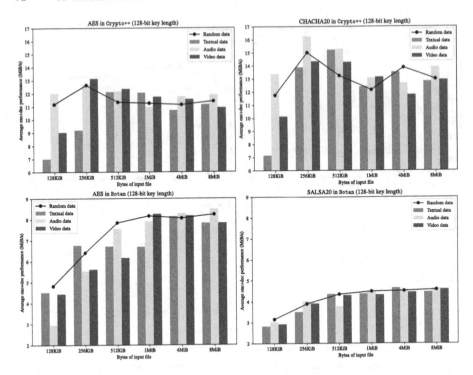

Fig. 2. Performance of the best block and stream cipher in `Crypto++` (top figures) and `Botan` (bottom).

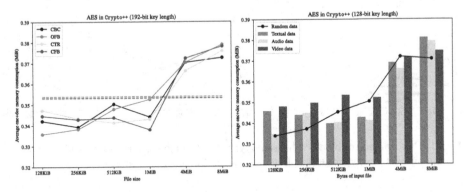

Fig. 3. Average memory usage for AES in `Crypto++`.

4.4   Limitations

A main limitation of our work is the measurement. Since we are working at the user-space level, monitoring and measurement of resource usage is restricted to polling methods. While running a specified program to retrieve the resource usage for each time period and average computation may seem appropriate, we may be skipping consumption variations (high or low) that may occur during execution. Using a kernel space level monitoring tool would allow us to provide more accurate measurements.

Besides, our results are limited in terms of how the libraries were compiled (we only evaluated one compiler) and the optimizations they were compiled with (we used the default optimization flag). Also, we evaluated only CPU usage and RAM consumption, when there are other crucial measurements like latency, power consumption, or battery drainage.

5   Conclusions and Future Work

The results showed that the higher performance rates are achieved with larger files in `Botan`, unlike `Crypto++`, in which the input size has no major impact. In all our experiments, `Crypto++` clearly outperforms `Botan`. Let us remark that we have empirically observed small variations on performance between different runs of the same configuration, which may indicate that external factors, such as the processor's heat, can be affecting its performance. This is an important issue for resource-constrained devices that requires further research. The best algorithm, in terms of performance, is ChaCha20. Regarding memory consumption, there is no difference between any of the algorithms. Our results also showed that the type of input data has no impact on the performance of the cryptographic primitives, with few exceptions that we believe require further research.

Our immediate step continuing this work is to evaluate the performance and memory consumption considering different optimization flags and different C++ compilers, such as `Clang` and `Intel C++ Compiler`. Our preliminary results with `g++` show that the executions with the default optimizer flag, O3, do not have the shorter execution time, while memory consumption are equal across all the executions. Moreover, we plan to extend our evaluation so as to cover asymmetric encryption algorithms and also extend the study to other IoT devices, such as Arduino boards and ESP8266 chips.

In addition, we also aim to assess the power consumption of the tested devices, since power consumption is key in the context of resource-restrained devices. Particularly, in battery-powered devices battery drain is critical. The power consumption of cryptographic primitives has already been measured in the literature [10,13,21,25,29], showing that the optimal algorithm for a given device is not necessarily the most efficient in terms of power consumption which, in turn, certifies that choosing the "best" algorithm implies more than just selecting the fastest.

References

1. Alrowaithy, M., Thomas, N.: Investigating the performance of C and C++ cryptographic libraries. In: Proceedings of the 12th EAI International Conference on Performance Evaluation Methodologies and Tools, VALUETOOLS 2019, pp. 167–170. Association for Computing Machinery, New York (2019)

2. Aumasson, J.P.: Serious Cryptography: A Practical Introduction to Modern Encryption. No Starch Press, San Francisco (2017)
3. Babovic, Z.B., Protic, J., Milutinovic, V.: Web performance evaluation for internet of things applications. IEEE Access **4**, 6974–6992 (2016)
4. Balsamo, S., Di Marco, A., Inverardi, P., Simeoni, M.: Model-based performance prediction in software development: a survey. IEEE Trans. Software Eng. **30**(5), 295–310 (2004)
5. Barker, E., Mouha, N.: Recommendation for the Triple Data Encryption Algorithm (TDEA) Block Cipher. techreport NIST Special Publication 800-67. Revision 2, National Institute of Standards and Technology, November 2017
6. Bernstein, D.J.: ChaCha, a variant of Salsa20. resreport, University of Illinois (2008)
7. Bernstein, D.J.: The Salsa20 family of stream ciphers. In: Robshaw, M., Billet, O. (eds.) New Stream Cipher Designs. LNCS, vol. 4986, pp. 84–97. Springer, Heidelberg (2008). https://doi.org/10.1007/978-3-540-68351-3_8
8. Bingmann, T.: Speedtest and Comparsion of Open-SourceCryptography Libraries and Compiler Flags, July 2008. https://panthema.net/2008/0714-cryptography-speedtest-comparison/. Accessed 11 Dec 2020
9. Dai, W.: Crypto++ version 8.4, January 2021. https://github.com/weidai11/cryptopp. Accessed 11 Jan 2021
10. Fotovvat, A., Rahman, G.M.E., Vedaei, S.S., Wahid, K.A.: Comparative performance analysis of lightweight cryptography algorithms for IoT sensor nodes. IEEE Internet Things J. **8**(10), 8279–8290 (2021). https://doi.org/10.1109/JIOT.2020.3044526
11. Freier, A., Karlton, P., Kocher, P.: The Secure Sockets Layer (SSL) Protocol Version 3.0. techreport RFC 6101, Internet Engineering Task Force (IETF), August 2011. https://tools.ietf.org/html/rfc6101. Accessed 28 Apr 2021
12. Haque, M.E., Zobaed, S., Islam, M.U., Areef, F.M.: Performance analysis of cryptographic algorithms for selecting better utilization on resource constraint devices. In: 2018 21st International Conference of Computer and Information Technology (ICCIT), pp. 1–6 (2018)
13. Hatzivasilis, G., Fysarakis, K., Papaefstathiou, I., Manifavas, C.: A review of lightweight block ciphers. J. Cryptogr. Eng. **8**(2), 141–184 (2017). https://doi.org/10.1007/s13389-017-0160-y
14. Katz, J., Lindell, Y.: Introduction to Modern Cryptography. CRC Press, Boca Raton (2020)
15. Krasnov, V.: It takes two to ChaCha (Poly), April 2016. https://blog.cloudflare.com/it-takes-two-to-chacha-poly/. Accessed 30 Apr 2021
16. Lloyd, J.: Botan version 2.17.3, March 2021. https://github.com/randombit/botan. Accessed 11 Mar 2021
17. Lucas, H., Jr.: Performance evaluation and monitoring. ACM Comput. Surv. (CSUR) **3**(3), 79–91 (1971)
18. Menascé, D.: Security performance. IEEE Internet Comput. **7**(3), 84–87 (2003)
19. Panda, M.: Performance analysis of encryption algorithms for security. In: 2016 International Conference on Signal Processing, Communication, Power and Embedded System (SCOPES), pp. 278–284 (2016)
20. Patil, P., Narayankar, P., Narayan D.G., Meena S.M.: A comprehensive evaluation of cryptographic algorithms: DES, 3DES, AES, RSA and blowfish. Procedia Comput. Sci. **78**, 617–624 (2016). 1st International Conference on Information Security & Privacy 2015

21. Pereira, G.C., Alves, R.C., Silva, F.L.D., Azevedo, R.M., Albertini, B.C., Margi, C.B.: Performance evaluation of cryptographic algorithms over IoT platforms and operating systems. Secur. Commun. Netw. **2017** (2017)
22. Peter, D.: Hyperfine version 1.11.0, January 2021. https://github.com/sharkdp/hyperfine. Accessed 19 Jan 2021
23. Raducu, R.: Evalme, January 2021. https://github.com/reverseame/evalme. Accessed 19 Jan 2021
24. Rodola, G.: psutil (version 5.8.0), January 2021. https://pypi.org/project/psutil/. Accessed 19 Jan 2021
25. Saraiva, D.A.F., Leithardt, V.R.Q., de Paula, D., Sales Mendes, A., González, G.V., Crocker, P.: PRISEC: comparison of symmetric key algorithms for IoT devices. Sensors **19**(19), 4312 (2019). https://doi.org/10.3390/s19194312
26. Secretary of Commerce: Advanced Encryption Standard. Techreport Federal Information Processing Standards Publication 197, National Institute of Standards and Technology, November 2001
27. Sheikh, M.F.A., Gaur, S., Desai, H., Sharma, S.K.: A study on performance evaluation of cryptographic algorithm. In: Rathore, V.S., Worring, M., Mishra, D.K., Joshi, A., Maheshwari, S. (eds.) Emerging Trends in Expert Applications and Security. AISC, vol. 841, pp. 379–384. Springer, Singapore (2019). https://doi.org/10.1007/978-981-13-2285-3_44
28. Tamimi, A.K.A.: Performance Analysis of Data Encryption Algorithms (2006). https://www.cs.wustl.edu/~jain/cse567-06/ftp/encryption_perf/index.html. Accessed 11 Dec 2020
29. Thakor, V.A., Razzaque, M.A., Khandaker, M.R.A.: Lightweight cryptography algorithms for resource-constrained IoT devices: a review, comparison and research opportunities. IEEE Access **9**, 28177–28193 (2021). https://doi.org/10.1109/ACCESS.2021.3052867
30. Woodside, M., Franks, G., Petriu, D.C.: The future of software performance engineering. In: Future of Software Engineering (FOSE 2007), pp. 171–187. IEEE (2007)

Authentication Protocol

A Secure Lightweight RFID Mutual Authentication Protocol Without Explicit Challenge-Response Pairs

Keke Huang[1,2], Changlu Lin[1,2,3(✉)], and Yali Liu[2,4]

[1] College of Computer and Cyber Security, Fujian Normal University,
Fuzhou 350117, Fujian, China
hkk@yjs.fjnu.edu.cn
[2] Fujian Provincial Key Lab of Network Security and Cryptology,
Fuzhou 350007, Fujian, China
[3] School of Mathematics and Statistics, Fujian Normal University,
Fuzhou 350117, Fujian, China
cllin@fjnu.edu.cn
[4] College of Computer Science and Technology, Jiangsu Normal University,
Xuzhou 221116, Jiangsu, China
liuyali@jsnu.edu.cn

Abstract. Radio Frequency Identification (RFID) has been widely deployed to various scenarios, but its security and privacy issues need to be concerned due to the tag's limited computing and storage resources. While benefiting from the great convenience and advantages of RFID systems, security is still a considerable threat to their applications, such as desynchronization attacks and cloning attacks. In this paper, we propose a secure lightweight mutual authentication protocol based on the configurable tristate physical unclonable functions and the cryptographic primitive of verifiable secret sharing to solve these issues. More specifically, the tag equipped with the configurable tristate physical unclonable functions structure can enhance the tag's security and effectively resist machine learning modeling attacks. Verifiable secret sharing plays the role of decentralized storage of secrets, and ensures the verifiability of the correctness of the each shares. The verifiability provided by verifiable secret sharing is effective against tag impersonation attacks, and

Supported by the National Natural Science Foundation of China (U1705264, 61702237, 61872168); Natural Science Foundation of Fujian Province (2019J01275); Guangxi Key Laboratory of Trusted Software (KX202039); the Opening Foundation of Guangxi Key Laboratory of Cryptography and Information Security (Guilin University of Electronics Technology) (GCIS202114); the Ministry of Education University-Industry Collaborative Education Program of China (CXHZ-GWebRAY-202002-18); the Special Foundation of Promoting Science and Technology Innovation of Xuzhou City (KC18005); the Natural Science Foundation of Jiangsu Province (BK20150241); the Natural Science Foundation of the Higher Education Institutions of Jiangsu Province (14KJB520010); the Scientific Research Support Project for Teachers with Doctor's Degree of Jiangsu Normal University (14XLR035); the Jiangsu Provincial Government Scholarship for Overseas Studies.

J. Lin and Q. Tang (Eds.): AC3 2022, LNICST 448, pp. 79–107, 2022.
https://doi.org/10.1007/978-3-031-17081-2_6

the validity of the each share provided by the tag has to be verified before it is adopted. Finally, the correctness of our protocol is analyzed formally using BAN-logic and the its security is verified informally by the Scyther. In addition, we analyze security properties including data integrity, data confidentiality, anonymity, mutual authentication, forward security and resistance to various malicious attacks. The results show that the proposed protocol satisfies various security properties and resistance to diverse malicious attacks.

Keywords: Radio Frequency Identification (RFID) · Configurable Tristate PUF (CT PUF) · Verifiable Secret Sharing (VSS) · BAN logic · Scyther

1   Introduction

The main principle of Radio Frequency Identification (RFID) technology is to automatically identify and track objects, people, and other objects in an open environment through radio frequency signals [1]. RFID has the following advantages: the non-contact, the high reliability, the fast certification, the waterproof, the anti-magnetic, the heat-resistant, the long service life, the long contact distance and so on. With the development of the Internet of Things (IoT), RFID technology has been widely used in various industries and scenarios, such as supply chain management systems [2], the healthcare environment [3,4], the vehicle identification [5], the unmanned aerial vehicle (UAV) [6].

The structure of a typical RFID system [7] is depicted in Fig. 1. The back-end server, which is a powerful device that maintains a database with tag information, communicates with the reader via a secure channel, while the reader and the tag is a wireless communication channel that is vulnerable to adversary attacks, such as the desynchronization attacks [8], the replay attacks [2], the man-in-middle attacks [6], the physical and cloning attacks [9], etc. To address the critical challenges of low-cost RFID tag secure authentication, many lightweight authentication schemes based on different technologies and from different perspectives have been proposed. Some research works are reviewed as follows.

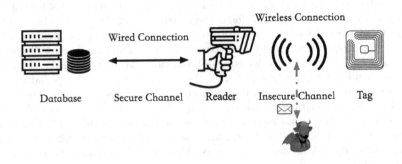

Fig. 1. The structure of a typical RFID system

Peris-Lopez et al. first proposed a family of authentication protocols (LMAP [10], EMAP [11], M^{2}AP [12]) that only involve simple bit-wise operations, such as XOR, AND, OR, and addition modulo 2^m (mod $2^m(+)$) for ultra-lightweight RFID authentication protocols in 2006. However, these protocols are vulnerable to both active and passive attacks [13,14]. Chien et al. proposed the SASI protocol [15], an ultra-lightweight protocol which defines a new bitwise transformation operation, the left cyclic shift operation in 2007. However, the weaknesses of SASI protocols were analyzed in [16,17], respectively, and the results showed that it suffers from the tracking attack, the key leakage attack, and the denial-of-service attack. Tian et al. proposed a RAPP protocol based on $Per(X,Y)$ operation in [18] in 2012; however, the protocol is vulnerable to the desynchronization attack [19], as well as cannot be resistant to the impersonation attacks and full exposure of its secret information by eavesdropping on the collected communication messages [20].

In recent years, numerous research efforts on Physically Unclonable Functions (PUF)-based RFID secure authentication protocols have been proposed. Pappu et al. [21] first introduced the concept of PUFs in 2002, which are based on physical systems to achieve one-way outputs. PUFs as an emerging lightweight hardware security primitive which can provide a secure lightweight cryptographic computational for resource-constrained devices such as RFID has received increasing concern. The idea of the PUF-based authentication protocol is to employ the PUF module to pre-generate a large number of Challenge-Response Pairs (CRPs), and the CRPs are stored in the server's database. The existing PUF-based RFID secure authentication protocols are based on pre-computing multiple sets of CRPs and storing them in a reader (server) database, which makes them vulnerable to the machine learning attacks [25].

Akgün et al. [23] proposed a PUF-based authentication scheme for RFID systems, however, the scheme could not ensure the forward security [9] in 2015. Liang et al. [24] proposed a double PUF-based RFID identity authentication protocol in service-centric internet of things environments, however, the scheme suffers from the possibility of tag counterfeiting and cannot robust against the desynchronization attacks (Denial-of-Service attacks, DoS) [25] and the replay attacks [22] in 2019. Gope et al. [6] proposed a PUF-based RFID secure authentication protocol for UAV applications in 2021. Multiple sets of CRPs are pre-generated and stored in the server during the setup phase to accomplish the subsequent process PUF-based RFID authentication communication. In addition, the storage cost of tags is too expensive and vulnerable to the potential multi-round desynchronization attacks in this protocol (See Appendix A for detailed analysis).

Our Contributions. In this paper, we focus on the requirements of security properties and the potential malicious attacks in RFID systems, as well as the vulnerabilities from previous research. To solve the vulnerability of RFID systems to various malicious attacks we propose a secure lightweight RFID mutual authentication protocol based on the configurable tristate physical unclonable functions (CT PUF) and the cryptographic primitive of verifiable secret sharing (VSS). The main contributions of this paper are summarized below:

- This paper flexibly combines three techniques, CT PUF, VSS and Hash Table, on which a secure lightweight authentication protocol is proposed. The proposed protocol addresses the performance and security issues of RFID authentication protocols, while low-cost RFID tags can achieve a compromise between security and performance. More specifically, the server takes advantage of VSS to enable that it does not require the storage of explicit challenge-response pairs for CT PUF but instead stores a secret share of $CRPs_{Arbiter_T}$. The tags are equipped with CT PUF structures to ensure more security against the machine learning attacks.
- In previous studies, it is necessary for the server to perform an exhaustive search when identifying the tag. In particular, there is no fine scalability with a large number of the tags. For each record entry of the tag's secret parameters, our protocol is not to store them directly in chronological order but to take advantage of the hash table storage mechanism. This mechanism can effectively reduce the complexity of search time. The time complexity of the server to perform the search under ideal conditions is $\mathcal{O}(1)$ only. Therefore, it can effectively reduce the time overhead of the server in searching and updating the tag's secret parameter.
- The formal analysis of the proposed protocol using BAN logic shows that the correctness of authentication communication between the server and the tag can be guaranteed. We also verify the security of the proposed protocol using the Scyther, and the simulation results show that no attacks are detected. In addition, We analyze security properties and resistance to malicious attacks. The results show that our protocol satisfies various security properties such as data integrity, data confidentiality, mutual authentication, anonymity, forward security and is resistant to malicious attacks such as the man-in-the-middle attacks, the replay attacks, the desynchronization attacks, and the physical attacks and cloning attacks, the impersonation attacks.

1.1 Structure of the Paper

The rest of this paper is organized as follows. The underlying preliminaries are introduced in Section 2. The proposed CT PUF and VSS-based lightweight RFID authentication protocol is presented detailed in Sect. 3. The informal security and formal security of the proposed scheme is analyzed in Sect. 4 and Sect. 5, respectively. Then, in Sect. 6, we give the performance evaluation of the proposed scheme. Finally, we present the conclusion of the paper and look to the future in Sect. 7.

2 Preliminaries

In this section, we present a brief description of the background required to build the proposed protocol. Due to space constraints, the detailed description of physical unclonable functions and Feldman's (t, n)-threshold verifiable secret sharing scheme are presented in Appendix B and C, respectively.

Here, we summarize the security properties and potential malicious attacks by RFID system security requirements as well as other researches [6,9,23,24], as follows.

- **Data Integrity.** It refers to the integrity of the communication messages during the authentication process as well as the secret parameters stored by the reader and tag. The proposed authentication scheme should provide an integrity confirmation mechanism that can verify whether the communication message has been tampered with by an adversary.
- **Data Confidentiality.** It refers to the communication message transmitted between the reader (the server), and the tag should be a ciphertext message generated by obfuscating or encrypting secret parameters. Hence, even if the adversary intercepts the message by means of eavesdropping, etc., it is impossible to obtain valuable information from it.
- **Anonymity.** It is mainly for tags, which have a unique identifier. Once that identity is captured by an adversary, then the tag can be continuously identified and tracked with that identity.
- **Mutual authentication.** Since there is a forgery attack in the potential attack, where the adversary impersonates as a reader or disguises as a tag. Therefore, the reader and tag are not trusted by each other in the authentication process, and mutual authentication between them is a necessary requirement for RFID authentication protocols.
- **Forward security.** Satisfying forward security means that even though all authentication messages between the reader and the tag during the authentication process are intercepted by the adversary, no authentication information or other secret parameters of the previous authentication session can be inferred from these messages.
- **Man-in-Middle attack.** This attack is undetectable to the readers and the tags; thus, the adversary can take control of the communication channel without being detected. The adversary establishes the communication channel with the reader and the tag respectively and intercepts the communication channel between the reader and the tag simultaneously. In this way, the communication messages in the system are forwarded by the adversary.
- **Replay attack.** This attack is an active attack that an adversary intercepts and replays communication messages during the authentication session. The adversary first eavesdrops on the communication channel, then he/she waits for authentication communication between a valid reader and a tag, and finally intercepts and holds the authentication session messages. In the future, the adversary impersonates as a legal reader or tag and replays the authentication messages for authentication.
- **Desynchronization attack.** The purpose of a desynchronization attack is to desynchronize shared key parameters that the reader and the tag require synchronization, and the attack occurs during the final update phase of a legitimate reader and a tag authentication communications.

- **Impersonation attack.** The adversary impersonates a legitimate tag or server by counterfeiting the tag's or server's identity and secret parameters, or even utilizing the forged parameters to generate authentication messages for authenticated communication in order to spoof the valid tag or server as a legitimate one.
- **Cloning attack.** This attack is a malicious attack on a tag in which an adversary clones a completely identical tag by detecting the tag's circuit or trying other mechanical methods to analyze the tag's circuit. Further, once the attack is successful, the adversary can initiate other malicious attacks.

3   The Proposed Protocol

In this section, we first explain the relevant notations and descriptions involved in our protocol. Next, the system model and the adversary model are described. Then the assumptions that the proposed scheme relies on are depicted. Finally, our protocol composes of the initialization phase and the authentication phase, which are described in detail step by step according to the authentication sequence.

3.1   Notations

The notations and descriptions involved in the protocol are detailed listed in Table 1.

3.2   Assumptions of Our Proposed Protocol

The basic assumptions followed in our protocol are as follows.

(a) The reader communicates with the back-end server over a secure channel, and therefore consider both as one unit. The reader (server) communicates with the tag over an open and insecure wireless channel, which is vulnerable to various malicious attacks, such as the man-in-middle attacks, the impersonation attacks and the replay attacks.

(b) The tag is a low-cost device with limited computing and storage resources, i.e., a low-cost passive RFID tag. Therefore, the tag can only perform lightweight or ultra-lightweight operations.

(c) The PUFs module is embedded in the Tag, and the PUFs structure refers specifically to the new Configurable Tristate PUF (CT PUF) proposed by Zhang et al. in [29]. The CT PUF can effective against a variety of machine learning attacks, such as logistic regression (LR), support vector machines (SVM), covariance matrix adaptation evolutionary strategies (CMA-ES), and artificial neural networks (ANN).

Table 1. Notations and descriptions

Notation	Descriptions	Notations	Descriptions
T	RFID Tags	S	Server and reader unit
CT PUF$_T(\cdot)$	CT PUF module embedded in T	$M_{\text{CT PUF}_T}$	A soft model of CT PUF$_T$ trained on S
SID_T^{i-1}	$i-1$ round shadow identity of T	SID_T^i	i round shadow identity of T
SID_T^{i+1}	$i+1$ round shadow identity of T	$PRNG(\cdot)$	Pseudo-random number generator
$C_{Arbiter_T}$	Stable challenge of CT PUF$_T(\cdot)$	$R_{Arbiter_T}$	The stable response of CT PUF$_T(\cdot)$
C_{XOR_i}	The challenge of Tristate PUF in the bitwise XOR obfuscation mechanism	R_{XOR_i}	Temporary response of Tristate PUF in the bitwise XOR obfuscation mechanism
C_i	i round random challenge of CT PUF$_T(\cdot)$	R	The real response of CT PUF$_T(\cdot)$
$\hat{R}$	An obfuscated response of $M_{\text{CT PUF}}$	τ	Difference threshold of FHD$(R,\hat{R})$
N_S	The random number generated by S	N_T	The random number generated by T
$M_i, i = \{1,2,3,4\}$	Authentication message	S_1, S_2	Shares of the $R_{Arbiter_T}$
K_T^{i-1}	$i-1$ round secret key of T	K_T^i	i round secret key of T
K_T^{i+1}	$i+1$ round secret key of T	K_S	The secret key of S
$Index_T$	T's storage index in database	$h(\cdot)$	A lightweight cryptographic Hash functions
$\parallel$	String conjunction operations	$\oplus$	Bitwise XOR
VSS.Share$(\cdot)$	A distribution algorithm for verifiable secret sharing	ht$(\cdot)$	The Hash algorithm that generates $Index_T$
VSS.Rec$(\cdot)$	A reconstruction algorithm for verifiable secret sharing	VSS.Verify$(\cdot)$	A verification algorithm for verifiable secret sharing
$\alpha = \{\alpha_i\}, i = \{1,\cdots,t-1\}$	The commitments of polynomial coefficients	FHD$(\cdot)$	The Fuzzy Hamming Distance
Sea$(\cdot)$	A function to find string information	match$(\cdot)$	A function to match strings
Pad$(\cdot)$	A function for bit-wise padding	$P(\cdot)$	PUF module embedded in T

3.3 Authentication Process

In this subsection, we fist present the authentication process of the proposed protocol based on CT PUF and the cryptographic primitive of verifiable secret sharing. The whole authentication process is divided into two phases: the setup phase and the authentication phase.

Setup Phase. During the setup phase server (reader) unit and tag communicate with each other over a secure channel in a secure environment. This phase completes the initialization and sharing of secret parameters between server and tag. For a tag's CT PUF_T, it has some stable $CRPs : CR_{Arbiter} = \{C_{Arbiter}, R_{Arbiter}\}$, assuming that server has acquired and stored the $CRPs$ during the initialization phase. The server register a tag's CT PUF_T by collecting R_{XOR} and training a soft model $M_{CT\ PUF_T}$ for each tag's CT PUF_T. The detailed process of communication interaction during the setup phase is depicted in Fig. 2. The detailed initialization steps of the proposed protocol are as follows.

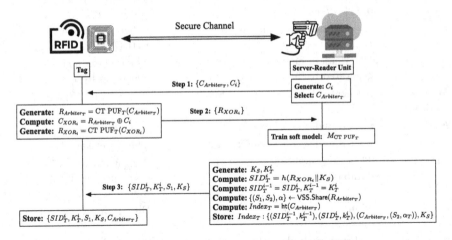

Fig. 2. Setup phase of the proposed protocol.

Step1: The server sends messages to the tag as $S \xrightarrow{\{C_{Arbiter_T}, C_i\}} T$

(1) First, S randomly selects a pair of $CR_{Arbiter_T}$ from some stable $CRPs$ of the CT PUF_T, and generates a random challenge C_i for the current round session.
(2) Then S sends $\{C_{Arbiter_T}, C_i\}$ to T.

Step2: The tag sends messages to the server as $T \xrightarrow{\{R_{XOR_i}\}} S$

(1) By default, the CT PUF_T of a unenroled T is in the Arbiter PUF working state. Once T receives the message $\{C_{Arbiter_T}, C_i\}$, it first takes $C_{Arbiter_T}$ as the input to the CT PUF_T, and then generates the response $R_{Arbiter_T} = $ CT $PUF_T(C_{Arbiter_T})$.

(2) Then, the real input challenge $C_{XOR_i} = R_{Arbiter_T} \oplus C_i$ of CT PUF_T is computed by the obtained $R_{Arbiter_T}$ to XORing C. Then, the C_{XOR_i} as the input of CT PUF to obtain the $R_{XOR_i} = $ CT $PUF_T(C_{XOR_i})$ in Arbiter PUF, RO PUF or BR PUF working states, T sends R_{XOR_i} to S.

(3) Finally, T sends $\{R_{XOR_i}\}$ to S.

Step3:   The   server   sends   messages   to   the   tag   as
$$S \xrightarrow{\{SID_T^i, K_T^i, (C_{Arbiter_T}, S_1), K_S\}} T$$

(1) Once S receives R_{XOR_i} and then S uses R_{XOR_i} to train a software model $M_{CT\ PUF_T}$ for CT PUF_T.

(2) Next, S generates a secret i-round session key K_T^i for T and a secret key K_S for itself. Then, S computes the shadow identity $SID_T^i = h(R_{XOR_i} \| K_S)$.

(3) To keep off the desynchronization attacks, S stores secret parameters shared with T for two authentication session. Therefore, S performs the following computing: $SID_T^{i-1} = SID_T^i, K_T^{i-1} = K_T^i$.

(4) To prevent the $R_{Arbiter_T}$ of CT PUF from being directly accessed after setup pahse, we make advantage of the verifiable secret sharing scheme with $(2,2)$ threshold to store $R_{Arbiter_T}$ instead of the explicit storage. S computes: $\{(S_1, S_2), \alpha_T\} \leftarrow$ VSS.Share$(R_{Arbiter_T})$:

① S generates two primes numbers p and q such that $q|(p-1)$, and $g \in \mathbb{Z}_p*$ an element of order q.

② S generates the random polynomial $P(x) = a_0 + a_1 x$ over $\mathbb{Z}_q$ such that $a_0 = R_{Arbiter_T}$, and makes commitment $\alpha_T = \{\alpha_i = g^{a_i} \bmod p, i = 0, 1\}$.

③ S computes $S_1 = P(1)$ and $S_2 = P(2)$, where S_1 is sent securely to T after with the other parameters, S_2 is stored by itself.

(5) When all secret parameters are generated, S takes advantages of hash table to store these parameters as a record entry. Here, the storage index $Index_T = $ ht$(C_{Arbiter_T})$ is generated by the $C_{Arbiter_T}$. The storage structure of S is shown in Fig. 3.

(6) Then, S stores: $Index_T : \{(SID_T^{i-1}, k_T^{i-1}), (SID_T^i, k_T^i), (C_{Arbiter_T}, (S_2, \alpha_T)), K_S\}$ and sends $\{SID_T^i, K_T^i, S_1, K_S\}$ to T.

(7) Once T receives $\{SID_T^i, K_T^i, S_1, K_S\}$, then T stores $\{SID_T^i, K_T^i, S_1, K_S, C_{Arbiter_T}\}$

Authentication Phase. After the initialization phase, the tag enters an open insecure real-world usage scenario in which S and T communicate over an insecure wireless channel. Therefore, the security and privacy of authentication during communication need to be guaranteed as the communication interaction

$Index_{T_k} = ht(C_{Arbiter_{T_k}})$	$\{(SID_{T_k}^{i-1}, K_{T_k}^{i-1}), (SID_{T_k}^i, K_{T_k}^i), (C_{Arbiter_{T_k}}, S_{T_{k2}}), K_S\}$
Null	Null
⋮	⋮
Null	Null
$Index_{T_i} = ht(C_{Arbiter_{T_i}})$	$\{(SID_{T_i}^{i-1}, K_{T_i}^{i-1}), (SID_{T_i}^i, K_{T_i}^i), (C_{Arbiter_{T_i}}, S_{T_{i2}}), K_S\}$
⋮	⋮
$Index_{T_j} = ht(C_{Arbiter_{T_j}})$	$\{(SID_{T_j}^{i-1}, K_{T_j}^{i-1}), (SID_{T_j}^i, K_{T_j}^i), (C_{Arbiter_{T_j}}, S_{T_{j2}}), K_S\}$

Fig. 3. The storage structure of S.

between S and T is vulnerable to various malicious attacks, such as Man-in-Middle attack, desynchronization attack, replay attack, etc. The detailed process of communication interaction during the authentication phase is depicted in Fig. 4. The detailed authentication steps of the proposed protocol are as follows.

Step1: The tag sends messages to the server as $T \xrightarrow{M_1:\{SID_T^i, C_T, N_T^*\}} S$

(1) Each new round of authentication session is initiated by T. T first selects SID_T and K_S, and generated random nonce N_T by $PRNG(\cdot)$ for the i-round authentication session, respectively.
(2) Next, T computes $N_T^* = N_T \oplus K_S$, $C_T = C_{Arbiter_T} \oplus N_T$.
(3) Finally, T sends a messages $M_1 : \{SID_T^i, C_T, N_T^*\}$ to S.

Step2: The server sends messages to the tag as $S \xrightarrow{M_2:\{C_i, N_S^*, Res_S\}} T$

(1) Once S receives message $M_1 : \{SID_T^i, C_T, N_T^*\}$, it first extracts the random number $N_T = N_T^* \oplus K_S$ generated by T from N_T^* and then uses N_T to extract $C_{Arbiter_T} = C_T \oplus N_T$ from C_T.
(2) Then, S computes the stored index $Index_T = ht(C_{Arbiter_T})$ of T using $C_{Arbiter_T}$, then reads the record entry$\{(SID_T^i, K_T^i), S_2\}$. Note that if the SID_T^i in the read record entry does not match the one received, then continue reading from the index until a match is found.
(3) Next, S randomly generates a challenge C_i and random number N_S by $PRNG(\cdot)$, and then computes $N_S^* = K_T^i \oplus N_S$, $Res_S = h(C_i, N_T \| K_T^i \| N_S^*)$.
(4) Finally, S sends a messages $M_2 : \{C_i, N_S^*, Res_S\}$ to T.

Step3: The tag sends messages to the server as $T \xrightarrow{M_3:\{R_T, S_{T_x}, S_{T_y}, Res_T\}} S$

(1) Once T receives $M_2 : \{C_i, N_S^*, Res_S\}$, it first checks the integrity of M_2. T computes $Res'_S = h(C_i \| N_T \| K_T^i \| N_S^*)$ using the received N_S^* and C_i and its locally stored K_T^i, N_T. The integrity of Res_S is verified by checking the equation $Res'_S \overset{?}{=} Res_S$. If the equation holds, the expected S is authenticated, and then T continues with the subsequent authentication process. Otherwise, Res_S can not be authencated by T and the protocol terminates.

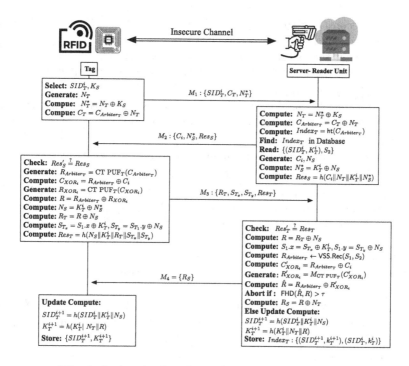

Fig. 4. Authentication phase of the proposed protocol.

(2) Then, T first takes $C_{Arbiter}$ as the input of the CT PUF_T to generate the response $R_{Arbiter_T} = \mathrm{CT}\ \mathrm{PUF}_T(C_{Arbiter_T})$. Then the tag's CT PUF_T Computes the real input challenge $C_{XOR_i} = R_{Arbiter_T} \oplus C_i$. And then, the C_{XOR_i} as the input to obtain the $R_{XOR_i} = \mathrm{CT}\ \mathrm{PUF}_T(C_{XOR_i})$. Then, the real response $R = R_{Arbiter_T} \oplus R_{XOR_i}$ of CT PUF_T is generated.

(3) Next, T extracts the random number $N_S = K_T^i \oplus N_S^*$ generated by S from N_S^* and then computes $R_T = R \oplus N_S$, $S_{T_x} = S_1.x \oplus K_T^i$, $S_{T_y} = S_{T_1}.y \oplus N_S$ and $Res_T = h(N_S\|K_T^i\|R_T\|S_{T_x}\|S_{T_y})$.

(4) Finally, T sends a messages $M_3 : \{R_T, S_{T_x}, S_{T_y}, Res_T\}$ to S.

Step4: The server sends messages to the tag as $S \xrightarrow{M_4:\{R_S\}} T$

(1) Once S receives $M_3 : \{R_T, S_{T_x}, S_{T_y}, Res_T\}$, it first checks the integrity of M_3. S computes $Res_T' = h(N_S\|K_T^i\|R_T\|S_{T_x}\|S_{T_y})$ using the received R_T, S_{T_x}, S_{T_y} and its locally stored K_T^i, N_S. The integrity of Res_T is verified by checking the equation $Res_T' \overset{?}{=} Res_T$. If the equation holds, the expected T is authenticated, and then S continues with the subsequent authentication process. Otherwise, Res_T can not be authencated by S and the protocol terminates.

(2) Then, S extracts the real response $R = R_T \oplus N_S$ of CT PUF_T from R_T, and then, S computes $R_T = R \oplus N_S$, $S_1.x = S_{T_x} \oplus K_T^i$, $S_1.y = S_{T_y} \oplus N_S$.

(3) Next, S reconstruct the $R_{Arbiter}$ by the obtained $S_1 = (S_1.x), S_1.y)$ and S_2 stored by itself.

    (a) Note that the validity of S_1 needs to be verified by VSS.Verify($\cdot$). S can verify the correctness of the share S_1 by checking the equation g^{S_1} mod $p \stackrel{?}{=} \prod_{j=0}^{1} \alpha_j^{1^j}$ mod p.

    (b) If the equation holds, then S_1 is valid and S could reconstruct $R_{Arbiter}$. Otherwise it is fail, and the protocol terminates.

(4) Next, S computes $C'_{XOR_i} = R_{Arbiter_T} \oplus C_i$, and then takes C'_{XOR_i} as input of the trained soft model $M_{CT\ PUF_T}$ to generates $R'_{XOR_i} = M_{CT\ PUF_T}(C'_{XOR_i})$, then computes $\hat{R} = R_{Arbiter_T} \oplus R'_{XOR_i}$. And then, S computes the hamming distance $\mathsf{FHD}(R, \hat{R})$. If $\mathsf{FHD}(R, \hat{R}) \leq \tau$ holds, T is verified successfully by S, otherwise it is fail and the protocol terminates.

(5) Then, S computes $SID_T^{i+1} = h(SID_T^i \| K_T^i \| N_S)$, $K_T^{i+1} = h(K_T^i \| N_T \| R)$ for the next authentication session round, and then stores $Index_T$: $\{(SID_T^{i+1}, K_T^{i+1}), (SID_T^i, K_T^i)\}$.

(6) Then, S computes $R_S = R \oplus N_T$ and sends a message $M_4 : \{R_S = R \oplus N_T\}$ to T.

(7) Once T receives $M_4 : \{R_S = R \oplus N_T\}$, it first extracts $R' = R_S \oplus N_T$ from R_S, and checks the correctness of $R' \stackrel{?}{=} R$. If it holds, then T computes $SID_T^{i+1} = h(SID_T^i \| K_T^i \| N_S)$, $K_T^{i+1} = h(K_T^i| N_T \| R)$ for the next round authentication session, and stores $\{SID_T^{i+1}, K_T^{i+1}\}$. Otherwise, T terminates the protocol and does not update the key parameters.

4   BAN Logic Analysis and Simulation Using the Scyther

In this section, we analyze the correctness and security of the proposed protocol using the BAN [31] logic formally, and simulate the proposed protocol using the Scyther informally. Note that we only analyze the correctness and security of communication for the authentication phase and not for the initialization phase which is in a secure environment.

4.1   BAN Logical Analysis

Authentication protocol is described by enumerating their communication messages, so the protocol communication sessions are first described formally in the BAN logic language. Inevitably, the protocol must make initial assumptions and build the set of initial assumptions. Then, the communication messages of the protocol are converted into formal formulas that the BAN logic can recognize to create an idealized protocol model. Next, the proving goals to be proved are specified. Finally, these proving goals are proved according to the BAN logical postulates. The BAN logical formal analysis of the proposed protocol is specified as follows.

Basic Notations and Logical Postulates. The basic BAN-logic proof notations as shown in Appendix D.1 Table 7. The five BAN logical postulates are used when we analysis the protocol, as shown in Appendix D.2.

Idealized Model of the Protocol. According to the basic notation of BAN logic listed in Table 7, the authentication communication interaction messages of the proposed protocol are converted into an idealized model. There are four authentication message: **M1:** $S \triangleleft \{SID_T^i, \{C_T\}_{N_T}, \{N_T^*\}_{K_S}\}$, **M2:** $T \triangleleft \{C_i, \{N_S^*\}_{K_T^i}, \{Res_S\}_{K_T^i}\}$, **M3:** $S \triangleleft \{\{R_T\}_{N_S}, \{S_T\}_{K_T^i}, \{Res_T\}_{K_T^i}\}$. **M4:** $T \triangleleft \{R_S\}_{N_T}\}$, With the BAN logical postulates R4, we have the idealized model of session messages between S and T in the protocol. The detailed session message are listed in the Table 2.

Table 2. The idealized model of the protocol

Message	Message	Message
M1: $S \triangleleft \{N_T^*\}_{K_S}$	**M2:** $S \triangleleft \{C_T\}_{N_T}$	**M3:** $S \triangleleft \{Res_S\}_{N_T, K_T^i}$
M4: $T \triangleleft \{N_S^*\}_{K_T^i}$	**M5:** $T \triangleleft \langle C_i \rangle_{K_T^i, N_T}$	**M6:** $S \triangleleft \{Res_T\}_{K_T^i, N_S}$
M7: $T \triangleleft \{R_T\}_{N_S}$	**M8:** $S \triangleleft \{S_{T_x}\}_{K_T^i}$	**M9:** $S \triangleleft \{S_{T_y}\}_{N_S}$
M10: $T \triangleleft \{R\}_{N_T}$		

Initiated Assumptions of Protocol. The basic initial assumptions followed in the protocol are shown in Table 3.

Table 3. The initial assumptions of the protocol

Assumption	Assumption	Assumption
A1: $S \mid\equiv S \xleftrightarrow{K_S} T$	**A2:** $T \mid\equiv T \xleftrightarrow{K_S} S$	**A3:** $S \mid\equiv S \xleftrightarrow{K_T^i} T$
A4: $T \mid\equiv T \xleftrightarrow{K_T^i} S$	**A5:** $S \mid\equiv \#(N_T)$	**A6:** $T \mid\equiv \#(N_S)$
A7: $S \mid\equiv \#(N_S)$	**A8:** $T \mid\equiv \#(N_T)$	**A9:** $S \mid\equiv T \mid\Rightarrow N_T^*$
A10: $S \mid\equiv T \mid\Rightarrow C_T$	**A11:** $T \mid\equiv S \mid\Rightarrow C_i$	**A12:** $T \mid\equiv S \mid\Rightarrow N_S^*$
A13: $T \mid\equiv S \mid\Rightarrow Res_S$	**A14:** $S \mid\equiv T \mid\Rightarrow R_T$	**A15:** $S \mid\equiv T \mid\Rightarrow S_{T_x}$
A16: $S \mid\equiv T \mid\Rightarrow S_{T_y}$	**A17:** $S \mid\equiv T \mid\Rightarrow Res_T$	**A18:** $S \mid\equiv T \mid\Rightarrow S_{T_y}$
A19: $T \mid\equiv S \mid\Rightarrow R_S$		

Proving Goals of the Protocol. The proving goals of the protocol are listed in Table 4. The detailed process of proving the goals is as follows.

- **For G1:** $S \mid\equiv N_T^*$: With the A1, M1, and R1, we have Result1: $S \mid\equiv T \mid\sim N_T^*$. Then, with the A5 and R5, we have Result2: $S \mid\equiv \#(N_T^*)$. Then, with the Result1, Result2 and R3, we have Result3: $S \mid\equiv T \mid\equiv N_T^*$. Finally, with A9, Result3 and R2, we have G1: $S \mid\equiv N_T^*$.

Table 4. The proving goals of the protocol

Proving goal	Proving goal	Proving goal	Proving goal
G1: $S \mid\equiv N_T^*$	**G2**: $S \mid\equiv C_T$	**G3**: $T \mid\equiv Res_S$	**G4**: $T \mid\equiv C_i$
G5: $T \mid\equiv N_S^*$	**G6**: $S \mid\equiv Res_T$	**G7**: $S \mid\equiv R_T$	**G8**: $S \mid\equiv S_{T_x}$
G9: $S \mid\equiv S_{T_y}$	**G10**: $T \mid\equiv R_S$		

- **For G2:** $S \mid\equiv C_T$**:** With the **G1**,M2 and R1, we have Result1: $S \mid\equiv T \mid\sim C_T$. Then, with the A5 and R5, we have Result2: $S \mid\equiv \#(C_T)$. Then, with the Result1, Result2 and R3, we have Result3: $S \mid\equiv T \mid\equiv C_T$. Finally, with A10, Result3 and R2, we have G2: $S \mid\equiv C_T$.
- **For G3:** $T \mid\equiv Res_S$**:** With the A4, M3 and R1, we have Result1: $T \mid\equiv S \mid\sim Res_S$. Then, with the A8, and R5, we have Result2: $T \mid\equiv \#(Res_S)$. Then, with the Result1, Result2 and R3, we have Result3: $T \mid\equiv S \mid\equiv Res_S$. Finally, with A13, Result3 and R2, we have G3: $S \mid\equiv Res_S$.
- **For G4:** $T \mid\equiv C_i$**,G5:**$T \mid\equiv N_S^*$**:** The security of G4 and G5 is equivalent to that of G5, so as long as the security of G3 is proved, the security of G4 and G5 is also proved.
- **For G6:** $S \mid\equiv Res_T$**:** With the A3, M6 and R1, we have Result1: $S \mid\equiv T \mid\sim Res_T$. Then, with the A7, and R5, we have Result2: $T \mid\equiv \#(Res_T)$. Then, with the Result1, Result2 and R3, we have Result3: $S \mid\equiv T \mid\equiv Res_T$. Finally, with A17, Result3 and R2, we have G6: $S \mid\equiv Res_T$.
- **For G7:** $S \mid\equiv R_T$, **G8:** $S \mid\equiv S_{T_x}$, **G9:** $S \mid\equiv S_{T_y}$**:** The security of G7, G8 and G9 is equivalent to that of G6, so as long as the security of G6 is proved, the security of G7, G8 and G9 is also proved.
- **For G10:** $T \mid\equiv R_S$**:** With the AX, M10 and R1, we have Result1: $T \mid\equiv S \mid\sim R_S$. Then, with the A8, and R5, we have Result2: $T \mid\equiv \#(R_S)$. Then, with the Result1, Result2 and R3, we have Result3: $T \mid\equiv S \mid\equiv R_S$. Finally, with A19, Result3 and R2, we have G10: $S \mid\equiv R_S$.

4.2   Simulation Using the Scyther

The Security Protocol Description Language (SPDL) description for function and messages, the SPDL description for role S and for role T in Appendix E. The verification result of Scyther simulation as shown in Appendix E Fig. 6.

5   Security Analysis

In Sect. 2, we provide the security requirements and potential attacks of the RFID system. In this section, we present an detailed analysis of the security of the proposed protocol according to the above security requirements.

Proposition 1 (Data Integrity). *The proposed protocol provides an effective verification mechanism for the data integrity of communication interaction messages.*

Proof. The data integrity of the communication message is an evidence to verify that the session information has not been tampered with by the adversary. The mutual authentication communication messages $M_2 : \{C_i, N_S^*, Res_S\}$, $M_3 : \{R_T, S_{T_x}, S_{T_y}, Res_T\}$ between S and T not only hide the key parameters, but also the Res_S and Res_T provide assurance for the integrity of M_1 and M_2, respectively. $Res_S = h(C_i \| N_T \| K_T^i \| N_S^*)$ is a hash value which is obtained by hashing $C_i \| N_T \| K_T^i \| N_S^*$, where C_i, N_T^* are part of M_1, and K_T^i and N_T are the parameters shared by S and T. Relying on the one-way nature of the hash function, the adversary cannot efficiently compute the matching Res_S when it can only tamper with C_i and N_S^* but does not gain access to K_T^i and N_T. For $Res_T = h(N_S \| K_T^i \| R_T \| S_{T_x} \| S_{T_y})$, the same applies. Thus, the integrity of the communication messages during mutual authentication of S and T is efficiently detected whenever they suffer from tampering damage. Therefore, we claim that the proposed protocol can effectively ensure data integrity.

Proposition 2 (Data Confidentiality). *The proposed protocol is able to ensure the confidentiality of the communication messages.*

Proof. Our protocol contains four communication messages, $M_1 : \{SID_T^i, C_T, N_T^*\}$, $M_2 : \{C_i, N_S^*, Res_S\}$, $M_3 : \{R_T, S_{T_x}, S_{T_y}, Res_T\}$ and $M_4 : \{R_S\}$. All messages except SID_T^i and C_i are transmitted after obfuscated encryption, See Sect. 3.3 for details. In addition, the obfuscated key parameters are shared only by the legitimate T and S, so the adversary cannot obtain valid secret data through the authentication message. Therefore, the proposed protocol can guarantee the data confidentiality of communication messages.

Proposition 3 (Anonymity). *The proposed protocol utilizes an updated pseudonymous identity mechanism to effectively protect the identity privacy of the tag, and an adversary cannot infer the true identity of the tag through authentication messages.*

Proof. Anonymity also means untraceability, and T does not specify a unique identity in our protocol. The shadow identity SID_T^i is only a momentary value in communication session round i. $SID_T^{i+1} = h(SID_T^i \| K_T^i \| N_S)$ will be updated according to the newly generated random number N_S and key parameters K_T^i as long as the authentication communication is successfully executed. The adversary cannot infer the tag's identity from the session messages M_1, M_2, M_3, M_4. In particular, according to the update mechanism SID_T^i of M_1 in two different rounds $(SID_T^i, SID_T^{i+1}|)$ are distinct and without direct correlation. Once T receives $M_4 = \{R_S\}$ and the contained R is successfully checked, then T computes $SID_T^{i+1} = h(SID_T^i \| K_T^i \| N_S)$, $K_T^{i+1} = h(K_T^i \| N_T \| R)$, and stores $\{SID_T^{i+1}, K_T^{i+1}\}$. Therefore, the adversary cannot identify T based on the SID_T^i and performs constant tracking attacks.

Proposition 4 (Mutual Authentication). *It is crucial in detecting adversaries disguised as legitimate entities in untrustworthy environments. The proposed protocol implements mutual authentication between S and T. The authentication terminates once one party cannot be authenticated by the other party.*

Proof. The **Step3 and Step4 of the authentication phase** in our protocol accomplish S and T mutual authentication. In Step3, T validates the validity of S by computing $Res'_S = h(C_i\|N_T\|K_T^i\|N_S^*)$, where N_S^* and C_i are received messages, K_T^i and N_T are locally stored shared key. As only a legitimate S holds the key parameter K_T^i and N_T shared with T to generate the matching message $Res_S = h(C_i\|N_T\|K_T^i\|N_S^*)$ with Res'. Therefore, if the equation $Res'_S \stackrel{?}{=} Res_S$ verifies successfully, it means that T verifies S as a legitimate server. Similarly, in step4 S first verifies whether the equation $Res'_T \stackrel{?}{=} Res_T$ holds or not. If it holds, then S has access to the secret share used to reconstruct $\hat{R}$ and the real response R of CT PUF_T. Then the final response $\hat{R}$ of $M_{\mathrm{CT\ PUF}_T}$ is generated. Finally, the validity of R is determined by comparing the hamming distance $\mathsf{FHD}(R, \hat{R})$. Obviously, according to the natural characteristics of CT PUF_T, only a legitimate tag can generate R that satisfies $\mathsf{FHD}(R, \hat{R}) \leq \tau$. If $\mathsf{FHD}(R, \hat{R}) \leq \tau$ verifies successfully, it means that S verifies T as a legitimate Tag. Therefore, the proposed protocol achieves mutual authentication of S and T.

Proposition 5 (Forward Security). *The interactive session messages for the authenticated communication of the proposed protocol ensure forward security.*

Proof. Our protocols have remarkable characteristics to ensure forward security. Authenticated communication of all messages are generated with a fresh random number N_S or N_T; moreover, S and T have not stored these nonces. Therefore, an adversary who intercepts the communication message but has no access to the random numbers N_S or N_T and key parameters K_T^i, K_S cannot effectively guess the exact valid key parameters.

Proposition 6 (Against the Man-in-Middle Attack). *The proposed protocol ensures security even if the authenticated communication is subject to the man-in-the-middle attacks.*

Proof. As we analyzed in the **Data Integrity** security property, our protocol provides verification of the integrity of communication messages. The integrity of the communication interaction messages M_2 and M_3 during mutual authentication between S and T can be effectively verified. For M_2, sent by the legitimate S suffers from a man-in-the-middle attack and is tampered with as $M'_2 : \{C'_i, N_S^{*\prime}, Res'_S\}$. In our protocol, M_2 contains three messages C_i, N_S^* and Res_S. The adversary can only effectively tamper with messages C_i, N_S^* and not Res_S, because the hash function ensures the security of Res_S. In turn, $Res_S = h(C_i, N_T\|K_T^i\|N_S^*)$ is generated by C_i, N_S^* as parameters, so C_i, N_S^*, and Res_S integrity are bound together. Hence, an adversary cannot tamper against the entire M_2 without being detected. Similarly, an adversary cannot tamper against the entire M_3 without being detected. Therefore, our protocol can effectively resist man-in-the-middle attacks.

Proposition 7 (Against the Replay Attack). *The proposed protocol ensures that a round of communication messages can only be validly applied for the authentication round. The adversary cannot replay the captured communication messages to spoof T or S and be authenticated.*

Proof. In our protocol, the generation of all the authentication communication messages and the updating of secret parameters utilize random numbers N_S, N_T freshly generated by S and T in each round of the session. The freshness of the authenticated message is guaranteed using a new random number generated each round session so that the adversary cannot be authenticated by S or T by replaying the captured message. Therefore, our protocol can effectively resist replay attacks.

Proposition 8 (Against the Desynchronization Attack). *The proposed protocol can ensure proper authenticated communication in subsequent session rounds even if it suffers from the desynchronization attacks.*

Proof. In our protocol, to resist potential desynchronization attacks, T does not initiate the update immediately after sending the message M_3. Instead, T needs to wait for $M_4 : \{R_S\}$ sent by S and performs the update only after the correctness of $R' = R_S \oplus N_T$ extracted from M_4 is verified($R' \overset{?}{=} R$). The adversary blocks M_4 to launch a desynchronization attack. S has completed the update operation when sending M_4, but T will not be updated because it does not correctly receive M_4. To solve this problem, S stores not only the updated secret parameters $SID_T^{i+1} = h(SID_T^i \| K_T^i \| N_S)$, $K_T^{i+1} = h(K_T^i \| N_T \| R)$ for communication session round $i+1$ but also the secret parameter (SID_T^i, k_T^i) of the successful authentication round i. After suffering a desynchronization attack, S initiates a new authentication session round $i+1$ with T. Since T does not update synchronously with S, the SID_T^{i+1}(actually SID_T^i) sent by T in $M1$ cannot match the SID_T^{i+1} in S. At this point, S tries to match it with SID_T^i and can successfully match. Then S continues the subsequent authentication process. Finally, if the authentication communication round $i+1$ is executed completely and successfully, S and T will synchronously update. Therefore, our protocol can effectively resist desynchronization attacks.

Proposition 9 (Against the Cloning Attack). *The proposed protocol ensures the security of the T in case of the physical attacks or the cloning attacks.*

Proof. In our protocol, the PUF structure equipped by the tag is the CT PUF structure, which uses the bitwise XOR mechanism to hide the relationship between the real challenge and the real response. ($R_{Arbiter_T} = $ CT $PUF_T(C_{Arbiter_T})$, $C_{XOR_i} = R_{Arbiter_T} \oplus C_i$, $R_{XOR_i} = $ CT $PUF_T(C_{XOR_i})$, $R = R_{Arbiter_T} \oplus R_{XOR_i}$) In addition, we do not explicitly store the $CRPs$ of CT PUF_T in S, but take advantage of VSS to store the $R_{Arbiter_T}$ in a decentralized method. (see Sect. 3.3 Setup Phase for detailed.) Therefore, our protocol can effectively resist cloning attacks (machine learning attacks).

Proposition 10 (Against the Impersonation Attack). *The proposed protocol ensures security against the impersonation attacks.*

Proof. Counterfeiting attacks are divided into tag impersonation and server impersonation. For S impersonation, the adversary first blocks the message

$M_2 : \{C_i, N_S^*, Res_S\}$, then personates to be a legitimate S' to communicate with T. In our protocol, if the adversary tries to impersonate S' by forging the message M_2', the output is "failed" when T checks $Res_S \stackrel{?}{=} Res_S'$, since the secret parameters N_T, K_T, N_S shared by S and T are hidden in M_2. The adversary does not have access to these parameters and relying on the one-way nature of the hash function Res_S cannot be modified. Similarly, for T impersonation, the adversary first blocks the message $M_3 : \{R_T, S_{T_x}, S_{T_y}, Res_T\}$, then personates to be a legitimate S' to communicate with T. The counterfeit message M_3 cannot be verified. Therefore, our protocol can resistance to impersonation attacks.

A detailed comparison of the security properties and resistance to some malicious attacks among our protocol and existing PUF-based RFID authentication protocols [6, 23, 24] is listed in the Table 5.

Table 5. Security comparison

Security properties	Akgün et al. [23]	Liang et al. [24]	Gope et al. [6]	Our protocol
SP1	●	●	●	●
SP2	●	●	●	●
SP3	●	●	●	●
SP4	●	●	●	●
SP5	○	●	●	●
SP6	●	●	●	●
SP7	●	○	●	●
SP8	◐	○	◐	●
SP9	○	●	○	●
SP10	●	○	●	●
SP11	●	●	○	●
SP12	●	○	○	●

Notes: **SP1**: Data Integrity; **SP2**: Data Confidentiality; **SP3**: Anonymity; **SP4**: Mutual Authentication; **SP5**: Forward Security; **SP6**: Against Man-in-Middle Attacks; **SP7**: Against Replay Attacks; **SP8**: Against Desynchronization Attacks; **SP9**: Against Cloning Attacks; **SP10**: Against Impersonation Attacks; **SP11**: Without explicit $CRPs$ in S(reader/verifier); **SP12**: Scalability;
●: satisfied SP; ◐: partially satisfied SP; ○: not satisfied SP;

6   Performance Evaluation

In this section, we compare our protocol with existing typical RFID authentication schemes such as Akgün et al. [23], Liang et al. [24], Gope et al. [6] in terms of cost of storage space for tags, communication overhead, and tag computation overhead for tags. The length of each parameter in our protocol is 96-bit.

The parameters stored by T in the proposed protocol include a shadow identity SID_T^i, a secret key K_T^i of T, a secret key K_S of S, a secret share S_1 of the secret $R_{Arbiter_T}$, and a challenge $C_{Arbiter}$ of CT PUF$_T$. As a result, the total storage cost of T is 580-bit.

In our protocol, the computation methods involved in the process of T generation of authentication messages and verification of communication messages contain four types, which are lightweight hash function operation $h(\cdot)$, pseudo-random number generator operation $PRNG(\cdot)$, XOR operation $\oplus$, and CT PUF response generation operation CT PUF$_T(\cdot)$.

To complete the mutual authentication between S and T, there are four interactive communication messages as $M_1 : \{SID_T^i, C_T, N_T^*\}$, $M_2 : \{C_i, N_S^*, Res_S\}$, $M_3 : \{R_T, S_{T_x}, S_{T_y}, Res_T\}$, and $M_4 : \{R_S\}$, which are transmitted during a complete round of authentication session. As a result, the total communication overhead to successfully complete a communication session between S and T is 1056-bit.

In summary, the detailed comparison results of the performance evaluation of the proposed protocol with other protocols [6,23,24] are listed in Table 6.

Table 6. Performance comparison

	Akgün et al. [23]	Liang et al. [24]	Gope et al. [6]	Our protocol
Cost of storage space for tags	512-bit	0-bit	*$(2L+2L \cdot n)$-bit	580-bit
Communication overhead	896-bit	2048-bit	*$8L$-bit	1056-bit
Computation overhead for tags	$4h(\cdot) +$ $2P(\cdot) +$ $1PRNG(\cdot)$	$2\oplus+2P(\cdot)+$ $2PRNG +$ $1\text{Pad}(\cdot) +$ $1\text{Sea}(\cdot) +$ $1\text{Match}(\cdot)$	$3 \oplus +6h(\cdot) +$ $2P(\cdot) +$ $1PRNG(\cdot) +$ $1\text{FE.Gen}(\cdot)$	$8 \oplus +4h(\cdot) +$ $2\text{CT PUF}_T(\cdot) +$ $1PRNG(\cdot)$

Notes: *:Not specified, $L = m$-bit;

7   Conclusion

In this paper, we concentrate on RFID system security requirements and potential malicious attacks, and in particular, we analyze the performance and security of the scheme by Gope et al. We investigate and analyze that cannot provide all the security requirements of the described RFID system. To address these security vulnerabilities and performance flaws, we propose a secure lightweight authentication scheme based on CT PUF, VSS and hash table mechanism. In our protocol, the server takes advantage of the hash table mechanism to store the tag entries and thus avoid exhaustive search during query and update. And with the help of VSS to achieve no explicit storage of $CRPs(CRPs_{Arbiter_T})$ at the server. The CT PUF utilizes the bit-wise XOR obfuscation mechanism to hide the mapping relationship between challenge and response pairs. Therefore, the CT PUF structure built into the tag can further enhance the security of the tag against machine learning attacks. In the future, we will further explore mutual authentication protocols based on distributed storage such as blockchain technology and further extend the application scenarios.

Appendix

A   Analysis of the Gope et al.'s Scheme

In this section, we analyze the high storage cost of tag and the security vulnerabilities of the authentication scheme proposed by Gope et al. in [6],

A.1   Performance and Security Analysis of Gope's Scheme

In this subsection, we analyze the performance and security issues of the Gope et al.'s scheme [6]. Specifically, the excessive storage overhead of low-cost tags and potential asynchronous attacks are analyzed, respectively. A detailed process is provided below.

Performance Analysis. We observe that S generates a set of shadow identities and emergency key pairs (SID, K_{em}) for T in the initialization phase of the protocol proposed by Gope et al. Specifically, a set of key pairs is pre-stored in order to resist desynchronization attacks, which is actually n sets of shadow identity identities sid and secret keys sk. The key parameters stored in T include $\{(SID_T^i, sk)\}$ and $(SID, K_{em}) = \{(sid_1, k_{em1}), (sid_2, k_{em2}), \ldots, (sid_n, k_{em})\}$. Obviously, the pre-stored set of contingency key pairs directly increases the storage overhead of the tag. In order to make the scheme more robust against desynchronization attacks, a larger number of pre-stored emergency key pairs must be required. The storage overhead of tag increases linearly as the number of contingency key pairs increases, which is unfriendly to low-cost RFID tags. And we also note that S stores all the CRPs of tag's PUF module, which is also a potential threat for tag's PUF module to be subjected to machine learning attacks. We also note that S stores all the CRPs of the PUF module of tag, which is also a potential threat to the PUF module of tag, such as an adversary initiates a machine learning modeling attack by collecting CRPs. There have been research works on machine learning attacks against various PUF structures such as Arbiter PUFs, Configurable RO PUFs, SRAM PUFs, etc.

Security Analysis. The communication of the protocol suffers from a desynchronization attack, more specifically, the adversary blocks the session message M_3, and S cannot receive M_3 correctly. In this point, T performs the update computation immediately after sending the session message M_3, which is blocked by the adversary so that S does not receive the message properly and does not perform any computation. The adversary successfully performs a desynchronization attack on S and T. The key parameter of both is not updated synchronously. Then S and T initiate a new authenticated communication round, the other party cannot successfully authenticate the session message generated by one party because their key parameters lose synchronization. In this case, S and T initiate a new authentication session using the pre-stored (SID, K_{em}) and (C_{em}, R_{em}). Specifically, T randomly selects one of the unused pairs of $(sid_x, k_{emx}) \in (SID, K_{em})$ from the pre-stored (SID, K_{em}), and similarly, S randomly selects a pair of $CRPs \in (C_{em}, R_{em})$ from the pre-stored (C_{em}, R_{em}) for authentication communication. Once each time a pair is $(sid_x, k_{emx}) \in (SID, K_{em})$ or $CRPs \in (C_{em}, R_{em})$ used, it needs to be deleted from both S and T respectively, which is important because no update mechanism is provided for contingency pairs. Obviously, according to the (SID, K_{em}) and (C_{em}, R_{em}) pre-stored by T and S respectively, so the communication between S and T can only resist at most n desynchronization attacks. Although Gope states that their scheme can resist desynchronization attacks, our analysis shows that the scheme cannot resist n consecutive desynchronization attacks. Specifically, T appends a "Re-Load" message to M_1 in the $i + n$ authentication session round after it has suffered $n - 1$ desynchronization attacks. When S receives the "Re-Load" message, it generates a new set of pairs and sends them to T with session key K_i encryption. According to the protocol authentication procedure, the session key $K_i = \mathsf{FE.Rec}(R_i, hd_i)$ is reconstructed by S after receiving M_3. However, the adversary initiates a desynchronization attack that precisely blocks M_3, hence S cannot reconstruct the K_i shared with T. Therefore, the scheme cannot resist the desynchronization attack.

B   Physical Unclonable Functions

According to the number of Challenge-Response Pairs $(CRPs)$ generated, PUF can be divided into strong PUF and weak PUF types. Since only a limited number of $CRPs$ can be generated for weak PUFs, once an adversary gains access to $CRPs$, the adversary can easily clone all $CRPs$, which is impossible with strong PUFs. The static random access memory PUF (SRAM PUF) is classified as weak because only a limited number of $CRPs$ can be generated. In contrast, traditional PUFs with large $CRPs$ (such as arbitrator PUFs) are classified as strong PUFs, which are commonly used in authentication protocols [26–28]. The PUF structure selected for placement in the tag is the SRAM PUF in the Gope et al. scheme. However, Talukder et al. point out that memory-based PUFs are vulnerable as well in [28].

Configurable Tristate Physical Unclonable Function (CT PUF). Zhang et al. [29] proposed configurable tristate PUF (CT PUF) to solve the vulnerability of PUF against the machine learning modeling attack. To improve its security, the CT PUF use the bit-wise XOR obfuscation mechanism to hide the mapping relationship between challenge and response pairs. The XOR bit-wise obfuscation mechanism consists of two phases, the Preparation phase and the Obfuscation phase. The detailed as depicted in Fig. 5.

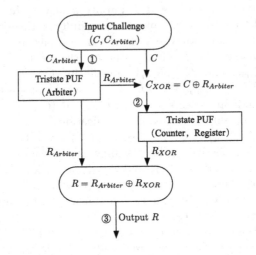

Fig. 5. The bitwise XOR obfuscation mechanism [29].

C   Feldman's (t, n)-threshold Verifiable Secret Sharing Scheme

Feldman proposed a non-interactive scheme for achieving verifiability in Shamir's threshold secret sharing scheme in [30]. The following three algorithms are included.

- VSS.Share($\cdot$): For a secret s. First, the dealer selects a random polynomial $(a_0 = s)$:

$$F(x) = a_0 + a_1 x + a_2 x^2 + \cdots + a_{t-1} x^{t-1}, a_0, a_1, \cdots, a_{t-1} \in_R \mathbb{Z}_n.$$

Next, the dealer distributes $s_i = F(i), i = 1, 2, \cdots, m$ to the P_i over a secure channel. Meanwhile, the dealer broadcasts the commitments $\alpha = \{\alpha_j = g^{a_j}, 0 \le j \le t - 1\}$.
- VSS.Verify($\cdot$): Then, once P_i receives s_i, the validity of the each share can be verified by the Eq. (1).

$$g^{s_j} = \prod_{i=0}^{t-1} \alpha_i^{j^i}. \tag{1}$$

– VSS.Rec($\cdot$): t parties can reconstruct the secret. The parties first check the validity of the received share s_i by comparing the Eq. (1). If it holds, then the s can be reconstruct with Lagrange Interpolation (the Eq. (2)).

$$P(0) = \sum_{i=0}^{t-1} P(x_i) \prod_{\substack{j=0 \\ j \neq i}}^{t-1} \frac{(0 - x_j)}{x_i - x_j} = s. \tag{2}$$

D Basic Notations and Logical Postulates of BAN Logical

D.1 Basic Notations

The basic notations and descriptions of BAN logic are listed in Table 7.

Table 7. Basic notations of BAN logical

Notation	Description	Notation	Description
$P \models X$	P believes X	$P \triangleleft X$	P sees X
$P \mid\sim X$	P once said X	$P \mid\Rightarrow X$	P has jurisdiction over X
$\#(X)$	X is freshness	$P \xleftrightarrow{K} Q$	P and Q share the K
$\{X\}_K$	X encrypted under the K	$\langle X \rangle_K$	X hasded by the K

D.2 Logical Postulates

The logical postulates and descriptions of BAN logic are shown as follows.

Lemma 1 (R1:The message-meaning rules). *If P believes that the key K is shared with Q and receives a message X encrypted by K: $\{X\}_K$, then P believes that Q once said the message X.*

$$\frac{P \models P \xleftrightarrow{K} Q, P \triangleleft \{X\}_K}{P \models Q \mid\sim X} \tag{R1}$$

Lemma 2 (R2:The jurisdiction rule). *If P believes that X could have been uttered only recently and that Q once send message X, then P believed that Q believes the message X.*

$$\frac{P \models Q \mid\Rightarrow X, P \models Q \models X}{P \models X} \tag{R2}$$

Lemma 3 (R3: The nonce-verification rule). *If P believes that X could have been uttered only recently (in the present) and that Q once said X (either in the past or in the present), then P believes that Q believes X.*

$$\frac{P \mid\equiv \#(X), P \mid\equiv Q \mid\sim X}{P \mid\equiv Q \mid\equiv X} \tag{R3}$$

Lemma 4 (R4: The belief rule). *If P believes that Q sends the tuple $\{X, Y\}$, then P believes message X was sent by Q.*

$$\frac{P \triangleleft \{X, Y\}}{P \triangleleft X} \tag{R4}$$

Lemma 5 (R5: The freshness rule). *If P believes that part of the X is fresh, then P believes that the entire $\#(X, Y)$ must also be fresh.*

$$\frac{P \mid\equiv \#(X)}{P \mid\equiv \#(X, Y)} \tag{R5}$$

E   Security Simulation Using Scyther

In this subsection, we evaluate the security level of our protocols using Scyther, a widely accepted tool for analyzing and verifying the security of protocols. The tool provides a user-friendly graphical user interface to facilitate the analysis and verification of complex attack scenarios on protocols.

The Security Protocol Description Language (SPDL) description for function and messages, the SPDL description for role S and the SPDL description for role T as follows. When the protocol model is established, two roles S and R are defined, representing the communication parties server and tag, respectively. In addition, a secret declaration for each message sent and received by the two communication parties. Figure 6 shows the verification result of Scyther simulation, which shows that no attack against the proposed protocol can be detected.

SPDL description for function and messages

```
1   //PUF-Based RFID authentication scheme
2   hashfunction H;              /*Secure Hash function*/
3   const XOR      : Function; /*Bitwise XOR function*/
4   const CTPUF    : Function; /*PUF function */
5   const MTCTPUF  : Function; /*Soft Model function */
6   const CON      : Function; /* Conjunction function*/
7   macro CT        = XOR( CArbiter , NT);
8   macro NTstar    = XOR(NT, KS);
9   macro M1        = CON(SID , CT, NTstar );
10  macro NT'       = XOR(NTstar ,KS);
11  macro CArbiter '= XOR(CT,NT);
```

```
12   macro  NSstar      = XOR(KT,NS);
13   macro  ResS        = H( Ci ,NT' ,KT, NSstar );
14   macro  M2          = CON( Ci , NSstar , ResS );
15   macro  ResS '       = H( Ci ,NT,KT, NSstar );
16   macro  RArbiter    = CTPUF( CArbiter );
17   macro  CXOR        = XOR( RArbiter , Ci );
18   macro  RXOR        = CTPUF(CXOR);
19   macro  R           = XOR( RArbiter ,RXOR);
20   macro  NS'         = XOR(KT, NSstar );
21   macro  RT          = XOR(R, NS');
22   macro  STX         = XOR( S1x ,KT);
23   macro  STY         = XOR( S1y , NS');
24   macro  ResT        = H(NS' ,KT,RT,STX,STY);
25   macro  M3          = CON(RT,  STX,  STY,  ResT );
26   macro  ResT '       = H(NS,KT,RT,STX,STY);
27   macro  R'          = XOR(RT,NS);
28   macro  S1x '        = XOR(STX,KT);
29   macro  S1y '        = XOR(STY,NS);
30   macro  RArbiter '= VSSRec( S1 , S2 );
31   macro  CXOR'       = XOR( RArbiter ' ,Ci );
32   macro  RXOR'       = CTPUF(CXOR');
33   macro  RHat        = XOR( RArbiter ', RArbiter ');
34   macro  RS          = XOR(R, NT');
35   macro  M4          = CON(RS);
36   macro  R'          = XOR(RS, NT);
```

SPDL description for roles S

```
1    role T{
2    var    NS : Nonce;
3    var    Ci : Nonce;
4    fresh NT : Nonce;
5    const KT,KS, CArbiter , RArbiter ,CXOR,RXOR,
6    R, S1x , S1y , SID ,RS, ResS   : Ticket ;
7    send_1 (T,S, M1);
8    recv_2 (S ,T,M2);
9    match ( ResS , ResS ');
10   send_3 (T,S ,M3);
11   recv_4 (S ,T,M4);
12   claim (T, Secret ,CT);
13   claim (T, Secret , NTstar );
14   claim (T, Secret , RArbiter );
15   claim (T, Secret ,R);
16   claim (T, Secret ,RT);
17   claim (T, Secret ,STX);
```

```
18  claim (T, Secret ,STY);
19  claim (T, Secret , ResT );
20  claim (T, Secret ,NT);
21  claim (T, Niagree );
22  claim (T, Nisynch );
23  claim (T, Alive );
24  claim (T, Weakagree );
25  }
```

SPDL description for roles R

```
1   role  S{
2   var    NT  :  Nonce;
3   fresh NS  :  Nonce;
4   fresh Ci  :  Nonce;
5   const KT, KS, C Arbiter , R Arbiter , CXOR, RXOR, R,
6   S1x , S1y , SID , RS , ResS  :  Ticket;
7   recv_1 (T, S,  M1);
8   send_2 (S, T, M2);
9   recv_3 (T, S, M3);
10  match (ResT , ResT ' );
11  send_4 (S, T, M4);
12  claim (S, Secret , NSstar );
13  claim (S, Secret , ResS );
14  claim (S, Secret , RS);
15  claim (S, Secret , NS);
16  claim (S, Niagree );
17  claim (S, Nisynch );
18  claim (S, Alive );
19  claim (S, Weakagree );
20  }
```

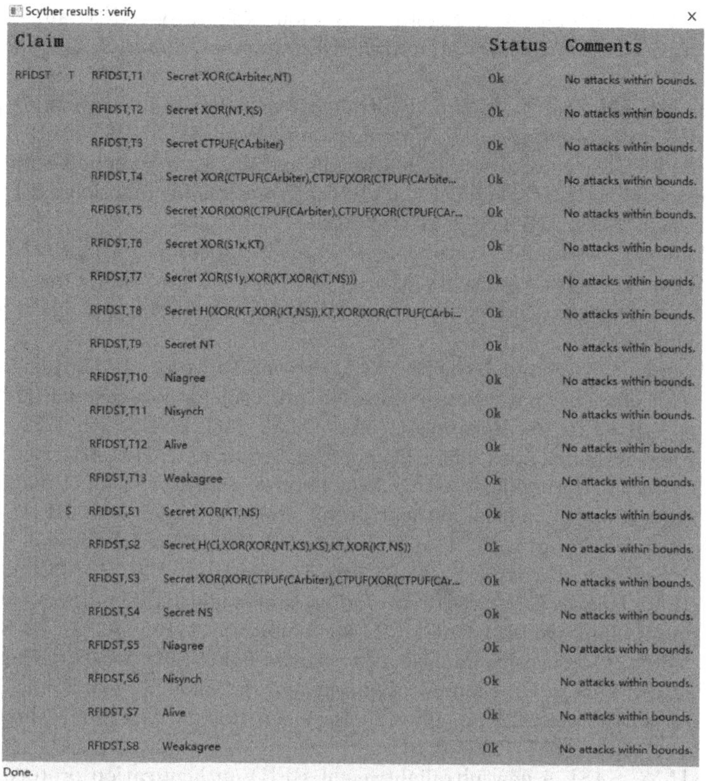

Scyther results : verify

Claim				Status	Comments
RFIDST	T	RFIDST,T1	Secret XOR(CArbiter,NT)	Ok	No attacks within bounds.
		RFIDST,T2	Secret XOR(NT,KS)	Ok	No attacks within bounds.
		RFIDST,T3	Secret CTPUF(CArbiter)	Ok	No attacks within bounds.
		RFIDST,T4	Secret XOR(CTPUF(CArbiter),CTPUF(XOR(CTPUF(CArbite...	Ok	No attacks within bounds.
		RFIDST,T5	Secret XOR(XOR(CTPUF(CArbiter),CTPUF(XOR(CTPUF(CAr...	Ok	No attacks within bounds.
		RFIDST,T6	Secret XOR(S1x,KT)	Ok	No attacks within bounds.
		RFIDST,T7	Secret XOR(S1y,XOR(KT,XOR(KT,NS)))	Ok	No attacks within bounds.
		RFIDST,T8	Secret H(XOR(KT,XOR(KT,NS)),KT,XOR(XOR(CTPUF(CArbi...	Ok	No attacks within bounds.
		RFIDST,T9	Secret NT	Ok	No attacks within bounds.
		RFIDST,T10	Niagree	Ok	No attacks within bounds.
		RFIDST,T11	Nisynch	Ok	No attacks within bounds.
		RFIDST,T12	Alive	Ok	No attacks within bounds.
		RFIDST,T13	Weakagree	Ok	No attacks within bounds.
	S	RFIDST,S1	Secret XOR(KT,NS)	Ok	No attacks within bounds.
		RFIDST,S2	Secret H(Ci,XOR(XOR(NT,KS),KS),KT,XOR(KT,NS))	Ok	No attacks within bounds.
		RFIDST,S3	Secret XOR(XOR(CTPUF(CArbiter),CTPUF(XOR(CTPUF(CAr...	Ok	No attacks within bounds.
		RFIDST,S4	Secret NS	Ok	No attacks within bounds.
		RFIDST,S5	Niagree	Ok	No attacks within bounds.
		RFIDST,S6	Nisynch	Ok	No attacks within bounds.
		RFIDST,S7	Alive	Ok	No attacks within bounds.
		RFIDST,S8	Weakagree	Ok	No attacks within bounds.

Done.

Fig. 6. Verification result of Scyther simulation.

References

1. Huang, Y.J., Yuan, C.C., Chen, M.K., et al.: Hardware implementation of RFID mutual authentication protocol. IEEE Trans. Ind. Electron. **57**(5), 1573–1582 (2009)
2. Aghili, S.F., Mala, H., Schindelhauer, C., et al.: Closed-loop and open-loop authentication protocols for blockchain-based IoT systems. Inf. Process. Manag. **58**(4), 102568 (2021)
3. Salem, F.M., Amin, R.: A privacy-preserving RFID authentication protocol based on El-Gamal cryptosystem for secure TMIS. Inf. Sci. **527**, 382–393 (2020)
4. Agrahari, A.K., Varma, S.: A provably secure RFID authentication protocol based on ECQV for the medical internet of things. Peer-to-Peer Netw. Appl. **14**(3), 1277–1289 (2021)
5. Kumar, V., Ahmad, M., Mishra, D., et al.: RSEAP: RFID based secure and efficient authentication protocol for vehicular cloud computing. Veh. Commun. **22**, 100213 (2020)
6. Gope, P., Millwood, O., Saxena, N.: A provably secure authentication scheme for RFID-enabled UAV applications. Comput. Commun. **166**, 19–25 (2021)

7. Park, H., Roh, H., Lee, W.: Tagora: a collision-exploitative RFID authentication protocol based on cross-layer approach. IEEE Internet Things J. **7**(4), 3571–3585 (2020)
8. Gao, L., Ma, M., Shu, Y., et al.: An ultralightweight RFID authentication protocol with CRC and permutation. J. Netw. Comput. Appl. **41**, 37–46 (2014)
9. Gope, P., Lee, J., Quek, T.Q.S.: Lightweight and practical anonymous authentication protocol for RFID systems using physically unclonable functions. IEEE Trans. Inf. Forensics Secur. **13**(11), 2831–2843 (2018)
10. Peris-Lopez, P., Hernandez-Castro, J C., Estévez-Tapiador, J M., et al.: LMAP: a real lightweight mutual authentication protocol for low-cost RFID tags. In: CONFERENCE 2006, the 2nd Workshop on RFID Security, vol 6, pp. 1–12. Springer, Heidelberg (2006)
11. Peris-Lopez, P., Hernandez-Castro, J.C., Estevez-Tapiador, J.M., Ribagorda, A.: EMAP: an efficient mutual-authentication protocol for low-cost RFID tags. In: Meersman, R., Tari, Z., Herrero, P. (eds.) OTM 2006. LNCS, vol. 4277, pp. 352–361. Springer, Heidelberg (2006). https://doi.org/10.1007/11915034_59
12. Peris-Lopez, P., Hernandez-Castro, J.C., Estevez-Tapiador, J.M., Ribagorda, A.: M^2AP: a minimalist mutual-authentication protocol for low-cost RFID tags. In: Ma, J., Jin, H., Yang, L.T., Tsai, J.J.-P. (eds.) UIC 2006. LNCS, vol. 4159, pp. 912–923. Springer, Heidelberg (2006). https://doi.org/10.1007/11833529_93
13. Chien, H.Y., Huang, C.W.: Security of ultra-lightweight RFID authentication protocols and its improvements. ACM SIGOPS Oper. Syst. Rev. **41**(4), 83–86 (2007)
14. Li, T., Wang, G.: Security analysis of two ultra-lightweight RFID authentication protocols. In: Venter, H., Eloff, M., Labuschagne, L., Eloff, J., von Solms, R. (eds.) SEC 2007. IIFIP, vol. 232, pp. 109–120. Springer, Boston, MA (2007). https://doi.org/10.1007/978-0-387-72367-9_10
15. Chien, H.Y.: SASI: a new ultralightweight RFID authentication protocol providing strong authentication and strong integrity. IEEE Trans. Dependable Secur. Comput. **4**(4), 337–340 (2007)
16. Cao, T., Bertino, E., Lei, H.: Security analysis of the SASI protocol. IEEE Trans. Dependable Secur. Comput. **6**(1), 73–77 (2008)
17. Sun, H.M., Ting, W.C., Wang, K.H.: On the security of Chien's ultralightweight RFID authentication protocol. IEEE Trans. Dependable Secur. Comput. **8**(2), 315–317 (2009)
18. Tian, Y., Chen, G., Li, J.: A new ultralightweight RFID authentication protocol with permutation. IEEE Commun. Lett. **16**(5), 702–705 (2012)
19. Li, W., Xiao, M., Li, Y., Mei, Y., Zhong, X., Tu, J.: Formal analysis and verification for an ultralightweight authentication protocol RAPP of RFID. In: Du, D., Li, L., Zhu, E., He, K. (eds.) NCTCS 2017. CCIS, vol. 768, pp. 119–132. Springer, Singapore (2017). https://doi.org/10.1007/978-981-10-6893-5_9
20. Wang, S H., Han, Z J., Liu, S J., et al.: Security analysis of RAPP an RFID authentication protocol based on permutation. College of computer, Nanjing University of Posts and Telecommunications, pp. 293–308 (2012). (in Chinese)
21. Pappu, R., Recht, B., Taylor, J., et al.: Physical one-way functions. Science **297**(5589), 2026–2030 (2002)
22. Li, T., Liu, Y.L.: A double PUF-based RFID authentication protocol. J. Comput. Res. Dev. **58**(8), 1801 (2021). (in Chinese)
23. Akgün, M., Çağlayan, M.U.: Providing destructive privacy and scalability in RFID systems using PUFs. Ad Hoc Netw. **32**, 32–42 (2015)

24. Liang, W., Xie, S., Long, J., et al.: A double PUF-based RFID identity authentication protocol in service-centric internet of things environments. Inf. Sci. **503**, 129–147 (2019)
25. Nimmy, K., Sankaran, S., Achuthan, K.: A novel lightweight PUF based authentication protocol for IoT without explicit CRPs in verifier database. J. Ambient Intell. Humaniz. Comput. 1–16 (2021). (Published online)
26. Herder, C., Yu, M.D., Koushanfar, F., et al.: Physical unclonable functions and applications: a tutorial. Proc. IEEE **102**(8), 1126–1141 (2014)
27. Rührmair, U., Sölter, J., Sehnke, F., et al.: PUF modeling attacks on simulated and silicon data. IEEE Trans. Inf. Forensics Secur. **8**(11), 1876–1891 (2013)
28. Talukder, B.M.S.B., Ferdaus, F., Rahman, M.T.: Memory-based PUFs are vulnerable as well: a non-invasive attack against SRAM PUFs. IEEE Trans. Inf. Forensics Secur. **16**, 4035–4049 (2021)
29. Zhang, J., Shen, C., Guo, Z., et al.: CT PUF: configurable tristate puf against machine learning attacks for IoT security. IEEE Internet Things J. **9**(16), 14452–14462 (2022)
30. Feldman, P.: A practical scheme for non-interactive verifiable secret sharing. In: 28th Annual Symposium on Foundations of Computer Science FOCS 1987, pp. 427–438. IEEE, Los Angeles, CA, USA (1987)
31. Burrows, M., Abadi, M., Needham, R M.: A logic of authentication. Proc. R. Soc. Lond. A Math. Phys. Sci. **426**(1871), 233–271 (1989)

bisAUTH: A Blockchain-Inspired Secure Authentication Protocol for IoT Nodes

Cherif Diallo$^{(\boxtimes)}$ (ID)

Laboratoire Algèbre, Cryptographie, Codes et Applications (LACCA),
UFR Sciences Appliquées et de Technologies (UFR SAT),
Université Gaston Berger, 234 Saint-Louis, Senegal
`cherif.diallo@ugb.edu.sn`

Abstract. Some existing methods for authentication of IoT nodes are based on blockchain technology which has limitations that must be taken into account. In this paper, our contribution consists in proposing a new authentication protocol, named bisAUTH, for IoT objects inspired on certain characteristics of the blockchain technology. Our main objective is to propose a mechanism allowing neighboring IoT nodes of a network to authenticate in a decentralized and secure way. Evaluation of our proposed protocol against several criteria, its resistance to various attacks and its comparison with recent protocols, show that it brings significant improvements compared to the existing ones.

Keywords: IoT · Blockchain · Authentication · Lightweight security

1 Introduction

The advent of connected objects is one of the major innovations of the Internet. It is a technology that brings together a set of physical objects integrated with sensors, software and other technologies with the aim of collecting information and allowing internet communication between devices, thus offering a multitude of services. The IoT is therefore developing rapidly. However, it presents many challenges that arise from its inherent characteristics. It presents a heterogeneous, uncontrolled environment made up of vulnerable objects with limited resources in terms of computing capacity and storage space. Security-related issues therefore represent major challenges that require effective solutions for the development and deployment of certain IoT applications. In this context, authentication is an essential aspect to guarantee good security in IoT environments, where objects process and exchange data without human intervention. Therefore, it is essential to develop secured authentication mechanisms to avoid possible threats. Many works have proposed several types of object authentication mechanisms suitable for the IoT environment. Most of these works are based on centralized authentication whereby all devices must contact a single entity. When this one is compromised, this creates a major inconvenience. Such issue can be overcome by using blockchain technology which allows the trusted

© ICST Institute for Computer Sciences, Social Informatics and Telecommunications Engineering 2022
Published by Springer Nature Switzerland AG 2022. All Rights Reserved
J. Lin and Q. Tang (Eds.): AC3 2022, LNICST 448, pp. 108–119, 2022.
https://doi.org/10.1007/978-3-031-17081-2_7

third party to be replaced with a transparent and untampered block of records available through a distributed form, so that trust is moved from a single entity to decentralized nodes. Thus, the object of our work is therefore to propose an efficient and secure mutual authentication protocol for IoT objects inspired on the blockchain technology to guarantee a high level of resistance to attacks.

2   Related Works

For most of IoT use cases, securing authentication between nodes is critical. We give here a brief review of some works that offer blockchain-based authentication methods in IoT environments. These schemes have their own specificity such that using a one-way hash chain for authentication [1], creating virtual trust bubbles [2], proposing a decentralized web authentication system [3], integrating the constraints of WSN sensor networks [4] or using Fog Nodes to allow devices to be relieved of some heavy lifting [5]. In terms of performance, some previous works try to reduce computational load, power consumption and latency [1,2,4]. Then [5] tries to avoid congestion. But these methods have their shortcomings. Thus [3] suffers from a slow user account creation process. [3] and [4] do not offer mutual authentication. Moreover [4] does not guarantee integrity and is not compatible with heterogeneous environments; [6] requires lot of messages sending and verification, which can quickly flood all the communication mediums; [7] and [8] need lot of memory, and lead to greater energy consumption, but [8] uses timestamping which allows resistance against replay attack. Finally, the Table 1 shows an assessment of these protocols in relation to their resistance to attacks. As we can see, each of them is vulnerable to at least two or more attacks. Considering all these weaknesses, we propose, in the following, a protocol with its lightweight version to address the shortcomings of existing solutions.

Table 1. Resistance to attacks of some protocols

Types of attacks	[1]	[2]	[3]	[4]	[5]	[6]	[7]	[8]
DoS/DDoS attack	Yes	No	Yes	Yes	No	No	Yes	No
Sybil attack	No	Yes	No	No	Yes	No	No	Yes
Impersonation attack	No	Yes	Yes	No	Yes	Yes	No	No
Man in the middle	Yes	No	No	Yes	No	Yes	Yes	No
Replay attack	Yes	Yes	Yes	No	Yes	Yes	No	Yes
Insertion of malicious nodes	Yes	Yes	Yes	No	No	Yes	No	Yes
Brute force attack	Yes	Yes	Yes	Yes	Yes	Yes	No	No

3   bisAUTH: A New Blockchain-Inspired Secure Authentication Protocol for IoT Nodes

As in the blockchain, our approach guarantees trust between the different nodes of the network in a consensual way. It is decentralized, and is characterized by a mechanism for distributing blocks of secrets to the different nodes. This allows them to authenticate new objects wishing to join the network. The solution also relies on the use of asymmetric cryptography. In addition, it has two versions, one of which offers a lightweight authentication function with a very high level of security.

3.1   Main Components of the bisAUTH Protocol

Server. The protocol is mainly characterized by a server (Fig. 1), hosted in the cloud, which contains in particular a set of blocks of secrets containing information that is only accessible by authorized objects. This server does not intervene in the authentication process, but it is used in the initialization phase of the objects before the deployment of the network. It contains other information such as the fingerprints or hashes of the blocks of secrets, those of the nodes, but also other useful information for an administrator such as logs and timestamping system. In addition, this server will have to store the public keys of the nodes to which it will assign blocks. It has its own public key which allows it to distribute blocks of secrets to different nodes. In the initialization phase, the server will encrypt the secret message contained in the block with a secret key which will be distributed to the nodes.

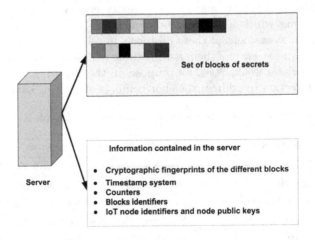

Fig. 1. Server for managing and distributing blocks of secrets.

Secret Blocks. Here, the secret blocks form an unlinked list of blocks independent of each other. Each secret block has its own fingerprint or hash through the use of a hash function. This ensures the integrity of a message and its authenticity. In our protocol, the use of hash function to generate a hash will allow nodes that have blocks in common to be able to authenticate in two different ways:

- In the lightweight version, the nodes will rely solely on the fingerprints of their blocks to be able to validate an authentication.
- In the full version, in addition to the fingerprints of their blocks, the nodes will also verify the secret message with the secret key distributed during the initialization phase in order to validate an authentication.

3.2   Main Phases of the bisAUTH Protocol

The bisAUTH Initialization Phase. Our approach begins with an initialization phase of the different IoT nodes. This phase is common to both lightweight and full versions of the protocol. The different blocks of secrets created in the server are distributed to the nodes, following this process:

1. A node requests the server public key.
2. The server sends its public key to the node.
3. Then, the node sends an encrypted message with the public key of the server containing its identifier and its public key.
4. The server calculates and assigns a list of secret blocks to the node.

The secret blocks are assign to the objects in such a way that to guarantee a certain rate of similarity between objects (Fig. 2). Indeed, by considering any two objects, the probability that these two objects have blocks in common must be greater than or equal to the fixed rate of similarity ($Prob_{SimBlocks}$). Each node will be assigned several blocks. The nodes do not necessarily have the same number of blocks. The node will first send a request to the server to ask for its public key. This node will then send a registration message containing its identifier and its public key encrypted with the public key of the server. Then the server will send the secret blocks to the nodes through an encrypted message with the public key of the node. When a node receive its list of secret blocks, it will also store the fingerprints of each block. At each allocation of secret blocks, the nodes will generate a private/public key pair to encrypt and decrypt messages. The nodes are very limited in terms of storage, we use elliptic curves public keys. The Fig. 3 shows the flowchart of the initialization phase.

The bisAUTH Authentication Phase. Our approach aims to guarantee that IoT legitimate nodes will be able to authenticate each other, and not allow malicious nodes to enter the network. Firstly, a node which would like to be authenticated, has to request the public keys of its neighbors who will authenticate it later. Then, the node encrypts with these public keys a message for its authentication request. This message will contain its identifier, the identifiers of secret blocks with their fingerprints. After this step, the different neighboring nodes will then decrypt the received message with their own private keys and calculate the hash function to check if the message has not been modified by an

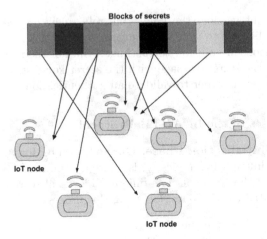

Fig. 2. Allocation of secret blocks to different IoT nodes.

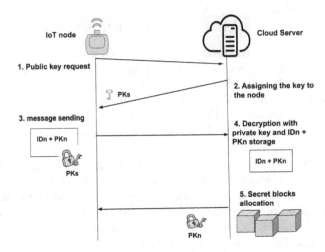

Fig. 3. Flowchart of the bisAUTH protocol initialization phase.

attacker node. If this information is correct, neighboring nodes will then see if they have one or more block fingerprints corresponding to the fingerprints they hold in their keyrings. Therefore, if a neighboring node recognizes one or more fingerprints, it will send a notification with the public key of the node to indicate to the node that it recognizes its block. In the lightweight version of the protocol, the authentication process stops at this step when the percentage of neighbors considered for consensus is reached. While, in its full version, the authentication process continues with other steps. Once a neighboring node has recognized and verified the information (hash and secret block), it has therefore been able to authenticate the node. Then, it sends a confirmation message encrypted with the public key of the requesting node (Fig. 4). The confirmation message contains its identifier as well as the fingerprint of the block, its public key and a hash (Fig. 4). The authentication phase will be complete only when the percentage of neighbors considered for consensus is reached, i.e. a certain number of nodes possessing blocks in common with the requesting node. In the event that the neighboring nodes fail to recognize the secret blocks, they will relay the request to their neighbors which in turn check whether they recognize one or more of these blocks. This process is repeated until authentication succeeds, or until all neighbors are reached. The figure (Fig. 5) shows the flowchart of the of the lightweight version of the protocol, whereas the figure (Fig. 6) gives the flowchart of the full version. Finally, the Algorithm 1 shows the overall process of the authentication phase for any requesting node.

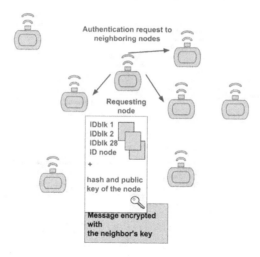

Fig. 4. Authentication request to neighbors.

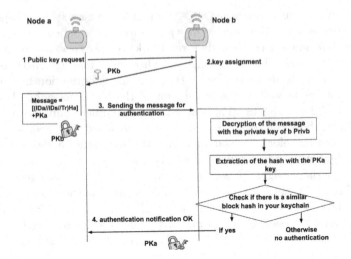

Fig. 5. Flowchart of the lightweight version of bisAUTH protocol.

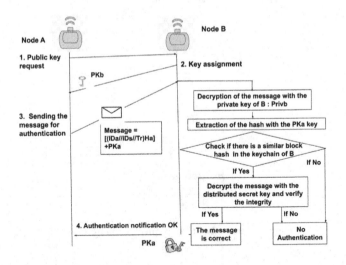

Fig. 6. Flowchart of the full version of bisAUTH protocol.

Algorithm 1. The bisAUTH Authentication phase for any requesting node

---

$Consensus \leftarrow Percent\_of\_neighbors\_for\_consensus$
$N \leftarrow Number\_of\_neighbors\_of\_the\_node$
$M \leftarrow \lceil \frac{N*Consensus}{100} \rceil$
$Sb \leftarrow Number\_of\_secret\_blocks\_of\_the\_node$
$Lsb \leftarrow Secret\_blocks\_of\_the\_node$ ▷ Secret blocks list of the requesting node
$Na \leftarrow 1$ ▷ Number of authentication attempts
$Auth \leftarrow False$
while $((Na \leq Sb)$ and $(Auth \neq True))$ **do**
    diffusion of the secret block $Lsb[Na]$
    $Cc \leftarrow 0$ ▷ Consensus counter
    for $i = 1$ to N **do**
        neighbor[i] checks the received secret block
        if the received secret block is validated by neighbor[i] **then**
            $Cc \leftarrow Cc + 1$
        end if
    end for
    if $Cc \geq M$ **then**
        $Auth \leftarrow True$
    end if
    $Na \leftarrow Na + 1$
end while
if $Auth = True$ **then**
    Return successful authentication message
else
    $EndProc \leftarrow False$
    while $EndProc \neq True$ **do**
        $i \leftarrow 1$
        while $i \leq N$ **do**
            neighbor[i] relays the authentication request using the Lsb list
            if Successful authentication **then**
                $Auth \leftarrow True$
                $i \leftarrow N + 1$
                Return successful authentication message
                $EndProc \leftarrow True$
            else
                $i \leftarrow i + 1$
            end if
        end while
        if $Auth \neq True$ **then**
            Return failed authentication message
            $EndProc \leftarrow True$
        end if
    end while
end if

The bisAUTH Maintenance Phase. It corresponds to the management of the cryptography keys which have a lifetime each. The lifetime begins when the authentication phase begins and ends when the node has been successfully authenticated by a number of nodes (percent neighbors for consensus).

3.3   bisAUTH Protocol Assessment

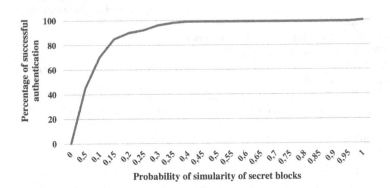

Fig. 7. Percentage of successful authentication of the node from its first request to neighbors according to the probability of similarity of secret blocks during the initialization phase. Here, the percent of neighbors for consensus is set to $\tau = 20\%$.

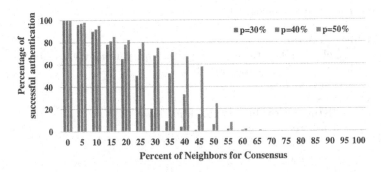

Fig. 8. Percentage of successful authentication of a node its immediate neighbors according to the percentage of neighbors for consensus when the probability of similarity of used secret blocks ($Prob_{SimBlocks}$) is p = 30%, p = 40% or p = 50%.

Simulation Results. The Fig. 7 plots the percentage of success from the first authentication request. This indicator is important because if many authentication requests are relayed by neighbors, this will increase traffic in the network, which will be harmful in terms of performance. The result shows that the curve converges quite quickly, which means that for our case, most of the requests are not relayed because the authentication is successfully performed by the immediate neighbors of the requesting node. As for the Fig. 8, it plots the percentage of success from the first authentication request as a function of the rate of similarity fixed for the secret blocks allocation process and the percentage of neighbors for the consensus. It is also an interesting result which shows that by increasing the initial similarity rate, we guarantee a good rate of authentication by the immediate neighbors. On the other hand, when the percentage of neighbors for consensus increases, the authentication conditions are toughened, and consequently, the success rate decreases. Which necessarily leads to the fact that more requests will be relayed by the neighbors who have not succeeded in authenticating the requesting node.

Analysis of bisAUTH Against Authentication Criteria. The bisAUTH protocol offers several features related to certain security criteria: privacy, integrity, mutual authentication, robustness and scalability. In terms of performance, the lightweight version guarantees a very good level of performance, while the full version could be a little wiped out when the average network density becomes too great. Moreover, bisAUTH could be considered as a Token-based authentication protocol since secret blocks can be considered tokens if embedded (Table 2). Even if it is not an authentication protocol based on physical hardware, secrets blocks could be burned in an inherently hardware-bound way. In addition, bisAUTH takes advantage of the performance offered by ECC cryptography which is considered as a natural modern successor of the RSA cryptosystem, because ECC uses smaller keys and signatures than RSA for the same level of security and provides very fast key generation, fast key agreement and fast signatures. Finally, [9] is resistant against many attacks, however it does not guarantee privacy whereas bisAUTH offers this important feature.

Table 2. Analysis of bisAUTH protocol against authentication criteria.

Criteria	bisAUTH features
Authentication factor	Shared secrets
Authentication procedure	Two-way or mutual authentication
Authentication based on physical hardware	Not used here, but possible
Authentication architecture	Decentralized
Integrity, privacy	Yes
Low computational and memory load	Yes
Scalability and efficiency	Yes
Cryptography technique	Use of ECC-type asymmetric keys
Lightweight version	Yes

Table 3. Analysis of bisAUTH in relation to its resistance to attacks

Types of attacks	Initialization phase	Authentication phase
DoS/DDoS attack	No	Yes
Sybil attack	Yes	Yes
Impersonation attack	Yes	Yes
Man in the middle	Yes	Yes
Replay attack	Yes	Yes
Insertion of malicious nodes	Yes	Yes
Brute force attack	Yes	Yes

Analysis of bisAUTH in Relation to Its Resistance to Attacks. The DoS/DDoS attack could occur during the initialization phase and the authentication phase. During the initialization phase, the server containing the secret blocks could be affected by this type of attack, preventing it from being able to carry out the collection of information from a node as well as the allocation process of the secret blocks to legitimate nodes. At the level of the authentication phase, this type of attack is not possible because requests from malicious nodes are ignored after a few unsuccessful authentication attempts. As for the sybil attack, an attacker cannot use fake identities to carry out this attack because each object, in our solution, has a unique identity that is intrinsically tied to its private/public key pair. Likewise, an attacker will be unable to impersonate a network node because he must have the node's private key in his possession. The Man in the middle attack cannot occur in our protocol because an attacker will not be able to put himself in the middle of a communication between two nodes and intercept messages coming from one of these nodes. He can generate his own private/public key pair but cannot hold the node's private key to decrypt the message sent to him. Indeed, this message will be encrypted with the public key of the recipient. So, the attacker must hold the private key of the recipient to read the message. For the same reason, an attacker will not be able to perform a replay attack because he must hold the node keys.

During the authentication phase, it is possible that malicious nodes try to be authenticated by the legitimate nodes of the network (Table 3). These malicious nodes which have not been initialized by the server will attempt to generate fingerprints in order to be authenticated and these fingerprints must match the fingerprints contained in the keyring of the legitimate nodes. A malicious node could generate a good number of fingerprints before being finally authenticated in the network. The probability that a node could be authenticated must depend on a certain number of parameters such as: the average number of secret blocks that exist in the vicinity of the node, the size of the hash (n), the average density of the network but also the percent of neighbors for consensus. The probability that a malicious node finds a legitimate node fingerprint is equal to:

$$P = \frac{Nb\_blocks}{2^n} * Average\_density * Percent\_of\_Neighbors\_for\_Concensus$$

This indicates that the probability that a malicious node integrates the network is very low. So, we can conclude that the protocol offers a very high level of security against this type of threat. To reinforce its resistance, one could use larger fingerprints (n). As for the brute force attack, it could happen when a malicious node manages to get all possible fingerprints. Therefore it would send a lot of requests to achieve this goal. The solution to avoid this attack is that, after a few unsuccessful attempts, neighboring nodes will blacklist this malicious node and simply ignore its future authentication requests.

4   Conclusion

In [9], the protocol did not guarantee confidentiality. In this paper, we have proposed a new authentication mechanism for IoT objects inspired by blockchain technology. We presented our new protocol and its lightweight version which ensure privacy. Finally, we assess it against several security challenges and attacks. Clearly, this protocol meets several criteria that an authentication method must guarantee to properly secure IoT nodes. Moreover, it brings important improvements, and it is better than the existing ones on various aspects that we have evaluated it.

References

1. Panda, S.S., Jena, D., Mohanta, B.K., Ramasubbareddy, S., Daneshmand, M., Gandomi, A.H.: Authentication and key management in distributed IoT using blockchain technology. IEEE Internet Things J. **8**(16), 12947–12954 (2021)
2. Hammi, M.T., Hammi, B., Bellot, P., Serhrouchni, A.: Bubbles of trust: a decentralized blockchain-based authentication system for IoT. Comput. Secur. J. **78**, 126–142 (2018)
3. Mohanta, B.K., Sahoo, A., Patel, S., Panda, S.S., Jena, D., Gountia, D.: DecAuth: decentralized authentication scheme for IoT device using Ethereum blockchain. In: Proceedings of 2019 IEEE Region 10 Conference (TENCON 2019) (2019)
4. Moinet, A., Darties, B., Baril, J.-L.: Blockchain based trust & authentication for decentralized sensor networks. IEEE Secur. Priv. Issue Blockchain (2017)
5. Abdalah, A.N., Mohamed, A., Hefny, H.A.: Proposed authentication protocol for IoT using blockchain and fog nodes. Int. J. Adv. Comput. Sci. Appl. **11**(4), 710–716 (2020)
6. Aman, M.N., Chua, K.C., Sikdar, B.: A lightweight mutual authentication protocol for IoT systems. In: GLOBECOM 2017, pp. 1–6. IEEE (2017)
7. Li, D., Peng, W., Deng, W., Gai, F.: A blockchain-based authentication and security mechanism for IoT. In: 2018 27th International Conference on Computer Communication and Networks (ICCCN), pp. 1–6. IEEE (2018)
8. Alizai, Z.A., Tareen, N.F., Jadoon, I.: Improved IoT device authentication scheme using device capability and digital signatures. In: 2018 International Conference on Applied and Engineering Mathematics (ICAEM), pp. 1–5. IEEE (2018)
9. Diedhiou, O.N., Diallo, C.: An IoT mutual authentication scheme based on PUF and blockchain. In: Proceeding of the IEEE International Conference on Computational Science and Computational Intelligence (CSCI), Las Vegas, USA, pp. 1034–1040 (2020)

Real-World Applied Cryptography

X-FTPC: A Fine-Grained Trust Propagation Control Scheme for Cross-Certification Utilizing Certificate Transparency

Shushang Wen[1,3], Bingyu Li[2(✉)], Ziqiang Ma[4], Qianhong Wu[2],
and Nenghai Yu[1]

[1] School of Cyber Science and Technology, University of Science and Technology
of China, Hefei 230026, China
sswen@mail.ustc.edu.cn, ynh@ustc.edu.cn
[2] School of Cyber Science and Technology, Beihang University, Beijing 100191, China
{libingyu,qianhong.wu}@buaa.edu.cn
[3] Beijing Research Institute, University of Science and Technology of China,
Beijing 100193, China
[4] School of Information Engineering, Ningxia University, Yinchuan 750021, China
maziqiang@nxu.edu.cn

Abstract. Cross-certification plays a fundamental role in facilitating the interconnection between different root stores in public key infrastructure (PKI). However, the existing trust management schemes (e.g., *certificate extension*) cannot implement fine-grained control over the trust propagation caused by cross-signing. This leads to the fact that although cross-certification expands the trust scope of certificate authorities (CAs), it also brings new security risks to the existing PKI system: (*a*) makes the certification path in PKI more complicated and lacks effective control, resulting in the arbitrary propagation of trust, and (*b*) more seriously, may even cause a revoked Cross-signed CA to continue to issue certificates that still have valid trust paths, due to the presence of cross-certificates that have not been fully revoked. Certificate Transparency (CT) is proposed to detect maliciously or mistakenly issued certificates and improve the accountability of CAs, by recording all certificates in publicly-visible logs. In this paper, we propose *X-FTPC*, a fine-grained trust propagation control enhancement scheme for cross-certification based on the idea of transparency, combined with the publicly-accessible, auditable, and append-only features of the CT log. *X-FTPC* introduces a new certificate extension to force the cross-signed CA

This work was supported in part by the National Natural Science Foundation of China under Grant 62002011, Grant 61772518, Grant 61932011, Grant 61972019, and Grant U21A20467; in part by the Youth Top Talent Support Program of Beihang University under Grant YWF-22-L-1272; in part by the China Postdoctoral Science Foundation under Grant 2021T140042 and Grant 2021M690304; in part by the Key RD Plan of Shandong Province, China under Grant 2020CXGC010115; and in part by the Beijing Natural Science Foundation through project M21031.

J. Lin and Q. Tang (Eds.): AC3 2022, LNICST 448, pp. 123–138, 2022.
https://doi.org/10.1007/978-3-031-17081-2_8

to submit an end-entity certificate to the specified log for pre-verification before it can be finally accepted. Fine-grained control of cross-certificate trust propagation is achieved through real-time monitoring of the certificate issuing behavior of cross-signed CAs. Moreover, it is fully compatible with CT frameworks that are widely deployed on the Internet.

Keywords: Public key infrastructure · Certificate transparency · Cross certification · Cross-signing · Trust management

1   Introduction

Traditional X.509 public key infrastructure (PKI) plays a fundamental role in establishing trust on the Internet. Based on digital certificates, PKI provides basic security services including authentication, confidentiality and data integrity in secure communications [5]. The application of the PKI system is based on the certificate authorities (CAs) being fully trusted and responsible for issuing certificates. The vendors of operating systems (OSes) and browsers evaluated the CA practices and then pre-installed a small group of CAs which located in the root stores in OSes or browsers, such that certificates signed by them or their subordinate authorities can pass validation [17,31].

However, due to the different security policies and service targets of different countries, regions or organizations, they usually trust only part of the secure and controllable root CAs according to their respective business needs. Currently, several mainstream OSes and browser vendors maintain their own public lists of trusted root CAs respectively [31], including Mozilla, Microsoft, and Apple. As a result, a specific CA organization may usually only be trusted by PKI users within a certain scope, and the trust cannot be propagated between various PKI user domains. Therefore, certificates issued by CA may not be trusted and accepted by all PKI users, and then formed separate islands of trust.

Cross-certification (also called cross-signing) [30] is proposed and widely used to alleviate the problem of trust islands, and the lengthy and costly validation processes that CAs must undergo to gain the trust of OSes and browsers [10]. That is, trusted CAs (typically called *Issuing CA*) can cross-sign other CAs (typically called *Cross-signed CA*) to extend their trust to them, and the resulting certificates typically called *cross-certificate*. Cross-certification provides a way for a certificate to obtain signatures from multiple issuers. That is, cross-certification creates several CA certificates that share the subject and public key, but each of them has a different issuer. Besides, it enables new CAs to quickly establish trust and also ensures extensive validation of certificates in the face of divergent root stores of OSes or browsers [10]. For example, several CAs, including Let's Encrypt [12] and GoDaddy [21], apply for cross-signing from other already trusted CAs before their own root certificates are included in root stores.

While cross-certification expands the trust scope of CAs, it also brings new security risks to the current PKI system: (*a*) makes the certification path in PKI more complicated [22] and lacks effective control, leading to the arbitrary propagation of trust. That is, once a cross-certificate is issued, it is no longer restricted by the Issuing CA, but the credibility of any end-entity certificate issued by the cross-certificate is endorsed by the Issuing CA. A worse assumption is that a Cross-signed CA may arbitrarily expand its service scope and issue certificates for more applicants that are not anticipated by the Issuing CA, which will lead to the loss control of trust propagation during the cross-signing process; (b) may even cause a revoked CA certificate continues to issue certificates that still have valid trust paths, due to the presence of cross-certificates [13]. There are multiple trust paths for an end-entity certificate signed by a cross-signed CA, the trusted scope is greatly increased, and can be accepted as long as one of the trust anchors pointed to is trusted by the user. This extremely complicates alternative trust paths and increases the number of points for attack meanwhile. For example, suppose a root CA which has cross-signing relationships with other trusted root CAs is revoked, and then be removed from browser's root store. Theoretically, in this way, any certification path pointing to this CA will not be effective. However, if the browser does not strictly check the revocation status of the certificate, the revoked CA can still issue certificates trusted by browsers, and the certification paths of these certificates will eventually point to other trusted root CAs (e.g., DigiNotar in 2011 [13]) [10].

Unfortunately, the existing scheme for trust propagation control over cross-certification can only restrict trust propagation at a coarse-grained level, and cannot fundamentally solve the above problems. For example, certificate extensions including *Basic Constraints* extension, *Name Constraints* extension, etc. can only simply impose coarse-grained restrictions on the type, path length, and subject namespace of the certificate issued by a CA. Meanwhile, a Cross-signed CA can still issue a certificate that is not intended by the Issuing CA while meeting all of these certificate extension restrictions. Therefore, it's urgent for both browsers and CAs to construct a scheme which can control the trust propagation of cross-certificates in a fine-grained manner.

Certificate Transparency (CT) is proposed to detect fraudulent certificates and improve the accountability of CAs [8,14]. CT has been widely adopted by browsers and TLS software, including Chrome, Apple platforms, and Firefox, etc. In the CT framework, certificates are submitted to multiple public servers called logs by the CA that issues it. In response, the log generates a signed certificate timestamp (SCT), as the promise to make the certificate be publicly-visible in the logs, so that it is visible to monitors for further checking [17,18]. Then, the certificate is sent along with SCTs in TLS handshakes, otherwise, it will be rejected by CT-enabled browsers.

Inspired by the publicly-accessible and auditable features of CT, we propose *X-FTPC*, a CT-based fine-grained scheme for trust propagation control of cross-certificates and realize the enhancement of PKI certification at the same time. Through a new certificate extension, X-FTPC allows Issuing CA that issues cross-certificates to operate a designated CT log server (called *Mandatory-Log*), and can customize additional certificate verification criteria. The end-entity certificates issued by the Cross-signed CA must be submitted to the Mandatory-Log for recording and verifying. Only approved certificates can get the *mandatory SCT* (called *m-SCT*) returned by the Mandatory-Log, otherwise it will be rejected by CT-enabled browsers in the TLS handshake. It should be noted that the end-entity certificate needs to be submitted to all mandatory logs that appear in the certification path (to obtain m-SCTs). If either m-SCT is missing, the end-entity certificate will be rejected by the CT-enabled browser.

In summary, X-FTPC provides cross-certification with the following enhancements:

- Fine-grained. Based on the certificate extension and CT log, a fine-grained cross-certificate trust propagation control scheme is realized, which can effectively provide the Issuing CA with the ability to restrict the issuance of any end-entity certificate by the Cross-signed CA.
- Revocable. By controlling the list of approved Cross-signed CAs in the Mandatory-Log, the restriction on the revoked CA and all related Cross-signed CAs from continuing to issue certificates with valid trust paths is realized.
- Easily-deployed. X-FTPC can be implemented and deployed by conveniently adding a certificate extension and based on the existing mature CT framework. Both CT and certificate extension have been widely adopted by browsers and TLS software.

The rest of this paper is organized as follows. The CT framework and the challenges with trust propagation control in PKI are reviewed in Sect. 2. The X-FTPC design details are described in Sect. 3. Section 4 presents the discussion of the feasibility in X-FTPC. Section 5 surveys the related work and Sect. 6 draws the conclusions.

2   Background and Challenges

In this section, we discuss how cross-certificates bootstrap the trust to root store, and analyse the shortcomings of certificate extensions for trust propagation control over cross-certificates in the Web PKI. Then, we briefly overview the certificate transparency, with a focus on the role of some key components.

2.1   Cross-Certification

In the trust model of Web PKI, CA acts as the trust anchor and holds self-signed certificates that are used to issue digital certificates to other entities. For flexibility and security considerations, root CAs typically delegate their signing capabilities by issuing intermediate CA certificates to their subordinate organizations, which in turn sign end-entity certificates to the website [31]. Browsers and OSes typically preinstall the public root trust list they maintain into the local root stores [17]. During the TLS handshake phase, the TLS server (e.g., website) sends the certificates to the TLS client (e.g., browser) to prove its identity. After receiving the certificates, the browser needs to construct a certification path (also called *certificate chain*) and verifies that all certificates in the path are valid. For browser, a end-entity certificate passes verification only if it has a valid chain to a root certificate that exists in its local root store.

It takes time for a CA to be included in these root stores to satisfy the audit and certification process [10]. Before being accepted, in order to make the certificate issued by the *untrusted-CA* can be trusted by the browser, another *trusted-CA* whose root certificate is already contained in the root stores is usually used to cross-sign the root or intermediate certificate of the *untrusted-CA*, to create a trust path ending with the trusted root certificate of the *trusted-CA*. The certificate obtained through the above cross-signing is called cross-certificate.

As shown in Fig. 1, since root CA (R_3) is located outside the *Root Store*, the certificate (E_6) issued by intermediate CA (I_5) will not be trusted by browsers whose root stores as *Root Store*. Compare to I_5, I_4 is cross-signed by I_3. That is, I_3 issues a copy I'_4 which has the same subject name and public key with I_4. Therefore, both I_4 and I'_4 can verify the digital signature of E_5. Furthermore, since the root CA of I_3 (R_2) is stored in the root store, TLS client will accept the certificate E_5. In this way, the trust of cross-certificate is propagated to E_5. Similarly, CAs that are contained only in some root stores can use cross-signing to extend trust to further root stores. As a real-world example, Let's Encrypt has already issued a large number of certificates based on the cross-signing of IdenTrust before its own root was included in root store [12].

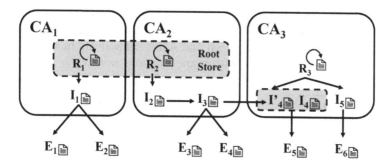

Fig. 1. An example of cross-signing in PKI system

2.2 Trust Propagation Challenge

Although the trust propagation control for cross-certification is a long-standing problem of traditional PKIs, until now there is no real perfect scheme to solve it from a fine-grained perspective.

In existing solutions, Issuing CA generally restricts the trust propagation scope and security level over cross-certificates through certificate extensions. For example, Basic Constraints as one of the most important extensions, although it works well in limiting the trust propagation scope, it only roughly limits the length in certificate chain as well and cannot prevent the issuance of non-compliant certificates. Policy Mapping extension describes the mapping relationship of certificate policies between Issuing CA and Cross-signed CA. Subscribers on both sides can evaluate the security level of their certificates to each other based on this extension. While, Name Constraints extension restricts the namespace in both the subject field and subject alternative name extensions to achieve more specific control of the certificate issuing behavior of the subordinate CA. However, in real-world scenarios, both Policy Mapping and Name Constraints extensions are rarely contained in certificates [6,7] and client applications few validate these extensions during the validation process. As a real-world example, Swiss Government has two intermediate CAs cross-signed by *QuoVadis* and *Baltimore* respectively [10]. The one cross-signed by Quo-Vadis set the Name Constraints which whitelist domains that certificates are allowed to issue. However, the other cross-signed by Baltimore did not set the extension and 9 of 756 certificates were found that out of the whitelist domains. Besides, for compatibility, Apple's secure transport library does not support Name Constraints prior to OSX/macOS 10.13.3 [25].

Therefore, it is urgent to design a scheme which is more controllable and transparent, so as to achieve fine-grained control of trust propagation over cross-certificates in PKIs.

2.3   Certificate Transparency

CT is proposed against fraudulent certificates which bind a domain name to a key pair held by MitM attackers. As shown in Fig. 2, in the CT framework, some new components have been introduced and some components in the traditional PKI system have been enhanced with extra functions as follows.

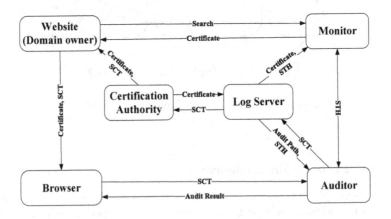

Fig. 2. The framework of certificate transparency

Log Server. A log is a public network service that records append-only certificates. Certificate is submitted by the CA to the log server, which responds with a signed certificate timestamp (SCT), as the promise to make the certificate be publicly-visible in the logs. Certificates in a log are organized as a Merkle hash tree, and the root node of the tree is periodically signed, called the signed tree head (STH), to facilitate the audits.

CA. CA submits the signed certificate to the log server to obtain the SCT. Then, the SCT is delivered to the website server along with the certificate. Alternatively, before signing the certificate, the CA creates a *precertificate* that binds the same data in a different format as the final certificate. Then, the precertificate is submitted to the log to return an SCT, and the SCT is embedded in the final certificate. According to the CT policy, a certificate may be submitted to multiple log servers to obtain multiple SCTs.

Website. In addition to the CA submitting the certificate to the log when issuing certificates, in the early stage of CT deployment, sometimes the website also needs to submit its own certificate to the log server to obtain the SCT by itself. Then, in the TLS handshake, the website sends SCTs along with the certificate to browsers [14], as the embedded certificate extensions or the TLS extensions (e.g., OCSP stapling).

Browser. In TLS handshakes, a CT-compliant browser verifies the certificate and SCTs based on the pre-installed public keys of CAs and approved log servers [9]. If the browser's CT policy is not met, for example, there are not enough valid SCTs, the browser will reject the certificate.

Monitor. Monitor is responsible for retrieving logs to find suspicious certificates issued by the CA incorrectly or maliciously. A monitor periodically obtains and decodes all records from the log, and then checks the certificate of interest.

Auditor. Auditor is responsible for auditing the compliance of the log server. The auditor periodically requests STHs from the log server to check whether the log is append-only and consistent. Besides, it also requests an audit path to check whether a certificate is recorded in the public log.

3   X-FTPC: Fine-Grained Trust Propagation Control for Cross-Certification

In this section we firstly give an overview of the X-FTPC. Then, we describe how the new-add components work and extend X-FTPC in different scenarios. Finally, we discuss the potential threats to browsers and websites with X-FTPC.

3.1   Overview

Our goal is to achieve fine-grained control over the trust propagation caused by cross-certificate. In this paper, we define the *fine-grained* as: for each end-entity certificate that the Cross-signed CA expects to issue, the Issuing CA can decide whether to approve the issuance. The core idea of X-FTPC is enabling the

Issuing CA can not only monitor the certificate issuing behavior of Cross-signed CA, just like the CT does, but also control whether it's permitted to issue. It's worth noting that the X-FTPC only works when cross-certificates exist in the end-entity certificate's certification path.

To do this, we design a new-add public log server which is called the *Mandatory-Log* (usually referred to as *M-Log* in this paper). The M-Log has the same storage structure (i.e., MerkleTree) and function (e.g., publicly auditable) as the CT log (usually referred to as *Regular-Log*). In particular, M-Log has the additional function of certificate verification which the specific verification criteria is customized by the Issuing CA. X-FTPC also borrows the spam control mechanism used in Regular-Log [14]. That is, each log holds an acceptable list of CAs and only accepts the (pre)certificates whose root CA belongs to the list [14,16]. But different from that in CT, each Issuing CA in X-FTPC operates its own M-Log and maintains a cross-signing list (called *X-List*) in the Log, which includes CA certificates cross-signed by the Issuing CA or the other CAs. In Sect. 3.2, we describe more details about the M-Log and the X-List.

For ease of understanding and highlighting the compatibility with CT, we take the common three-level certificate chain in the Web PKI as an example to describe the main process in X-FTPC as shown in Fig. 3.

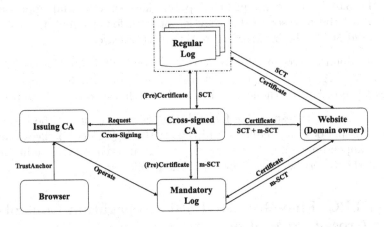

Fig. 3. The framework of X-FTPC

Cross-Signing. Issuing CA issues a cross-certificate with a new critical certificate extension (called MandatoryLogIdentifier) for the requested Cross-signed CA. Specifically, MandatoryLogIdentifier describes the information about the M-Log, e.g., gives its URL location in HTTP format. In Sect. 4, we'll discuss further about the security implications for browsers when this extension is set to "critical" or "non-critical". Then, Issuing CA adds the cross-certificate to the X-List in its M-Log actively. It is also important to note that if there are other cross-certificates present in the certification path, they should also request the Issuing CA to add them to the X-List.

Issuing the Compliant End-Entity Certificates. The SCT list of a compliant end-entity certificate in X-FTPC must have two types of SCT, which are returned by the Regular-Log and M-Log respectively. When the M-Log receives a submitted (pre)certificate chain, it checks whether the Cross-signed CA is included in its X-List and then verifies the end-entity certificate according to its verification criteria. The M-Log will return the m-SCT if and only if the above two requirements are met. Specifically, there are two methods for the Website to deliver the m-SCTs to browsers during a TLS handshake: (a) *TLS extensions.* After an end-entity certificate is issued, the Website or the Cross-signed CA submits it to logs to obtain an (m-)SCT and then delivers the SCT to browser as TLS extension. In this way, those Cross-signed CA issued certificates that have existed in the Internet in large quantities before the deployment of X-FTPC can still meet the policy requirements of X-FTPC; (b) *Certificate extensions.* Before an end-entity certificate is issued, Cross-signed CA submits a pre-certificate to the M-Logs to obtain m-SCTs. Then the certificate is issued with all the (m-)SCTs embedded as a certificate extension.

Validation. When browser validates the certificate chain sent by the websites or constructed by itself, it iterates all intermediate CA certificates so as to identify whether they have the `MandatoryLogIdentifier` extension. Then, browser validates whether the end-entity certificate contains m-SCTs returned by all the M-Logs given in the above extensions. After that, it further validates the other information in certificates according to the existing validation methods, e.g., the browser's CT policy.

3.2   Fine-Grained Control Based on Mandatory-Log in X-FTPC

In CT systems, each log holds an acceptable list of CAs and accepts only the (pre)certificates issued by these CAs [14,16]. Analogously, in X-FTPC, instead of the list of root CAs in Regular-Log, we propose the X-List in the M-Log, which is configured by the Issuing CA and includes CAs that are cross-signed by Issuing CA directly or indirectly. Here the indirect means that Cross-signed CA can continue to cross-sign other CAs to propagates trust further, which these CAs form an indirect cross-signing relationship with Issuing CA. Besides, the M-Log requires additional verification of the submitted certificate. Specifically, Issuing CA achieves the cross-certificate trust propagation control in fine-grained through the M-Log it operated from the following steps:

- Verifying the cross-certificates. For each certificate chain submitted to the M-Log, it verifies whether all CAs cross-signed by the Issuing CA directly or indirectly in the certificate chain are contained in the X-List. If one of the CAs is not in the X-list, then the end-entity certificates will be rejected for lack of the corresponding m-SCT.
- Verifying the end-entity certificate. Issuing CA customizes the additional verification criteria that the end-entity certificate must comply with.[1] If the end-

---

[1] In this paper, we do not restrict the specific format and content of the verification criteria. Issuing CA can define it according to their own application scenarios.

entity certificate fails to meet the criteria, it will be rejected and m-SCT will not be returned.

Combined with above, the M-Log in X-FTPC does need to do more work than Regular-Log in CT. On the other hand, however, the extra workload also solves part of the problems caused by the negligence of cross-certificates revocation (as mentioned in Sect. 1). In X-FTPC, when Issuing CA revokes a cross-certificate issued to a Cross-signed CA, it also removes the cross-certificate from the X-List in its M-Log. Since a X-FTPC-compliant certificate must contain all m-SCTs returned by the relevant M-Logs. Therefore, even if the others M-Logs in the certification path of the end-entity certificate that do not remove the revoked cross-certificates from their own X-List, it does not affect. In this way, X-FTPC enables browsers to avoid continuing to trust certificates issued by the revoked cross-signed CA as failure to perform the revocation checks.

In summary, Issuing CA centralizes the management of cross-certificates issued directly or indirectly through the X-List in M-Log and further achieves the fine-grained control of trust propagation by deciding whether to return the m-SCT.

3.3   Different Scenarios in X-FTPC

Based on the M-Log, we achieve fine-grained control of cross-certificate trust propagation in a high compatibility with CT meanwhile. Considering the different scenarios in practical application, we analyze the following scenarios, which demonstrate that X-FTPC can be easily extended. We take the CAs' trust relationships of Let's Encrypt [12] as a background for our scenario analysis. Let's Encrypt has already issued a large number of certificates based on the cross-signing of IdenTrust before their own root was included in the root store.

To begin with, as shown in Fig. 4, we assume that the following scenarios are based on the Web PKI and also make the definition as follows:

- E_x refers to the browser, website or end-entity certificate depending on the context.
- R_x is the trust anchor of E_x, which is already in-built in its root store, e.g., R_1 is the trust anchor of E_1 and E_2.
- I_x are the intermediate certificates issued by the root CAs. I'_x are the cross-certificates which cross-signed by another CAs, e.g., R_1 issues cross-certificates I'_{R_2} and I'_2 for R_2 and I_2, respectively.
- $M - Log_x$ means that the M-Log is operated by x.

Scenario 1 - Trust Propagation in Adjacent CAs. In this scenario, as shown in Fig. 4, assumed that user (e.g., E_1) requests to connect with the website (e.g., E_3), and then E_3 sends a certificate chain to E_1. To validate the identification of E_3, there are two ways for E_1 to do it: (a) validate the certificate chain sent by E_3; (b) construct the certification path by itself. There exists three alternative certification paths: (1) $E_3 - I_2 - R_2$, (2) $E_3 - I'_2 - R_1$,

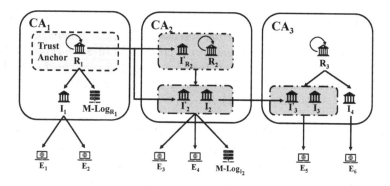

Fig. 4. Trust propagation among multiple CAs

and (3) $E_3 - I_2 - I'_{R_2} - R_1$. Since in Path (1), R_2 is out of the root store of E_1, so E_3 would not be accepted. In Path 2 and Path 3, as both I'_2 and I'_{R_2} have the $MandatoryLogIdentifier$ extension which presents the information of $M - Log_{R_1}$, so E_3 must be submitted to the $M - Log_{R_1}$ for additional verification. But it's also noted that I'_2 and I'_{R_2} are cross-signed by R_1 directly, so both of them are included in the X-List of $M - Log_{R_1}$ actively. Considering that user accepts E_3 only when the SCT list of E_3 includes the m-SCT from $M - Log_{R_1}$, so through this way, R_1 controls the trust propagation and certificate issuing behavior of I_2 in Path 2 and 3.

Scenario 2 - Trust Propagation Across Multiple CAs. Considering a more complicated scenario where there are multiple cross-signing between different CA domains along the certificate chain in Fig. 4. When the user (also E_1) communicates with E_5, it has the following alternative certification paths: (1) $E_5-I_3-R_3$, (2) $E_5 - I'_3 - I_2 - R_2$, (3) $E_5 - I'_3 - I'_2 - R_1$, and (4) $E_5 - I'_3 - I_2 - I'_{R_2} - R_1$. Different from the cross-signing directly in Scenario 1, I_2 also cross-signs I_3 and thus bootstraps the trust of E_5 to both R_1 and R_2 through I'_3, I'_2 and I'_{R_2}.

However, in Path 2, 3 and 4, as I'_3 has the $MandatoryLogIdentifier$ extension which points to $M-Log_{I_2}$, so E_5 also needs to be submitted to the $M-Log_{I_2}$ in addition to the $M-Log_{R_1}$ as Scenario 1 does. In particular, since I_3 is cross-signed by R_1 indirectly, I'_3 also needs to send a request to R_1 to be included in the X-List of $M - Log_{R_1}$. When $M - Log_{I_2}$ receives these certificate chains, it verifies whether the I'_3 is contained in its X-List and then verifies E_5 according to its verification criteria. The similar verification can be applied to $M - Log_{R_1}$. In Path 3, $M - Log_{R_1}$ verifies whether both I'_2 and I'_3 contained in its X-List. While in Path 4, I'_{R_2} and I'_3 are verified. Therefore, even I_3 cross-signed by R_1 indirectly, R_1 also has the ability to control the certificate issuing behavior of I_3 (or I'_3) in Path 3 and 4.

Scenario 3 - Internal Cross-Signing. In above scenarios, we only discuss the cross-signing between different PKI domains, e.g., the issuer of I'_{R_2} is attributed to CA_1 but the subject of I'_{R_2} is attributed to CA_2. On the contrary, internal cross-signs are that the cross-certificates' issuer and owner are attributed to the same PKI domain [10], e.g., both the issuer and subject of I_3' are attributed to CA_2, as shown in Fig. 5. We further discuss some of the differences between Scenario 1 and 2 when there exists internal cross-signs in Scenario 3. To begin with, we also assume that E_1 connects to the E_5 and then validates E_5 which has the following alternative certification paths: (1) $E_5-I_4-R_3$, (2) $E_5-I_4'-I_3-R_2$, (3) $E_5 - I_4' - I_3' - I_2 - R_2$, and (4) $E_5 - I_4' - I_3' - I_2' - I_1 - R_1$. Since E_1 only accepts E_5 in Path 4, so we do not discuss the other Paths here which their analysis are similar to the above scenarios. In Path 4, E_5 must be submitted to $M - Log_{I_1}$, $M - Log_{I_2}$ and $M - Log_{I_3}$ for additional verification.

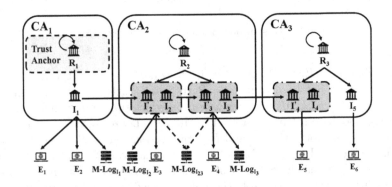

Fig. 5. Scenario of internal cross-signing

However, note that both I_2 and I_3 are governed within CA_2, we also propose that I_2 and I_3 can jointly operate an M-Log (called $M - Log_{I_{23}}$) to avoid resource redundancy and reduce the maintenance cost of CA. Correspondingly, whenever I_2 or I_3 cross-signs other CAs, only information about the $M - Log_{I_{23}}$ will be given in the $MandatoryLogIdentifier$ extension of the cross-certificate. For example, the $MandatoryLogIdentifier$ extension of I_4' can only give the information about the $M - Log_{I_{23}}$. Then, I_2 or I_3 adds the cross-signed CAs to the X-List of $M - Log_{I_{23}}$ respectively. In particular, the X-List also contains all CAs which cross-signed internally, e.g., the I_3'. When $M - Log_{I_{23}}$ receives the certificate chain of Path 4, it can verifies whether I_3' and I_4' are included in X-List meanwhile. Most importantly, because of the relative independence between M-Logs, it does not weaken the fine-grained control of trust propagation by I_1. For example, $M - Log_{I_1}$ also needs to verify whether I_2', I_3' and I_4' are included in its X-List.

3.4   Potential Threats in X-FTPC

Our primary goals in this paper are to design a scheme which can realize fine-grain control of cross-certificate trust propagation. Meanwhile, it can also provide sufficient security and will not introduce more potential threats than the existing CT. In particular, as X-FTPC is proposed based on CT, so it naturally inherits the proven security attributes of CT [14]. Fundamentally, a misbehavior from compromised or misoperated CA against the X-FTPC usually results in either one of the two outcomes: (1) to issue a certificate which is not conform to the verification criteria (also unauthorized) in the M-Log; (2) to issue a certificate which is fraudulent but meeting the verification criteria. Briefly, we analyze the security in X-FTPC against the following threat assumptions.

Case 1. Cross-signed CA may collaborate with the website to issue a certificate that is outside the scope of its authority and does not submit the certificate to the corresponding M-Log. However, this certificate will not be accepted by the X-FTPC-enabled browser because it lacks the m-SCT returned by M-log. It's important to note that the X-FTPC only works if cross-certificates exist in the certification path. Thus, for a regular certificate chain without cross-certificates, the certificate without m-SCT can still be accepted by browsers.

Case 2. There is another case where Cross-signed CA may issue a fraudulent certificate which conforms to the verification criteria customized by the Issuing CA. When browsers validate the fraudulent certificate, it can be accepted as its SCT list meets the requirements stated in X-FTPC. Fortunately, X-FTPC also uses publicly-accessible logs as CT does, meaning that both auditors and monitors can independently verify whether the certificate really present in the M-Log. Besides, as the M-Log is monitored by Monitors just like the Regular-Log, thus the domain owner can detect the fraudulent certificate through the third-party monitor in time.

4   Discussion in Feasibility of X-FTPC

In this section, we discuss the feasibility of X-FTPC in CT-based PKIs around browsers. Essentially, how X-FTPC is deployed and the impact of its deployment is very similar to the CT framework [26]. An important measure of one scheme's feasibility is its compatibility with users (e.g., browsers). In X-FTPC, the SCT list of a website's certificate consists of two parts: (1) SCTs returned by the Regular-Log, (2) m-SCTs returned by the M-Log. With the $MandatoryLogIdentifier$ extension that provides information about the M-Log, browsers can be informed which m-SCT should be validated.

On the one hand, if the browser is required to enforce the X-FTPC verification (i.e., set $MandatoryLogIdentifier$ extension critical), the false positive rate may be too high in the early stage of X-FTPC deployment, that is, many valid certificates issued by cross-certificates will be rejected by the browser. On the other hand, if the browser is not required to enforce the X-FTPC verification (i.e., set $MandatoryLogIdentifier$ extension non-critical), then the scheme is weakened to the CT, which is fully compatible with the existing browser's CT policy, but a degradation attack may occur [19], resulting in a high false negative rate, that is, the browser will accept the "problem" certificate issued by the cross-certificate. Therefore, CAs and websites with high security requirements can implement mandatory checks by setting a white-list in the browser similar to the CT mechanism [26]. For a wider scope of CAs and common domain names, we can achieve gradual deployment by setting deadlines.

In summary, as X-FTPC is based on the CT, so the deployment of it can be fully compatible and incrementally deployable. Besides, as X-FTPC-enabled browsers do not require much efforts to support its deployment, thus the feasibility and scalability are acceptable as well.

5   Related Work

With the abroad application of PKI, security researchers have studied a lot of work [1,3,4] around both CA ecosystem and certificate ecosystem. Among these works, there are few works involving the cross-signing or cross-certificate. As early as 2011, Holz et al. already noted the problem that once a untrusted CA is cross-signed by the other trusted CA which is contained in the root store may introduce heavy results [11]. Besides, the authors mentioned that the excessive issuance of intermediate certificates not only complicates the certification path, but also poses potential security risks. Durumeric et al. conducted an analysis of the HTTPS ecosystem and unexpectedly found a lot of cross-certificates among CA certificates which trusted by browsers in 2013 [7]. Roosa et al. believed that as CAs often do not disclose their cross-sign relationships when request to include in the root store, which exacerbates the opacity of the PKI system [22]. Hiller et al. systematically detailed the use and effect of cross-signing on the current web PKI, but did not analyze the behavior of cross-certificate issuance and discuss how to control it [10]. Casola et al. proposed an automatic methodology to enable CAs evaluate and compare the certificate policies for cross-certification [2]. However, most of above works have an emphasis on the measurement and analysis, but do not concentrate on the trust propagation control under the certification path, especially the trust originated from cross-certificates.

Based on the idea of transparency, several designs were proposed to improve the security and/or performance. A number of studies have reworked the log server structure to achieve more efficient transparency [23,24,29] and support more types of transparency [23,28], such as support for revocation transparency. PoliCert [27] records subject certificate policies and certificates in public logs, providing the cryptographic proofs of presence and absence. CONIKS [20] builds transparent key directories based on Merkle prefix trees, allowing users to audit their public keys while maintaining privacy. CTng [15] modifies the current CT design in a limited way to achieve transparency including certificate and revocation status without requiring any trusted third party.

6   Conclusion

In this paper, we analyze the problem of trust propagation with cross-certificates. We detail that the existing extension solution can only provide coarse-grained control over certificates. To achieve fine-grained control in cross-certificate trust propagation, inspired by the transparency in CT, we introduce the X-FTPC with a new certificate extension to force the Cross-signed CA to submit the end-entity certificate to the specified log for pre-verification before it can be finally issued. X-FTPC realizes the real-time monitoring of the certificate issuing behavior of the Cross-signed CA, and achieves the goal of fine-grained control of the trust propagation over cross-certificate. Our research and analysis show that X-FTPC is effective in a variety of scenarios. In addition, X-FTPC has good compatibility with the CT mechanism widely deployed at present, thus enabling incremental deployment.

References

1. Amann, J., Gasser, O., et al.: Mission accomplished? HTTPS security after DigiNotar. In: 17th IMC (2017)
2. Casola, V., Mazzeo, A., Mazzocca, N., Rak, M.: An innovative policy-based cross certification methodology for public key infrastructures. In: Chadwick, D., Zhao, G. (eds.) EuroPKI 2005. LNCS, vol. 3545, pp. 100–117. Springer, Heidelberg (2005). https://doi.org/10.1007/11533733_7
3. Chung, T., Liu, Y., et al.: Measuring and applying invalid SSL certificates: the silent majority. In: 16th IMC (2016)
4. Clark, J., van Oorschot, P.: SSL and HTTPS: revisiting past challenges and evaluating certificate trust model enhancements. In: 34th IEEE S&P (2013)
5. Cooper, D., Santesson, S., et al.: IETF RFC 5280 - Internet X.509 public key infrastructure certificate and certificate revocation list (CRL) profile (2008)
6. Debnath, J., Chau, S.Y., et al.: On re-engineering the X.509 PKI with executable specification for better implementation guarantees. In: 28th ACM CCS (2021)
7. Durumeric, Z., Kasten, J., et al.: Analysis of the https certificate ecosystem. In: 13th IMC (2013)
8. Google Inc.: Certificate transparency (2021). https://www.certificate-transparency.org/
9. Google Inc.: Known logs (2021). https://www.certificate-transparency.org/known-logs
10. Hiller, J., Amann, J., et al.: The boon and bane of cross-signing: shedding light on a common practice in public key infrastructures. In: 27th ACM CCS (2020)
11. Holz, R., Braun, L., et al.: The SSL landscape: a thorough analysis of the X.509 PKI using active and passive measurements. In: 11th IMC (2011)
12. Internet Security Research Group: Chain of Trust (2021). https://letsencrypt.org/certificates/
13. Johnathan Nightingale: Mozilla Security Blog - DigiNotar Removal Follow Up (2011). https://blog.mozilla.org/security/2011/09/02/diginotar-removal-follow-up/
14. Laurie, B., Langley, A., et al.: IETF RFC 6962 - Certificate transparency (2013)
15. Leibowitz, H., Ghalwash, H., et al.: CTng: secure certificate and revocation transparency. Cryptology ePrint Archive (2021)
16. Li, B., Lin, J., et al.: Certificate transparency in the wild: exploring the reliability of monitors. In: 26th AMC CCS (2019)
17. Li, B., Lin, J., et al.: Locally-centralized certificate validation and its application in desktop virtualization systems. IEEE TIFS 16, 1380–1395 (2020)
18. Li, B., Lin, J., et al.: The invisible side of certificate transparency: exploring the reliability of monitors in the wild. IEEE/ACM ToN 30(2), 749–765 (2021)

19. Matsumoto, S., Szalachowski, P., Perrig, A.: Deployment challenges in log-based PKI enhancements. In: 8th EuroSec (2015)
20. Melara, M.S., Blankstein, A., et al.: CONIKS: bringing key transparency to end users. In: 24th USENIX Security Symposium (2015)
21. Mozilla: Bug 403437 - Request Valicert/Starfield/GoDaddy Root Certificates be enabled for EV. https://bugzilla.mozilla.org/show_bug.cgi?id=403437
22. Roosa, S.B., Schultze, S.: Trust darknet: control and compromise in the internet's certificate authority model. IEEE Internet Comput. **17**(3), 18–25 (2013)
23. Ryan, M.D.: Enhanced certificate transparency and end-to-end encrypted mail. In: 21st NDSS (2014)
24. Singh, A., Sengupta, B., Ruj, S.: Certificate transparency with enhancements and short proofs. In: Pieprzyk, J., Suriadi, S. (eds.) ACISP 2017. LNCS, vol. 10343, pp. 381–389. Springer, Cham (2017). https://doi.org/10.1007/978-3-319-59870-3_22
25. StackExchange: Are X.509 nameConstraints on certificates supported on OS X? https://security.stackexchange.com/questions/95600/are-x-509-nameconstraints-on-certificates-supported-on-os-x
26. Stark, E., Sleevi, R., et al.: Does certificate transparency break the web? Measuring adoption and error rate. In: 40th IEEE S&P (2019)
27. Szalachowski, P., Matsumoto, S., et al.: PoliCert: secure and flexible TLS certificate management. In: 21st ACM CCS (2014)
28. Szalachowski, P., Chuat, L., et al.: PKI safety net (PKISN): addressing the too-big-to-be-revoked problem of the TLS ecosystem. In: 1st IEEE EuroS&P (2016)
29. Tomescu, A., Bhupatiraju, V., et al.: Transparency logs via append-only authenticated dictionaries. In: 26th ACM CCS (2019)
30. Turnbull, J.: Cross-certification and PKI policy networking. Entrust, Inc. (2000)
31. Zhang, Y., Liu, B., et al.: Rusted anchors: a national client-side view of hidden root CAs in the web PKI ecosystem. In: 28th ACM CCS (2021)

The Block-Based Mobile PDE Systems are Not Secure - Experimental Attacks

Niusen Chen[1], Bo Chen[1(✉)], and Weisong Shi[2]

[1] Department of Computer Science, Michigan Technological University,
Michigan, USA
bchen@mtu.edu

[2] Department of Computer Science, Wayne State University, Michigan, USA

Abstract. Nowadays, mobile devices have been used broadly to store and process sensitive data. To ensure confidentiality of the sensitive data, Full Disk Encryption (FDE) is often integrated in mainstream mobile operating systems like Android and iOS. FDE however cannot defend against coercive attacks in which the adversary can force the device owner to disclose the decryption key. To combat the coercive attacks, Plausibly Deniable Encryption (PDE) is leveraged to plausibly deny the very existence of sensitive data. However, most of the existing PDE systems for mobile devices are deployed at the block layer and suffer from deniability compromises.

Having observed that none of existing works in the literature have experimentally demonstrated the aforementioned compromises, our work bridges this gap by experimentally confirming the deniability compromises of the block-layer mobile PDE systems. We have built a mobile device testbed, which consists of a host computing device and a flash storage device. Additionally, we have deployed both the hidden volume-based PDE and the steganographic file system-based PDE at the block layer of our testbed and performed disk forensics to assess potential compromises on the raw NAND flash. Our experimental results confirm it is indeed possible for the adversary to compromise the block-layer PDE systems when the adversary can have access to the raw NAND flash in real world. We also discuss practical issues when performing such attacks in practice.

Keywords: PDE · Coercive attacks · NAND flash · Deniability compromises · Experimental attacks

1 Introduction

Mobile computing devices are widely used in our daily life nowadays and, with their increased use, more and more sensitive data are stored and processed in the mobile devices. Therefore, it turns to become an urgent need of protecting those sensitive data, and one of the most critical data security issues is confidentiality.

© ICST Institute for Computer Sciences, Social Informatics and Telecommunications Engineering 2022
Published by Springer Nature Switzerland AG 2022. All Rights Reserved
J. Lin and Q. Tang (Eds.): AC3 2022, LNICST 448, pp. 139–152, 2022.
https://doi.org/10.1007/978-3-031-17081-2_9

A straightforward approach to protect data confidentiality is to use encryption. Currently, Full Disk Encryption (FDE) has been deployed to the mainstream mobile operating systems including Android [1] and iOS [8]. In FDE, encryption and decryption are completely transparent to users. Without the key, the attacker cannot obtain any knowledge about the original sensitive data. However, FDE cannot defend against a novel coercive attack in which the attacker can force the device owner to disclose the key, and decrypt the ciphertext to obtain the original sensitive data. For example, a journalist or a human rights worker [15,34] who is working in a country of conflict or oppression, has captured some sensitive evidence of atrocities and tries to cross the border; to protect the evidence, he/she encrypts the evidence; the border inspector however, may be aware of the ciphertext and force the journalist to disclose the decryption key.

Plausibly Deniable Encryption (PDE) can be used to combat coercive attacks. In PDE, the plaintext is encrypted with a decoy key and a true key. When decrypting the cipher using the decoy key, we will obtain a decoy message and when decrypting the cipher using the true key, we will obtain the true message. Upon being coerced by the attacker, the device owner can only disclose the decoy key and keep the true key secret. In this way, the sensitive data can be protected against the coercive attackers as the attackers cannot notice the existence of the hidden sensitive data. Following the concept of PDE, a large number of PDE systems [14–16,18–21,23,26,30–32,34] have been designed for mobile devices. In general, the existing mobile PDE systems can be divided into three categories: C1) block-layer PDE systems [14–16,23,31,32,34]; C2) flash translation layer (FTL) PDE systems [20,26]; and C3) deniability aware flash file systems [19,30]. A majority of the existing mobile PDE systems belong to the category C1 which deploys PDE on the block layer. The reason is that deploying the PDE on the block layer could be achieved much more easily, resulting in a much better usability. However, the block-layer PDE systems are insecure, because: the hidden sensitive data will leave special traces in the underlying flash memory and such traces cannot be removed by the block-layer PDEs; by having access to the raw flash memory, the adversary may compromise the deniability [26]. The compromises have been analyzed theoretically by DEFTL [26], but none of the existing works have confirmed such compromises experimentally. This work thus aims to bridge this gap by conducting the first experimental study on understanding the deniability compromises of the existing block-layer PDE systems.

Comparison with DEFTL. Our work is different from that of the DEFTL [26] in a few aspects: First, DEFTL theoretically analyzes the potential deniability compromises when deploying the PDE on the block device layer. However, our work experimentally validates the deniability compromises in real-world devices. Especially, we have created a mobile device testbed which includes a host computing device (ARM architecture) and a self-made flash-based block device (using an open-source flash controller and a cheap USB development prototype board). This self-built mobile device follows the architecture of mainstream mobile devices in real world. We then deploy a few representative block-based PDE systems in our testbed, and perform forensic analysis over the raw NAND flash to study the deniability compromises. Second, DEFTL only focuses on the deniability compromises on the PDE systems which use hidden volume technique, but our work assesses both the hidden volume-based and the steganographic file system-based PDE. Third, we have identified extra deniability compromises which have not been discovered in DEFTL.

2   Background

2.1   Flash Memory

Flash memory especially NAND flash has been used broadly as the external storage of mobile computing devices nowadays. Flash memory usually consists of blocks, and each block consists of pages. Typically, each flash block is a few hundreds of kilobytes in size and each page is a few kilobytes in size. Compared to conventional hard disk drives (HDD), flash memory has a few different features: 1) The unit of a read/write operation is a page, but the unit of an erase operation is a block. 2) A flash page needs to be erased before it can be programmed. 3) Due to the unique features of 1) and 2), the in-place update in flash memory would be expensive. Therefore, the flash storage typically uses an out-of-place instead of in-place update strategy [24]. 4) Each block in the flash memory can only be programmed/erased for a limited number of times and, therefore, programmings and erasures should be distributed evenly across the entire flash to prolong the service life.

2.2   Flash Translation Layer

To manage flash memory, we can use a flash-specific file system like YAFFS or JFFS. However, the flash-specific file systems are rarely used in mobile computing devices today. Instead, a flash translation layer (FTL) is incorporated into the flash storage media (e.g., SD cards, UFS cards, MMC cards) to transparently handle the unique nature of NAND flash hardware, so that the flash storage media can expose a block access interface externally and the traditional block-based file systems can be deployed. The core functions implemented in the FTL include garbage collection, wear leveling, and bad block management.

Garbage Collection. As the flash storage media adopt the out-of-place update strategy, the flash pages storing old data may be invalidated. Garbage collection is typically used to reclaim those invalid pages. The garbage collection usually works as follows: The FTL selects a victim block which has the largest number of invalid pages. It then copies data stored in valid pages in the victim block to an empty block, and erases the victim block.

Wear Leveling. Each flash block only supports a limited number of program/erase (P/E) cycles. The main purpose of wear leveling is to distribute P/E cycles evenly across the entire flash. There are a lot wear leveling strategies

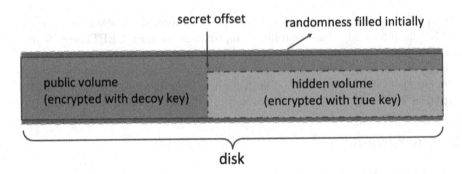

Fig. 1. The hidden volume-based PDE technique.

including static wear leveling and dynamic wear leveling. A fundamental idea is to swap hot and cold data, so that the hot data will be relocated to those blocks with least P/E cycles and the cold data will be relocated to those blocks with most P/E cycles.

Bad Block Management. Over time, a flash block may turn "bad" and cannot be used to reliably store data, as there were too many P/E cycles performed on this block in the past. Therefore, the FTL needs to keep track of those bad blocks and prevents them from being used to store data. Typically, a bad block table can be used to keep track of bad blocks. If a block turns bad, the FTL will copy data from this block to an empty block and add this bad block to the bad block table.

2.3 Plausibly Deniable Encryption

Plausibly deniable encryption can be leveraged to combat coercive attacks. Typically, there are two techniques which can be used to implement the PDE system, namely, the hidden volume technique [6,7] and the steganographic file system [9,28].

For the hidden volume technique (see Fig. 1), the entire disk is filled with random data initially. Two volumes—a public volume and a hidden volume—will be introduced. Correspondingly, two keys—a decoy key and a true key—are selected. The public volume is encrypted via the decoy key and placed across the entire disk, and the hidden volume is encrypted with the true key and placed to the end of the disk starting from a secret offset (derived from the true key). Upon being coerced, the victim will simply disclose the decoy key. Via the decoy key, the attacker can decrypt the public volume, but will not notice the existence of the hidden volume stored stealthily among the random data.

One implementation of the steganographic file system is to fill the disk with random data initially, and to encrypt and to hide the sensitive data at a secret location which can be derived from a secret key. To prevent loss of sensitive data, multiple copies of sensitive data are stored in multiple locations across the disk.

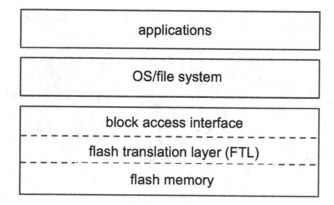

Fig. 2. The storage architecture of main-stream mobile computing devices

3 Model and Assumptions

System Model. We consider a mobile computing device which is equipped with flash memory (e.g., UFS cards, eMMC cards, microSD cards, etc.) as the external storage. The storage architecture of main-stream mobile devices is shown in Fig. 2. A mobile user directly communicates with apps (e.g., a PDF viewer app) running at the application layer. The OS/file system will manage storage hardware and provide system calls for the applications to access the data stored at the storage hardware. The underlying flash memory storage is typically used in the form of a block device. The FTL will handle special nature of flash memory, exposing a block access interface externally.

Adversarial Model. We assume the adversary can capture both the victim and his/her mobile device, and coerce the owner to disclose the decryption key. The adversary is rationale and will stop coercing the user once he/she believes that the decryption key is disclosed [15,16,26,31]. Using the disclosed key, the adversary will play with the mobile devices to compromise the PDE. In addition, the adversary can extract the raw image from the flash storage equipped with the victim device and obtain the hardware parameters (e.g., page size and block size) of the underlying flash memory chips. The adversary can then perform forensic analysis on the raw image—with the help of the disclosed key—to identify the existence of PDE.

4 Experimentally Attacking the Block-Layer PDE Systems

The hidden volume technique and the steganographic file system (Sect. 2.3) are two major techniques which have been leveraged to implement the PDE system at the block layer. We therefore focus on attacking those two types of PDE systems. For each type of PDE systems, we first deploy a representative

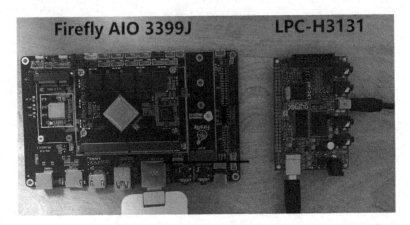

Fig. 3. A self-made mobile device testbed for our experiment. Firefly AIO-3399J is the host computing device and LPC-H3131 (with flash controller) is the flash-based block device.

PDE implementation on a self-built mobile device testbed, and then perform forensic analysis to identify any potential deniability compromises. We mainly concentrate on the deniability compromises in the underlying storage medium, which is typically NAND flash for mobile devices.

4.1   Experimental Setup

A challenge faced in our experiment was that, almost every commercially available mobile device (smartphones, tablets, smart watches, or the recent IoT devices like smart home assistants) uses a well encapsulated flash-based block device, e.g., UFS cards, eMMC, microSD cards. To facilitate our attacks, we have built a mobile device testbed, which consists of a flash-based block device and a host computing device (Fig. 3). The flash-based block device was built by porting [33] an open-sourced flash controller OpenNFM [22] to a USB header development prototype board LPC-H3131 [3] (Major hardware: ARM9 32-bit ARM926EJ-S, 180 Mhz, 32 MB RAM, and 512 MB NAND flash. The flash memory consists of 128 KB blocks, and each block consists of 2 KB pages). The host computing device was an embedded development board, Firefly AIO-3399J (Major hardware: Six-Core ARM 64-bit processor, 4 GB RAM). The Firefly AIO-3399J was managed by Linux kernel 4.4.194. This mobile device testbed shares a common architecture with mainstream mobile devices in real world.

We then deployed a block-based PDE system in the host computing device. For the hidden volume-based PDEs, we deployed VeraCrypt [7], a fork of the discontinued TrueCrypt project. Note that a large number of PDE systems deployed on the block layer (including PDE systems [6,11] designed for PCs as well as PDE systems [14–16,31,32,34] designed for mobile devices) have utilized the hidden volume technique, and our attack can be applied to most of them. For the steganographic file systems, we deployed stegfs [5], a recent open-source implementation of steganographic file systems [9, 28, 29] in user space[1]. For each deployed PDE system, we analyzed the raw NAND flash to identify the potential PDE compromises.

4.2 Experimental Attacks

Experimentally Attacking the Hidden Volume-based PDEs. We deployed VeraCrypt [7] in the host computing device, and manually created both a public and a hidden volume via VeraCrypt. The public volume occupies the entire disk (i.e., the flash-based block device built by porting OpenNFM to LPC-H3131) and the hidden volume is 200MB in size. The file system deployed in the public volume was exFAT, which writes data sequentially from the beginning of the disk to avoid overwriting the hidden volume stored stealthily in the second half of the disk. We also deployed exFAT in the hidden volume. We performed three tests to simulate behaviors of a device owner as follows:

Test #1: We entered the public mode, and wrote non-sensitive data to the public volume. The size of the non-sensitive data being written is small (i.e., the size is in the magnitude of a few kilobytes, and should be always smaller than the size of a flash block). We then quit the public mode, entered the hidden mode, and wrote a small amount of sensitive data to the hidden volume. The size of the sensitive data being written is similar to the size of the non-sensitive data being written to the public volume. We also repeated the aforementioned operations a few times. This behavior is reasonable. For instance, the user may write a short article to the public volume and then store a small secret audio record to the hidden volume.

Test #2: We entered the public mode and wrote non-sensitive data to the public volume. The size of the non-sensitive data being written should be large, e.g., always larger than the size of one flash block. Then, we quit the public mode, entered the hidden mode, and wrote a small amount of sensitive data to the hidden volume. The size of the sensitive data being written should be small, e.g., in the magnitude of a few kilobytes which is always smaller than the size of a flash block. This behavior is reasonable. For instance, the user may store a large video to the public volume and then store a small secret audio record to the hidden volume.

Test #3: We entered the hidden mode and wrote a small file (i.e., file 1) to the hidden volume. The size of file 1 is a few kilobytes (e.g., 3 KBs). We then modified a few randomly selected locations in file 1 and saved it. Next, we wrote a large file (i.e., file 2) to the hidden volume. The size of file 2 is more than 128 kilobytes. This behavior is reasonable. For instance, the user may create a small secret document in the hidden mode and modify it later; the user may then create another secret document which is large in size.

After each test, we analyzed the corresponding flash memory image. Note that the coercive adversary should have access to the decoy key.

---

[1] Note that the original implementation of the steganographic file system [2, 9, 28] was done in 1999 for Ext2, and has not been updated since then.

From the image obtained after running test #1, we have identified the first type of special flash blocks, i.e., "special block 1" in Fig. 4. Such a block is completely filled with random data, but a portion of pages among this block cannot be decrypted successfully. *Without the PDE deployed*, there are only two possibilities for a block completely filled with random data: 1) All data stored in it can be decrypted successfully, i.e., the block is filled with public data. 2) All data stored in it cannot be decrypted successfully, i.e., the block is completely occupied by random data filled initially. However, *with the PDE deployed*, some of the pages in the block are occupied by the hidden data and cannot be decrypted, as we wrote a small amount of data to the public volume and the hidden volume in turn repeatedly during the test #1. The existence of "special block 1" indicates the device owner has entered the hidden mode and committed hidden sensitive data to the external storage before.

From the image obtained after test #2, we have identified the second type of special blocks, i.e., "special block 2" in Fig. 4. Such a block has a few pages in the beginning storing random data and the remaining pages filling with all '1' bits; among the random data, those located in the end cannot be decrypted. *Without the PDE deployed*, a block is erased and then partially used by the public data which are all decryptable. However, *with the PDE deployed*, some of pages in this block may be used by the hidden data and hence cannot be decrypted. Especially in our test #2, the hidden data will occupy those pages before the empty pages (i.e., a page with all '1's) of the block. Therefore, the existence of "special block 2" also indicates the device owner has committed hidden sensitive data to the external storage before.

From the image obtained after running test #3, we have identified the third type of special blocks, i.e., "special block 3" in Fig. 4. Such a block is completely filled with undecryptable random data, but some of them (i.e., in arbitrary locations across the block) are marked as invalid. A snapshot of a portion of special block 3 is also provided in Fig. 5. This is because: *With the PDE deployed*, a flash block may have been used by the hidden volume, and arbitrary pages across the block may have been updated by the user and hence invalided by the FTL; in addition, the hidden data are encrypted by the true key and cannot be decrypted via the decoy key. However, *Without the PDE deployed*, the data being updated by the user and invalidated by the FTL will be the public data which are decryptable via the decoy key. Therefore, the existence of "special block 3" indicates the existence of the hidden volume. Note that the "special block 3" has not been discovered in the literature.

Experimentally Attacking The Steganographic File System-based PDEs. We deployed stegfs [5] in the host computing device. Note that the steganographic file system works differently from the hidden volume technique that: the file system is initially filled with randomness and the sensitive data are encrypted via a secret key and stored at random locations of the entire disk; it also needs to maintain a few copies of the hidden data across the disk to mitigate loss of hidden sensitive data as the public data may overwrite them over time. We performed one test to simulate the behavior of a device owner as follows:

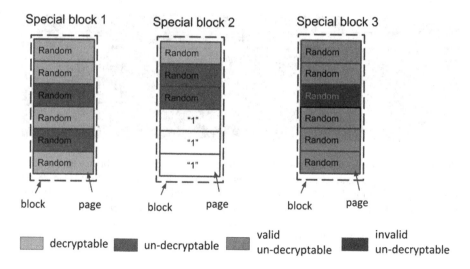

Fig. 4. Special blocks observed in raw NAND flash.

We first mounted the FAT file system on the flash device, and wrote a certain amount of public non-sensitive data. Then, we manually mounted the steganographic file system, and wrote a certain amount of sensitive data. This behavior is reasonable. For instance, the user may first store a few non-sensitive images to the disk via the public file system and then store some secret documents to the disk using the steganographic file system.

After the test, we extracted the corresponding flash memory image and analyzed it. We have identified a few special traces due to the existence of the PDE: 1) Trace #1: public data and random data are interleaving across the entire flash. However, *without the existence of the hidden sensitive data*, the distribution of the data across the flash should be public data followed by random data. This is because: The steganographic file system fills random data across the entire flash initially and, since the FTL uses log-structured writing, regardless how the file system writes public data at the upper layer, the FTL will always program flash blocks from the beginning. Therefore, the observed trace #1 indicates the existence of the hidden sensitive data. 2) Trace #2: public data and random data share the same flash block. Figure 6 shows a snapshot we obtained from one flash block after the test, in which we can observe some of the pages in a flash block store public data which are semantically meaningful, while some of the pages of the block store random undecryptable data. However, *without the existence of the hidden sensitive data*, the distribution of data in a flash block should be either i) public data, followed by all '1' bits, or ii) all public data. This is because: Without the existence of hidden data, each time when the FTL writes public data but cannot find empty pages, it will erase a flash block, and write public data sequentially from the beginning of the block due to the use of log-structured writing; if any pages in this block have not been filled, they

```
block 3897, page 28
a11b2b495e44c9842d2e8f375840961fac9ab9da04271aae9317226bae94f0cf4220358f45d1b6693f351bdd82c7c3bff6ebb53a838e46b
504a949f59312a46bb43f2633d316eda3b312d3740cff762bf31c0d0b67ffdfb7a97c2982f9ed4c74951d88c275aedbae20cf78b3d71e85
492e45c5b46ea7ae2091ae41c3e34da6209224417fe3ce55585b327abb8f95ffca3b2167ff78f91584f1d85ca4bbf96ae526b49e7c86b74
be789db252a5ed8cc6d99bfca19af8e46e1f64556e3a565f2c2b6dd2d025f182b3374b4243706160f548d0ec2095702af577907766983a6
571b398f2cc5a47be1d28fbf3f1b5a367a75da26167ed6957cb


block 3897, page 36
a11b2b495e44c9842d2e8f375840961fac9ab9da04271aae9317226bae94f0cf4220358f45d1b6693f351bdd82c7c3bff6ebb53a838e46b
504a949f59312a46bb43f2633d316eda3b312d3740cff762bf31c0d0b67ffdfb7a97c2982f9e3bf63c12fdc1ce7250986725633bfdb4388
59f6ea41591df2817a53453214b340a34d31d227324b5d7d6843cecf37a9f115e318fd1ca5989e1a218f25ca6feeca8a8d16bdbfbe9fb84
a6334714b713d49932a672e274911c296aeb892cba1cdbc967da1d733a97311529f75441798b7a2f7de72dc11f5c4b35b19fcbca46e6913
c7b961159ba7
```

Fig. 5. A snapshot (portion) of special block 3. Every 4 bits have been converted to the corresponding hexadecimal digit. In this snapshot, the data stored on page 28 has been updated and invalidated by the FTL, and the newly updated data are written to page 36. The data stored in the aforementioned pages are undecryptable.

```
block is 26, page is 12
int main(int argc, char *argv[]) {
        enableRawMode();
        initEditor();
        ...
}

block is 26, page is 13, content is ⍰⍰⍰⍰⍰⍰⍰⍰⍰⍰⍰⍰⍰⍰⍰⍰⍰    ⍰
⍰⍰⍰⍰⍰
⍰⍰⍰⍰⍰⍰⍰⍰⍰⍰⍰⍰⍰⍰⍰⍰⍰⍰⍰⍰⍰⍰⍰⍰⍰⍰⍰⍰⍰⍰⍰⍰⍰⍰⍰ ⍰!⍰"⍰#⍰$⍰%⍰&⍰'⍰(⍰)⍰*⍰+⍰,⍰-⍰.⍰/⍰0⍰
block is 26, page is 14, content is ⍰⍰⍰⍰⍰⍰⍰⍰⍰⍰⍰⍰⍰⍰⍰⍰⍰    ⍰
⍰⍰⍰⍰⍰
⍰⍰⍰⍰⍰⍰⍰⍰⍰⍰⍰⍰⍰⍰⍰⍰⍰⍰⍰⍰⍰⍰⍰⍰⍰⍰⍰⍰⍰⍰⍰⍰⍰⍰⍰ ⍰!⍰"⍰#⍰$⍰%⍰&⍰'⍰(⍰)⍰*⍰+⍰,⍰-⍰.⍰/⍰0⍰
block is 26, page is 15, content is E          ⍰
block is 26, page is 16, content is E          ⍰
block is 26, page is 17, content is E          ⍰
block is 26, page is 18, content is $警鳍⍰藴側尷瑞Y佩??1嬉]N1?N⍰1
⍰邡R龃蜂贩凳镨Y澶RQ?\蔣zz⍰鳩N??瓷        pXf?E?⍰mA?Y?c9??魇U4ゾ?壓
block is 26, page is 19, content is j⍰熠?舩6栅?A鱸tne??[[??TW)1Z{
婼   欵⍰鹗淨舫豎愍睍紎W赡k⍰??僿⍰=统=?⍰迮畴嗹⍰懿⍰到   籑⍰f:G蝬猢?臨'
那勒?菁j蜥?⍰黧€靫??稷W鼻⍰嵇鉦⍰嚣?VU扪c$鳑?tz?B罨?,
舠g\Z⍰Re?
```

Fig. 6. A snapshot (portion) from a flash block when attacking the steganographic file system

remain empty and contain all '1's. Therefore, the observed trace #2 indicates the existence of the hidden sensitive data.

5 Discussion

Assessing the Difficulty of Performing Our Attacks. To compromise the deniability by having access to the raw flash memory, the adversary needs to tackle two issues: 1) how to extract an image from the NAND flash memory given a victim mobile device, and 2) how to perform forensic analysis over the raw flash memory data. For the first issue, Breeuwsma et al. [12] introduced a few low-level data acquisition methods for flash memory, including flasher tools, using an access port commonly used for testing and debugging, etc. Chen et al. [20] mentioned a method of obtaining raw data from SSDs "by opening the covers and directly reading the memory chips with cheap off the shelf readers".

For the second issue, the adversary can use the existing digital forensic tools available on the market (e.g., Photorec [4], etc.) or develop new special tools to analyze the captured image.

Implications of Our Experimental Attacks. Our attacks performed in this work confirm that it is indeed feasible to compromise the block-based PDE systems in practice. Our results further justify that the deniability compromise in the lower storage medium is indeed a significant issue and should be considered seriously when designing any future PDE systems for mobile computing devices. An immediate remediation would be moving the entire PDE system design to the flash translation layer (FTL) [20,25] which however, would not be a good solution as it will impose a large burden on the FTL firmware. In addition, as the PDE integrated in the FTL firmware is far away from the user applications, making it user unfriendly. It is unclear how to design a PDE system which is 1) secure (i.e., eliminating deniability compromises in the flash memory), and 2) keeping the FTL lightweight, and 3) user-friendly. This is still an open problem in the literature.

Other Attacks on the PDE Systems. This work only focuses on the single-snapshot attack in which the adversary is only allowed to have access to the victim device once. A stronger adversary may conduct the multiple-snapshot attack by periodically accessing to the victim device [17,18,20]. By capturing different snapshots of the external storage over time and comparing the different snapshots, the adversary will detect changes of the hidden sensitive data, compromising the deniability. For example, if the hidden volume technique is used, by comparing different snapshots, the adversary may observe data changes performed in the space which is claimed empty but actually hides the hidden volume. Some of mitigation strategies can be accompanying public writes with dummy writes and hiding the sensitive data into the dummy writes [17,18], or using the WOM (write-once memory) code to encode the hidden data in a public cover [20]. In addition, this work only focuses on the deniability compromises in the external storage, but hidden sensitive data may leave traces in the internal memory, and such traces may be extracted by the adversary by performing memory forensics [13]. One potential solution is to power-off the device each time after quitting the hidden mode in which the user can manage the hidden sensitive data. Another solution could be leveraging trusted execution environments (TEE) like Arm TrustZone [27] so that the memory used to process the hidden sensitive data can be protected, avoiding being accessed by the adversary.

6   Related Work

In the following, we summarize the major PDE systems utilizing the hidden volume technique or the steganographic file systems. A thorough literature review of PDE system can be found in [35].

6.1   The Hidden Volume-Based PDE Systems

Skillen et al. proposed Mobiflage [31,32], which adapts the hidden volume technique to Android devices. There are a few variants of Mobiflage. One variant assumes the existence of an FAT32 SD card, and deploys the public volume/hidden volume to this SD card. Another variant releases the aforementioned assumption by using a modified Ext4 file system. Yu et al. proposed [34] MobiHydra to mitigate a booting-time attack faced by Mobiflage. In addition, MobiHydra allows the user to switch from the public to the hidden mode without rebooting the device and supports multi-level deniability. Chang et al. designed Mobipluto [14,15], the first file system friendly PDE system which allows any block-based file systems to be deployed on the public volume, by smartly integrating the hidden volume technique with thin provisioning. Chang et al. further extended the hidden volume technique to combat the multi-snapshot adversary by introducing dummy writes on the block layer [16]. Jia et al. proposed DEFTL [26], the first hidden volume-based PDE system integrated with the flash translation layer. Barker et al. [10] proposed Artifice, which can meet a few additional security requirements including: 1) information leakage resistance, and 2) deniable changes, and 3) deniable software.

6.2   The Steganographic File Systems

Anderson et al. [9] proposed the first steganographic file system. One of their constructions is to hide the secret data among the randomness. The system maintains several copies of secret data to reduce the possibility of losing them. Inspired by Anderson et al.'s construction, McDonald et al. [28] designed a more practical as well as efficient steganographic file system, in which secret files are hidden in unused blocks of a partition which also contains normal files. Pang et al. [29] proposed StegFS, a new steganographic file system which allows the user to hide his/her files or directories in a selective manner. A salient advantage of StegFS is that it can ensure integrity of files while maintaining effective disk utilization. Zhou et al. [36] further mitigate the attacks which may compromise the steganographic file system by analyzing data access of use applications.

7   Conclusion

In this work, we have experimentally confirmed the deniability compromises of the block-layer PDE systems deployed on the mobile computing devices. Our work conducts the first experimental attacks by 1) deploying both the hidden volume-based PDE and the steganographic file system on the block layer of a mobile device testbed, and 2) allowing the adversary to have access to the flash memory and to perform forensic analysis over the raw flash memory data. Our results strengthen the necessity of taking care of the deniability compromises in the lower storage layer when designing any future PDE systems for mobile devices.

Acknowledgments. This work was supported by US National Science Foundation under grant number 1928349-CNS, 1928331-CNS, 1938130-CNS, and 2043022-DGE.

References

1. Android full disk encryption. https://source.android.com/security/encryption/. Accessed 21 Apr 2022
2. Index. https://www.cl.cam.ac.uk/~mgk25/stegfs/. Accessed 21 Apr 2022
3. Lpc-h3131. https://www.olimex.com/Products/ARM/NXP/LPC-H3131/. Accessed 21 Apr 2022
4. Photorec. https://www.cgsecurity.org/wiki/PhotoRec. Accessed 28 Mar 2022
5. stegfs. https://sourceforge.net/projects/stegfs/. Accessed 21 Apr 2022
6. Truecrypt. https://truecrypt.sourceforge.net/. Accessed 21 Apr 2022
7. Veracrypt. https://www.veracrypt.fr/code/VeraCrypt/. Accessed 21 Apr 2022
8. How to encrypt your devices (2017). https://spreadprivacy.com/how-to-encrypt-devices/. Accessed 21 Apr 2022
9. Anderson, R., Needham, R., Shamir, A.: The steganographic file system. In: Aucsmith, D. (ed.) IH 1998. LNCS, vol. 1525, pp. 73–82. Springer, Heidelberg (1998). https://doi.org/10.1007/3-540-49380-8_6
10. Barker, A., Gupta, Y., Au, S., Chou, E., Miller, E., Long, D.: Artifice: data in disguise. In: Proceedings of the 36th International Conference on Massive Storage Systems and Technology (MSST 2020) (2020)
11. Blass, E.O., Mayberry, T., Noubir, G., Onarlioglu, K.: Toward robust hidden volumes using write-only oblivious ram. In: Proceedings of the 2014 ACM SIGSAC Conference on Computer and Communications Security, pp. 203–214. ACM (2014)
12. Breeuwsma, M., De Jongh, M., Klaver, C., Van Der Knijff, R., Roeloffs, M.: Forensic data recovery from flash memory. Small Scale Digital Device Forensics J. **1**(1), 1–17 (2007)
13. Burdach, M.: Physical Memory Forensics. Black Hat, USA (2006)
14. Blass, E.O., Mayberry, T., Noubir, G., Onarlioglu, K.: User-friendly deniable storage for mobile devices. Comput. Secur. 72:163–174 (2018)
15. Chang, B., Wang, Z., Chen, B., Zhang, F.: MobiPluto: file system friendly deniable storage for mobile devices. In: Proceedings of the 31st annual computer security applications conference, pp. 381–390 (2015)
16. Chang, B., et al.: Mobiceal: Towards secure and practical plausibly deniable encryption on mobile devices. In: 2018 48th Annual IEEE/IFIP International Conference on Dependable Systems and Networks (DSN), pp. 454–465. IEEE (2018)
17. Chen, B.: Towards designing a secure plausibly deniable system for mobile devices against multi-snapshot adversaries-a preliminary design. arXiv preprint arXiv:2002.02379 (2020)
18. Chen, B., Chen, N.: Poster: a secure plausibly deniable system for mobile devices against multi-snapshot adversaries. In: 2020 IEEE Symposium on Security and Privacy Poster Session (2020)
19. Chen, C., Chakraborti, A., Sion, R.: INFUSE: Invisible plausibly-deniable file system for NAND flash. Proc. Priv. Enhancing Technol. **4**, 239–254 (2020)
20. Chen, C., Chakraborti, A., Sion, R.: PEARL: plausibly deniable flash translation layer using WOM coding. In: The 30th Usenix Security Symposium (2021)

21. Chen, N., Chen, B., Shi, W.: MobiWear: a plausibly deniable encryption system for wearable mobile devices. In: Chen, B., Huang, X. (eds.) AC3 2021. LNICST, vol. 386, pp. 138–154. Springer, Cham (2021). https://doi.org/10.1007/978-3-030-80851-8_10
22. Google Code. Opennfm. https://code.google.com/p/opennfm/. Accessed 21 Apr 2022
23. Feng, W., et al.: MobiGyges: a mobile hidden volume for preventing data loss, improving storage utilization, and avoiding device reboot. Future Gener. Comput. Syst. **109**, 158–171 (2020)
24. Guan, L., et al.: Supporting transparent snapshot for bare-metal malware analysis on mobile devices. In: Proceedings of the 33rd Annual Computer Security Applications Conference, pp. 339–349. ACM (2017)
25. Jia, S., Xia, L., Chen, B., Liu, P.: NFPS: adding undetectable secure deletion to flash translation layer. In: Proceedings of the 11th ACM on Asia Conference on Computer and Communications Security, pp. 305–315. ACM (2016)
26. Jia, S., Xia, L., Chen, B., Liu, P.: DEFTL: implementing plausibly deniable encryption in flash translation layer. In: Proceedings of the 2017 ACM SIGSAC Conference on Computer and Communications Security, pp. 2217–2229 (2017)
27. Liao, J., Chen, B., Shi, W.: TrustZone enhanced plausibly deniable encryption system for mobile devices. In: 2021 IEEE/ACM Symposium on Edge Computing (SEC), pp. 441–447. IEEE (2021)
28. McDonald, A.D., Kuhn, M.G.: StegFS: a steganographic file system for Linux. In: Pfitzmann, A. (ed.) IH 1999. LNCS, vol. 1768, pp. 463–477. Springer, Heidelberg (2000). https://doi.org/10.1007/10719724_32
29. Pang, H., Tan, K. L., Zhou, X.: StegFS: a steganographic file system. In: Proceedings 19th International Conference on Data Engineering (Cat. No. 03CH37405), pp. 657–667. IEEE (2003)
30. Peters, T.M., Gondree, M.A., Peterson, Z.N.: DEFY: a deniable, encrypted file system for log-structured storage. In: 22th Annual Network and Distributed System Security Symposium, NDSS (2015)
31. Skillen, A., Mannan, M.: On implementing deniable storage encryption for mobile devices. In: 20th Annual Network and Distributed System Security Symposium, NDSS 2013, San Diego, California, USA, 24–27 February 2013
32. Skillen, A., Mannan, M.: Mobiflage: deniable storage encryption for mobile devices. IEEE Trans. Dependable Secure Comput. **11**(3), 224–237 (2014)
33. Tankasala, D., Chen, N., Chen, B.A.: A step-by-step guideline for creating a testbed for flash memory research via lpc-h3131 and opennfm (2020)
34. Yu, X., Chen, B., Wang, Z., Chang, B., Zhu, W.T., Jing, J.: MobiHydra: pragmatic and multi-level plausibly deniable encryption storage for mobile devices. In: Chow, S.S.M., Camenisch, J., Hui, L.C.K., Yiu, S.M. (eds.) ISC 2014. LNCS, vol. 8783, pp. 555–567. Springer, Cham (2014). https://doi.org/10.1007/978-3-319-13257-0_36
35. Zhang, Q., Jia, S., Chang, B., Chen, B.: Ensuring data confidentiality via plausibly deniable encryption and secure deletion-a survey. Cybersecurity **1**(1), 1 (2018)
36. Zhou, X., Pang, H., Tan, K.L.: Hiding data accesses in steganographic file system. In: Proceedings 20th International Conference on Data Engineering, pp. 572–583. IEEE (2004)

Black-Box Testing of Cryptographic Algorithms Based on Data Characteristics

Haoling Fan[1,2,3], Lingjia Meng[1,2,3], Fangyu Zheng[1,2,3(✉)], Mingyu Wang[1,2,3], and Bowen Xu[1,2,3]

[1] State Key Laboratory of Information Security, Institute of Information Engineering, Chinese Academy of Sciences, Beijing 100093, China
{fanhaoling,menglingjia,zhengfangyu,wangmingyu,xubowen}@iie.ac.cn
[2] Data Assurance and Communications Security Center, Chinese Academy of Sciences, Beijing 100093, China
[3] School of Cyber Security, University of Chinese Academy of Sciences, Beijing 100049, China

Abstract. Serving communications security, identity authentication, etc., cryptographic algorithms constitute the cornerstone of cyberspace security. During the past decades, cryptanalysts have proved that many once prevailing cryptographic algorithms (e.g., MD4, MD5, 3DES, RC4) are no longer secure now. However, insecure cryptographic algorithms are still widely deployed in practice, seriously endangering the security of cyberspace. The reasons for this dilemma are many-fold, one of which is difficult to detect the algorithms used in the legacy binaries. Most of the existing detecting methods of cryptographic algorithms, either require source code analysis (i.e., white-box testing) or depend on the dynamic execution information (i.e., dynamic testing), narrowing the testing scope where the source codes of commercial software are not provided and the running environment may be difficult to deploy. In this paper, we propose a method of static black-box testing of cryptographic algorithms, which can identify a specific algorithm based on the corresponding data characteristics. We have implemented the testing method and used it to check 150 binaries of three types, including cryptographic libraries, commonly-used programs that use cryptographic algorithms, and general-purpose Github projects without cryptographic algorithms. The empirical results demonstrate that 80.6% of the insecure cryptographic algorithm are implemented in the test files that contain the cryptographic algorithms. The false negative rate and false positive rate were 2.10% and 1.68% using our method. Moreover, we found that the insecure cryptographic algorithms (i.e., MD4, SHA-1) is still exist in some popular software, e.g., MbedTLS and 7-Zip.

Keywords: Black-box testing · Data characteristics · Algorithm identification

This work is supported in part by the National Natural Science Foundation of China No. 61902392 and CCF-Tencent Open Fund under Grant RAGR20210131. The corresponding author is Fangyu Zheng.

J. Lin and Q. Tang (Eds.): AC3 2022, LNICST 448, pp. 153–169, 2022.
https://doi.org/10.1007/978-3-031-17081-2_10

1   Introduction

The proliferation of the Internet has given rise to remote conferences, e-commerce, especially after the pandemic of COVID-19. Cryptography plays a vital role in cyberspace security, ensuring the confidentiality and the integrity of information, preventing information from being tampered and forged.

Built upon computational complexity theory, the practical cryptographic algorithms are not absolutely-secure.

We consider the reasons for the insecurity of cryptographic algorithms, including short keys, back doors, collision in hash algorithms, and so on. The widely-used insecure cryptographic algorithms are shown in Table 1.

Table 1. Insecure cryptographic algorithms

Cryptographic algorithm	Insecure reference
MD2	MD2 was obsoleted in RFC 6149 [24]
MD4	In 2011, RFC 6150 stated that RFC 1320 (MD4) is historic (obsoleted) [22]
MD5	Approved the information RFC 6151 to update the security considerations in MD5 [25]
SHA-1	NIST formally deprecated the use of SHA-1 in 2011 [23]
DES/3DES	NIST has deprecated DES and 3DES for new applications in 2017, and for all application by 2023 [18]
RC2	It is vulnerable to brute force attacks, the 40-bit cryptographic algorithm is outdated [11]
RC4	RC4 was banned from all versions of TLS in 2015 by RFC7465 [16]
RSA[a]	Insecure padding mode and insufficient key length [5]
ECC/DH	Based on unsafe elliptic curves [7]
Dual_EC_DRBG	NIST removed Dual_EC_DRBG from the pseudorandom number generator algorithm standard [21]

[a] When we use black-box testing tool to identify RSA as an insecure cryptographic algorithm, we can only detect the existence of a specific implementation of RSA, and further analysis is required for its padding mode and key length.

Any insecure cryptographic algorithm would seriously affect the overall security of the system. However, out of our expectation, such great risks do not seem to raise worldwide attention. Disabled cryptographic algorithms are still used: 25% of websites in 2011 are still using insecure MD5 [1], and 2015 statistics show that about 30% of network communications are still protected by disabled RC4 [2]. Outdated cryptographic algorithms in cryptographic libraries are abused, Lazar et al. found that 83% of cryptographic vulnerabilities are caused by misuse of cryptographic vaults [14], and Egele et al. found that about 88% of mobile applications (sampled from Google Play) involve a considerable degree of misuse of the cryptographic library [8]. Detection is the first step required to address the issue of insecure cryptographic algorithms and implementations. A straightforward method for cryptographic algorithm identification is code review. The manual detection method of cryptographic algorithm is time-consuming and laborious, and requires personnel with professional skills. Meanwhile, some software can not release source codes, and thus the code review method cannot apply. In order to detect cryptographic algorithms of closed-source software, researchers perform binary file detection, including dynamic analysis and static analysis. Static methods, e.g., Cipher hunting [10], CryptoGuard [20], CrySL [13], do not execute the program but require disassembly or decompilation of the file under test to check for the existence of an implementation of a cryptographic algorithm. The advantage of static analysis is that the program does not required actual executions. However, static analysis may fail to trigger some cryptographic algorithms in the code, resulting in a higher false negative rate and false positive rate. The methods of dynamic analysis include K-Hunt [15], Reformat [26], SMV-Hunter [9]. Dynamic analysis requires an encryption algorithm to be triggered at runtime for detection, and dynamic detection is relatively time-consuming.

In order to solve the problems of the existing detection methods, in this paper, we propose a cryptographic algorithm detection method that does not require open source or an execution environment, has a low false negative rate and false positive rate, and is highly efficient. According to this method, we have implemented a black-box testing tool for cryptographic algorithms based on characteristic data. This paper makes the following main contributions:

- **Characteristic data classification.** We perform artificial data characteristic extraction on the standard of cryptographic algorithms and implementations in common libraries, and then classify them, including a total of 10 categories (the categories on the right in Fig. 2) for the subsequent identification of cryptographic algorithms (Sect. 2).
- **Set properties for characteristic data.** 1) We set the **Weight** for the characteristic data to reduce the false negative rate. The **Weight** setting is based on three principles: *Length* - whether the length of the characteristic data is greater than 2 bytes; *Uniqueness* - whether the characteristic data is only used by one cryptographic algorithm; *Activeness* - whether the characteristic data participates in the calculation. 2) The **List** we set we set uses the relationship among different characteristic data as the basis for identification to reduce the false positive rate. The relationship of characteristic data includes two types of positional relationships: a set of characteristic data is in continuous position; a set of characteristic data occurs cyclically at the same interval (Sect. 3.2).
- **Implemented a cryptographic algorithm black-box testing tool.** We provide a method for black-box detection of cryptographic algorithms based on characteristic data, and then we make a tool based on this method. The tool includes a characteristic database (Sect. 3.2), a matching strategy module (Sect. 3.3), a decision module (Sect. 3.4), and a result output module.
- **Evaluation of black-box testing tool.** We evaluate the test tool by testing 150 binary executables of different sizes (1KB-4GB), including 23 popular cryptographic libraries, 8 cryptography-related programs, and 119 cryptography-independent programs. The final false negative rate is 2.10%, and the false positive rate is 1.68%.

The rest of the paper is organized as follows. Section 2 discusses the pre-required knowledge. In Sect. 3, we designed and implemented a black-box testing tool based on characteristic data. In Sect. 4, we evaluated the tool. Section 5 summarizes this paper.

2   Preliminaries

The data characteristics of cryptographic algorithms drive the cryptographic algorithm detection proposed in this paper. Due to the particularity of crypto-graphic algorithms, many cryptographic algorithms use special constants in the process of data processing. We divided the characteristic data into 10 *categories* (**C1–C10**).

The characteristic data of these three cryptographic algorithms are described below.

Hash Algorithms map an arbitrary finite-length input to a fixed-length output. The characteristic data of this type of cryptographic algorithms include *initialization vectors* (**C1**), *round constants* (**C2**) and *logical operation function constants* (**C3**). When implemented, *initialization vectors* are used to initialize the parameters in the hash calculation process, the *round constants* and *logical operation function constants* participate in the transformation of each round of encryption.

Symmetric Cryptographic Algorithms transform a data-to-be-encrypted into ciphertext under the control of the encryption key. *S-box* (**C4**), *permutation table* (**C5**) and *lookup table* (**C6**) for fast implementation of encryption are used in the implementation of symmetric cryptographic algorithms. These characteristic data are all used for data substitution, and are generally defined as a static array in software implementation. Symmetric cryptographic algorithms use these data in the implementation to increase the degree of confusion in the encryption process.

Asymmetric Cryptographic Algorithms in real-world applications are mainly divided into two categories: one is based on large integer factorization, such as RSA; The other is based on discrete logarithm problems, such as elliptic curve cryptography (ECC). For asymmetric cryptographic algorithms, we mainly focus on three aspects: 1) Diffie-Hellman key exchange algorithm. Through the study of its principle, we noticed that it uses *preset prime values* (**C7**), and these prime numbers can be used as its characteristic data. 2) ECC. We found that all the standards and implementations will use the recommended *elliptic curve related parameters* (**C8**), so the elliptic curve related parameters are used as the characteristic data of the elliptic curve. 3) *RSA*. Since the principle of RSA is based on the factorization of large integers, we found that it will generate many large prime numbers when it is implemented, and the code that generates large prime numbers often contains *a table of small prime numbers* (**C9**), and small prime numbers will appear in the data segment, we use the small prime number table as the characteristic data.

The pseudo-random number generator is also a class of algorithms that we need to detect, in which the implementation of Dual_EC_DRBG is based on an elliptic curve, and *elliptic curve related parameters.* (**C8**) can be used as characteristic data.

In addition to the above characteristic data, the *OID* (Object Identifier) (**C10**) of the cryptographic algorithm itself can also play an auxiliary role in the identification process of the cryptographic algorithm. We also use OID as a type of characteristic data.

3   Design and Implementation

We aim to achieve a fast, accurate, and comprehensive black-box testing tool for cryptographic algorithms. And the detection is mainly based on the characteristic data of cryptographic algorithms in binary executables. Therefore, it can support cryptographic algorithm detection for closed-source software without running binary executables. This section describes the design goals, outlines the black-box testing tool, and then introduces the design details of the characteristic data set, matching strategy, and determination method.

3.1   Overview

We design the architecture of a black-box testing tool for cryptographic algorithms based on characteristic data, as shown in Fig. 1. The tool follows a modular design, which can reduce the complexity of the tool design and ensure the relative independence between modules, which is convenient for development and modification. The black-box testing tool consists of three modules: I) characteristic data extraction and data set construction module; II) characteristic data matching module; III) cryptographic algorithm determination and output module. Figure 1 outlines the workflow of the tool as follows:

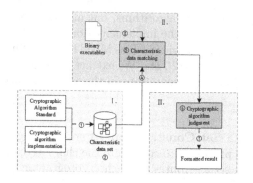

Fig. 1. Cryptographic algorithm black-box testing tool architecture

3.2 Characteristic Data Extraction and Data Set Construction

Characteristic data needs to be extracted and analyzed before using in cryptographic algorithm detection. The process of characteristic data extraction and data set construction is shown in Fig. 2.

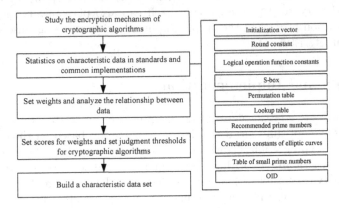

Fig. 2. Characteristic data set construction process

Characteristic Data Extraction The characteristics data of the cryptographic algorithms are the key to black-box testing. The selected characteristic data should be representative and remain unchanged when the environment changes. We researched and analyzed the implementation of cryptographic algorithms in standards and cryptographic libraries. It was discovered that cryptographic algorithms perform special operations on data, such as substitution and obfuscation. When performing special operations on data, the algorithm uses some specific constants. We use the specific constants used in the special data processing as the characteristic data of the cryptographic algorithm.

It's also worth noting that we not only analyze characteristic data from the standards of cryptographic algorithms, but also the popular cryptographic libraries. We have investigated the implementation of cryptographic algorithms in cryptographic algorithm libraries such as MbedTLS [19], OpenSSL [27], Botan [17], Crypto++ [6], libgcrypt [12], etc. We extract the characteristic data of the cryptographic algorithm implementations in the above cryptographic algorithm library.

Characteristic Data Set Construction After collecting the raw characteristic data, we need to process it to constitute the characteristic data set directly used by our tool. We set attributes for each cryptographic algorithm and each characteristic data. The meaning of each attribute is: **Algorithm** refers to the name of the cryptographic algorithm; **DataNum** refers to the total number of characteristic data of the cryptographic algorithm; **DataName** refers to the name of the characteristic data; **Weight** refers to the artificially set characteristic data weight; **List** is an attribute set for characteristic data with associated relationship. The associated relationship refers to the storage location of characteristic data that occurs next to each other or at cyclic intervals. Characteristic data with associated relationships has the same List value, represented as a group. The List value of characteristic data that is not associated with any characteristic data is 0; **Data** is the value of characteristic data.

For the characteristic data of the cryptographic algorithms, we set the weight and the association relationship, each weight corresponds to a score, and calculated the threshold of each cryptographic algorithm through the weight value.

Weight. After extracting the characteristic data, we made statistics on the characteristic data in different cryptographic algorithms and the length of the characteristic data. We found that multiple cryptographic algorithms use some characteristic data and some characteristic data is too short to act as a piece of strong evidence. Therefore, we set the individual weight for each characteristic data. We set the weights based on three principles: 1) Length. Whether the length of the characteristic data is greater than 2 bytes; 2) Uniqueness. Whether characteristic data is used by only one cryptographic algorithm; 3) Activeness. Whether the characteristic data is involved in the calculation. The characteristic weight information is initially determined manually and is divided into three levels: *high (H), medium (M),* and *low (L).*

- **High weight:** We specify that the characteristic data used by only one cryptographic algorithm has a high weight, that is, other cryptographic algorithms do not use the characteristic data, and the length of the characteristic data is greater than 2 bytes, such as the S-box of DES.
- **Medium weight:** Our research found that different cryptographic algorithms may use the same characteristic data. We set this shared characteristic data as medium weight. And the length of the characteristic data of the medium weight is greater than 2 bytes. For example, SHA-1 and MD5 have the same initialization vector, this initialization vector is medium-weight characteristic data in both cryptographic algorithms.
- **Low weight:** We experimented on the length of the characteristic data. The empirical result showed that the characteristic data with a length of one or two bytes has a great probability of appearing in the cryptography-irrelevant part of the binary executables, so we set this type as low weight. At the same time, the experiment also found that although the OID of the cryptographic algorithm can uniquely identify the cryptographic algorithm, there is a high possibility that the binary executable contains the data value of OID without the existence of the corresponding cryptographic algorithm, which leads to false positive. OID does not participate in the calculation. Therefore, OID only assists the testing of the cryptographic algorithm, and we set the OID to low weight.

Association Relationship. We noticed that some characteristic data has an association relationship. There are two types of association relationships here: one is that a group of characteristic data positions appear adjacently, for example, a group of S-boxes in DES are stored in the data segment adjacently; the other is that characteristic data appears cyclically, such as the round constant in the hash algorithm, because it requires multiple rounds of calculations, so it appears regularly in the code segment of the binary executable. We set the attribute *List* for the characteristic data of a cryptographic algorithm. The 0 value of *List* indicating that the characteristic data has no association relationship with other characteristic data, We set the *List* values to the same non-zero value for characteristic data with an associative relationship.

Score and Threshold. To facilitate the subsequent determination of the cryptographic algorithm, we assign scores based on each characteristic data's weight and association relationship and calculate the cryptographic algorithm determination threshold. In different cryptographic algorithms, the scores of each weight are different, we calculate the corresponding scores for the three weights of each cryptographic algorithm according to the following calculation principles:

- The score of high-weight (H) data is greater than that of low-weight data (M, L).
- The total score of middle-weight (M) data in an algorithm must not exceed the value of high-weight (H) data.
- The total score of the low-weight data (L) shall not exceed the score of medium-weight data (M).

The calculation formula of each weight score (S_H, S_M, S_L) is shown in formula (1), where N_H, N_M, N_L are the number of characteristic data with weights H, M, and L in a cryptographic algorithm, and n is the preset score of the H weight.

$$S_H = n; S_M = \lfloor n/(N_M + 1) \rfloor; S_L = \lfloor S_M/(N_L + 1) \rfloor; \tag{1}$$

The weights M and L scores are calculated according to the above regulations and the number of characteristic data contained in M and L in the algorithm. The weight of the characteristic data is assigned a specific score. For each cryptographic algorithm, the threshold is calculated based on the weight of its characteristic data. The weight scores of the characteristic data are sequentially accumulated as the threshold. T is the threshold, and its calculation formula is shown in formula (2).

$$T = S_H * N_H + S_M * N_M + S_L * N_L \tag{2}$$

The two most important parameters are the score of weight and threshold information of each characteristic data. The scores and threshold information are set manually. They are optimized through training to reduce the false negative rate and false positive rate during the testing process.

3.3   Characteristic Data Matching Strategy

The characteristic matching strategy is used to query the characteristic of the cryptographic algorithm in the target binary executable. The matching strategy consists of three parts: 1) binary executable information's extraction, including file format, machine word length and byte order, record position offset and size information of data segment, read-only data segment, and code segment; 2) characteristic data conversion, we will convert the byte order according to different data types before matching. In the matching module, different types of feature data are used as input in turn; 3) result record, we take the binary executable to be tested and the characteristic dataset as the input object of the matching strategy, and finally record the matching result.

3.4   Cryptographic Algorithm Determination

This module analyzes the characteristic information that is successfully matched under the characteristic matching logic and determines the existence of the cryptographic algorithm in the tested object by processing the weight and association relationship of the characteristic information. The cryptographic algorithm decision logic is responsible for processing the matched characteristics to verify the existence of specific cryptographic algorithm implementation.

Characteristic Data Relevance Detection. For characteristic data with an association relationship, the successful matching of a single characteristic data is often more likely to cause false positives. By detecting whether all the characteristic data that has an association relationship appears or not, assists in deciding whether the tested binary executable contains a cryptographic algorithm implementation. Suppose each data in a group of data with an association relationship is close to the position in the data segment or periodically appears in the code segment. In that case, it proves that the group of data conforms to the attribute of the association relationship.

Characteristic Data Matching Result Statistics. We design the score calculation to determine the cryptographic algorithm as a reward system. We score each cryptographic algorithm, based on the weight of the successfully matched entry and the existence of the association relationship. Subsequently, we compare the score with the threshold to determine the probability of the existence of the cryptographic algorithm implementation. Finally, we show the cryptographic algorithms supported by the tested file in the form of a list. The output result also includes the matching situation of each characteristic data.

4   Evaluation

To evaluate the effectiveness and efficiency of the proposed method, we employ the tool against various binary executables, which are of different types and sizes.

4.1 Experiments Setup

The evaluation was conducted on a ThinkCentre M920t PC with Intel i7-9700 CPU (3.00 GHz) and 8 GB RAM. The operating system is Ubuntu 16.04 LTS. The binary executable formats tested include PE and ELF. Binary executables come from Intel and ARM processors, and our tool supports detection of binaries in both 32-bit and 64-bit operating systems. Test files include popular crypto libraries, binaries with cryptography, and binaries without cryptography. The source of the test file is shown in the Table 2.

Table 2. File source for false negative testing

Popular crypto libraries	Binaries with cryptography	Binaries w/o cryptography
openssl-0.9.8 openssl-1.0.2u openssl-1.1.0l openssl-1.1.1c openssl-1.1.1k mbedtls-2.1.0 Botan-2.15.0 libgcrypt-20.2.6 crypto++-8.2	7z RAR KeePass ultrasurf	Files in this category are from 58 projects that are easy to obtain executable binary executables labeled by "tool", "release", "exe" and "C++" on GitHub according to the time sequence. See Appendix B for a detailed list

4.2 Effectiveness

We first recorded the cryptographic algorithm support of the test files before the test, then used the black-box testing tools to test the cryptographic algorithms on these test files, and compare and analyze the results with the actual conditions recorded. We evaluate the effectiveness of the tool under two important metrics: false negative rate and false positive rate.

False Negative Rate. Through black-box testing, we detect which cryptographic algorithms are in binaries with cryptography and prevalent cryptographic libraries.

We first count all the cryptographic algorithms in the test file. The total number of cryptographic algorithms is recorded as T. After the test, we add up the number of false negative cryptographic algorithms in each file to be tested. The number is recorded as t. The formula for calculating false negative rate is t/T. In our tests, the false negative rate is 2.10%. The false negatives mainly come from the following aspects:

- *Assembly code invalidates characteristic data.* We discover that if there is assembly code in the implementation of cryptographic algorithms the characteristic data would not work. We found assembly code implementations of Cast, AES and Camellia in OpenSSL.

- *Characteristic data generated at runtime cannot be detected.* The characteristic data will be generated only when the cryptographic algorithm is used. The detection of RC4 failed for this reason.
- *No characteristic data in the implementation of cryptographic algorithms.* Implementing some cryptographic algorithms does not require characteristic data in the software code form. The hardware implementation of AES in Botan does not require characteristic data and thus cannot be detected using our method.
- *Characteristic data detection capabilities are limited.* For RSA, we select a small prime table (used for key generation and prime detection) and OID as characteristic data. Still, OID can only play a supporting role, and other algorithms also use the small prime number table.

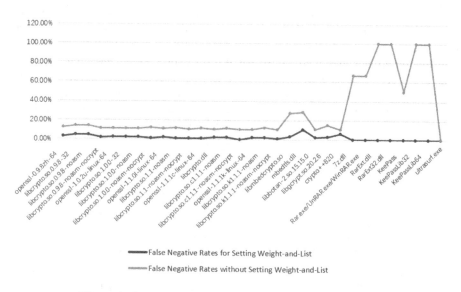

Fig. 3. Influence of weight-and-list on false negative rate

We set the *Weight-and-List* attribute for the characteristic data, Fig. 3 shows the comparison of false negative rates for setting *Weight-and-List* or not. We conclude that *Weight-and-List* is indeed effective in reducing the false negative rate. Multiple cryptographic algorithms use the characteristic data and the length of the characteristic data is different. After setting the *Weight-and-List* attribute for the data, the contribution of the characteristic data to the detection and the correlation between the characteristic data are taken into account, and the alarm leakage rate decreases.

False Positive Rate. We conduct black-box testing on binaries without cryptography and calculate the false positive rate based on whether a cryptographic algorithm is detected.

We use files that do not contain cryptographic algorithms for testing, the number of files to be tested is F, after the test, the number of files with cryptographic algorithms detected is f, and the formula for calculating the false alarm rate is f/F. In our tests, the false positive rate was 1.68%. False positive algorithms include RC4 and XTEA, and the reasons are as follows: 1) The characteristic data of RC4 is a numeric array from 0 to 255, which is commonly used and thus, easily collided with other regular valuables; 2) XTEA uses a constant δ as characteristic data, which is defined as $\delta = (\sqrt{5} - 1)2^{31}$ (0x9E3779B9). In addition to being used in XTEA, δ is often used in mathematical calculations, so it is easy to cause false positives.

4.3 Performance

The black-box testing tool only matches the characteristic data of the binary file data segment, read-only data segment, and code segment during detection, and performs page-by-page detection during implementation. By narrowing the matching range of characteristic data, the detection time is reduced and improved performance. Table 3 illustrates the time-consuming comparison of segment matching and full matching for binary executable files of different sizes. For larger files to be tested, as the size of the test file increases, the test time is shortened while ensuring the accuracy of the test results.

Table 3. Single file detection performance

File size	Segment match time	Full match time	STR[a]
3 KB	0.71 s	0.70 s	0.99
10 KB	0.72 s	0.71 s	0.99
100 KB	1.33 s	1.31 s	0.98
1 MB	7.61 s	7.82 s	1.03
10 MB	64.71 s	67.41 s	1.04
80 MB	451.79 s	490.83 s	1.08

[a]STR refers to the time-consuming ratio of detection under different methods for a single file, that is, the ratio of the time consumed by full matching to the time consumed by segment matching.

At the same time, the method of narrowing the matching range to the segment also has a significant performance improvement in batch detection. Table 4 shows the time-consuming comparison between segment and full matching for batch testing of different sizes.

Table 4. Batch file detection performance

Number	Test folder size	Number of files	Time for matching segment[a]	Time for matching total file	BTR[b]
1	10 MB	91	64.55 s	64.68 s	1.002
2	100 MB	109	394.89 s	400.03 s	1.013
3	200 MB	472	1093.93 s	1117.59 s	1.022
4	500 MB	630	3420.35 s	3550.83 s	1.038
5	1 GB	1734	6632.59 s	6902.62 s	1.041
6	2 GB	3468	13166.64 s	14206.78 s	1.079

a. Segments here refer to data segments, read-only data segments, and code segments in binary executables.
b. BTR refers to the time-consuming ratio of detection under different methods for batch file, that is, the ratio of the time consumed by full matching to the time consumed by segment matching.

4.4   Limitations

Although there are already many cryptographic algorithms that can be detected by our tool, there are also limitations. First, our tool does not support the accurate identification of the following cryptographic algorithms.

– The characteristic data is not applied in some implementations. For example, in the AES-NI implementation and the white-box implementation of AES [4] and SM4 [3], S-box no longer exists.
– Other algorithms completely share the characteristic data, for example, characteristic data of XTEA is fully shared by SEED, characteristic data of MD4 is fully shared by SHA-1.
– The characteristic data is generated at runtime, such as RC4.

In addition, for some algorithms, the tool is temporarily unable to distinguish its key length and working mode based on characteristic data. For example, we cannot distinguish between RSA-1024 and RSA-2048; we cannot recognize AES's CBC and CTR working modes. At last, if a shell processes the tested object, the characteristic data of the cryptographic algorithm will not be found. The location of the read-only data segment of the data segment code segment cannot be determined, as a result, our tool cannot be used.

5   Summary

In this paper, we propose and implement a black-box testing tool for cryptographic algorithms based on characteristic data. Characteristic data is extracted from the standard and general implementation of cryptographic algorithms. In particular, we set Weight and List for characteristic data and set a threshold for cryptographic algorithm determination to reduce the false positive and false negative rates. The tool can detect 15 symmetric cryptographic algorithms, 13 hash algorithms, RSA, 8 Diffie-Hellman key exchange algorithm prime numbers, 85 elliptic curves, and 1 pseudo-random number generator. The evaluation results show that the tool can accurately, comprehensively, and quickly detect cryptographic algorithms in binaries and supports the detection of non-open source software. In the future, we will train the Weights and thresholds to obtain a lower false positive rate and false negative rate Table 5.

A   Cryptographic Algorithm Supports

The cryptographic algorithms supported by the cryptographic algorithm blackbox testing tool include: 13 cryptographic hash algorithms, 15 symmetric cryptographic algorithms, 1 asymmetric cryptographic algorithm, 85 elliptic curves, 8 prime domains of Diffie-Hellman key exchange algorithm, three types of double elliptic curve pseudo-random number generators based on elliptic curves.

Table 5. Cryptographic Algorithm Detection Support

Category	Name			
Cryptographic hash algorithm	SHA-1	MD5	SHA-384/512	RIPEMD-160
	MD4	SHA-224/256	SHA-3	Blake2
	SM3	MD2	Siphash	
Symmetric cryptographic algorithm	AES	RC4	XTEA	Camellia
	RC2	ChaCha20	Cast	SEED
	ARIA	Blowfish	SM4	Gost
	DES	RC5	Seal	
RSA	RSA			
ECC	brainpoolP-(160/192/224/256/320/384/512)-(r/t)1			
	c2tnb-(163v1/163v2/163v3/176v1/191v1/191v2/191v3/208w1)			
	c2tnb-(239v1/239v2/239v3/272w1/304w1/359v1/368w1/431r1)			
	sect-(113r1/113r2/131r1/131r2/163k1/163r1/163r2)			
	sect-(233k1/233r1/239k1/283k1/238r1/409k1/409r1/571k1/571r1)			
	secp-(112r1/112r2/128r1/128r2/160k1/160r1/160r2)			
	secp192k1/192r1/224r1/224k1/256k1/256r1/384r1/521r1			
	wap-wsg-idm-ecid-wtls-(8/9/12)			
	Oakley-EC2N-(3/4)	prime192v-(1/2/3)	wapip192v1	M-(221/383/511)
	sm2p256v1	prime239v-(1/2/3)	gost-(256/512)	Curve-(448/25519)
	sm9bn256v1	prime256v1	frp256v1	
Diffie-Hellman key exchange algorithm	DH-dh-(1024_160/2048_224/2048_224)			
	DH-ffdhe-(2048/3072/4096/6144/8192)			
Dual_EC_DRBG	Dual_EC_DRBG-x9_62_prime_256v1		Dual_EC_DRBG-nist_prime_-(384/521)	

B   Test File Information

When we tested the false positive rate, we used "tool", "release" and "exe" as search keywords on Github, sorted the search results by year, and selected 58 projects that are not related to cryptographic algorithms for compilation to get the test file. Github project information is shown in the Table 6.

Table 6. Github project for testing the false positive rate

No	GitHub link	No	GitHub link
1	GH:/TonyChen56/HackerTools.git	30	GH:/v-star0719/MFC_ImageSlider.git
2	GH:/christopher5106/FastAnnotationTool.git	31	GH:/JoshCodesJava/Platform-Game.git
3	GH:/vedderb/bldc-tool.git	32	GH:/bjk12/LittleBird_TypeExercise.git
4	GH:/yasserhcn/MinCPT.git	33	GH:/zwang452/MGAFeedAssayProcessor.git
5	GH:/jptr218/bgp_hijack.git	34	GH:/L3cr0f/DccwBypassUAC.git
6	GH:/yoursunny/ndn6-tools.git	35	GH:/yanncam/exe2powershell.git
7	GH:/zouxiaofei1/TopDomianTools.git	36	GH:/aaaddress1/RunPE-In-Memory.git
8	GH:/MichaelKCortez/CrackMapExecWin.git	37	GH:/BeNhNp/CallOCRDLLDemo.git
9	GH:/blundar/analyze.exe.git	38	GH:/DiegoRicardo26/20-programas.git
10	GH:/QQProtectUdpInspector.git	39	GH:/loveemu/bin2psf1.git
11	GH:/ZisBoom/MsiInv.exe.git	40	GH:/crea7or/getwindowsversion.git
12	GH:/ps1337/getuser.git	41	GH:/matthiasg/zeromq-node-windows.git
13	GH:/PhilJollans/RegSpy.git	42	GH:/lordmulder/TimedExec.git
14	GH:/LGinC/ImageLadle.git	43	GH:/Valorant-AntiCheat-Disabler.git
15	GH:/yangjiechina/GB28181_Stress_Tools.git	44	GH:/areve/node2exe.git
16	GH:/chorushe/princekin.git	45	GH:/dolarsecurity/vurbana.git
17	GH:/Jiangxiaogang/FontMaker.git	46	GH:/codepongo/zshellext.git
18	GH:/aaaddress1/RunPE-In-Memory.git	47	GH:/hufuman/sym_size.git
19	GH:/liangfu/bet2.git	48	GH:/Arma-Remote-Code-Executor.git
20	GH:/PLohrmannAMD/update_check_api.git	49	GH:/Paulo-D2000/PNexe.git
21	GH:/TinkerEdgeR/release_tools.git	50	GH:/ethereum/aleth.git
22	GH:/district10/boost-tools.git	51	GH:/jptr218/bgp_hijack.git
23	GH:/A1kmm/usbrelease.git	52	GH:/HoI4-Map-Normalizer-Tool.git
24	GH:/vczh-libraries/Release.git	53	GH:/SergioMartin86/jaffar2.git
25	GH:/Win-LocalPriv-Escalation-polarbear.git	54	GH:/rnlf/rad2exe.git
26	GH:/kristiankoskimaki/vidupe.git	55	GH:/floooh/sokol-tools.git
27	GH:/z3r0d4y5/Simple-PE32-Packer.git	56	GH:/abreheret/PixelAnnotationTool.git
28	GH:/frankgorhamengard/SparkyBrain.git	57	GH:/kliment-olechnovic/voronota.git
29	GH:/alcan2jc/FlappyBird.git	58	GH:/arggscomputerecke/cmd_start.git

Note: "GH:" stands for "https://github.com"

References

1. A quarter of major CMSs use outdated MD5 as the default password hashing scheme. www.zdnet.com/article/a-quarter-of-major-cmss-use-outdated-md5-as-the-default-password-hashing-scheme/ (2020)

2. AlFardan, N., Bernstein, D.J., Paterson, K.G., Poettering, B., Schuldt, J.C.: On the security of RC4 in TLS. In: 22nd USENIX Security Symposium (USENIX Security 13), pp. 305–320 (2013)
3. Bai, K., Wu, C.: A secure white-box SM4 implementation. Secur. Commun. Netw. 9(10), 996–1006 (2016)
4. Billet, O., Gilbert, H., Ech-Chatbi, C.: Cryptanalysis of a white box AES implementation. In: Handschuh, H., Hasan, M.A. (eds.) SAC 2004. LNCS, vol. 3357, pp. 227–240. Springer, Heidelberg (2004). https://doi.org/10.1007/978-3-540-30564-4_16
5. Boneh, D., Joux, A., Nguyen, P.Q.: Why textbook ElGamal and RSA encryption are insecure. In: Okamoto, T. (ed.) ASIACRYPT 2000. LNCS, vol. 1976, pp. 30–43. Springer, Heidelberg (2000). https://doi.org/10.1007/3-540-44448-3_3
6. Dai, W.: Crypto++ library 5.1-a free c++ class library of cryptographic schemes. https://www.cryptopp.com/ (2004)
7. Daniel, J., Bernstein, T.L.: Safecurves: choosing safe curves for elliptic-curve cryptography. https://safecurves.cr.yp.to/
8. Egele, M., Brumley, D., Fratantonio, Y., Kruegel, C.: An empirical study of cryptographic misuse in android applications. In: Proceedings of the 2013 ACM SIGSAC Conference on Computer & Communications Security (2013)
9. Greenwood, D.S.J.S.G., Khan, Z.L.L.: SMV-HUNTER: large scale, automated detection of SSL/TLS man-in-the-middle vulnerabilities in android apps. In: Network and Distributed System Security Symposium (NDSS). Internet Society, San Diego, CA, pp. 1–14. Citeseer (2014)
10. Harvey, I.: Cipher hunting: how to find cryptographic algorithms in large binaries. NCipher Corporation Ltd., pp. 46–51 (2001)
11. Kessler, G.C.: An overview of cryptography (2003)
12. Koch, W., Schulte, M.: The libgcrypt reference manual. Free Software Foundation Inc, pp. 1–47 (2005)
13. Krüger, S., Späth, J., Ali, K., Bodden, E., Mezini, M.: CrySL: an extensible approach to validating the correct usage of cryptographic APIs. IEEE Trans. Softw. Eng. 47(11), 2382–2400 (2019)
14. Lazar, D., Chen, H., Wang, X., Zeldovich, N.: Why does cryptographic software fail?: a case study and open problems. In: APSys (2014)
15. Li, J., Lin, Z., Caballero, J., Zhang, Y., Gu, D.: K-hunt: pinpointing insecure cryptographic keys from execution traces. In: Proceedings of the 2018 ACM SIGSAC Conference on Computer and Communications Security, pp. 412–425 (2018)
16. Lindström, P., Pap, O.: Mapping the current state of SSL/TLS (2017)
17. Lloyd, J.: Botan: crypto and TLS for modern C++. https://botan.randombit.net/ (2018)
18. Mouha, N., Dworkin, M., et al.: Review of the advanced encryption standard (2021)
19. Paul Bakker, A.: mbedTLS. tls. mbed. org (2019)
20. Rahaman, S., et al.: Cryptoguard: high precision detection of cryptographic vulnerabilities in massive-sized java projects. In: Proceedings of the 2019 ACM SIGSAC Conference on Computer and Communications Security, pp. 2455–2472 (2019)
21. Rogers, M., Eden, G.: The Snowden disclosures, technical standards and the making of surveillance infrastructures. Int. J. Commun. 11, 802–823 (2017)
22. Sindhu, S., Sindhu, D.: Cryptographic algorithms: applications in network security. Int. J. New Innovations Eng. Technol. (2017). ISSN 2319-6319
23. Stevens, M., Bursztein, E., Karpman, P., Albertini, A., Markov, Y.: The first collision for full SHA-1. In: Katz, J., Shacham, H. (eds.) CRYPTO 2017. LNCS, vol.

10401, pp. 570–596. Springer, Cham (2017). https://doi.org/10.1007/978-3-319-63688-7_19

24. Turner, S., Chen, L.: MD2 to Historic Status. Technical report, RFC 6149, March (2011)

25. Turner, S., Chen, L.: RFC 6151: updated security considerations for the MD5 message-digest and the HMAC-MD5 algorithms. Internet Eng. Task Force (2011)

26. Wang, Z., Jiang, X., Cui, W., Wang, X., Grace, M.: ReFormat: automatic reverse engineering of encrypted messages. In: Backes, M., Ning, P. (eds.) ESORICS 2009. LNCS, vol. 5789, pp. 200–215. Springer, Heidelberg (2009). https://doi.org/10.1007/978-3-642-04444-1_13

27. Young, E.A., Hudson, T.J., Engelschall, R.S.: OpenSSL. World Wide Web. https://www.openssl.org/. Accessed September 2001 (2001)

Network Attack and Defense

IoT Devices Classification Base on Network Behavior Analysis

Lingan Chen[1]([✉]) [iD], Xiaobin Tan[1,2] [iD], Chuang Peng[2] [iD], Mingye Zhu[3] [iD], Zhenghuan Xu[3] [iD], and Shuangwu Chen[1,2] [iD]

[1] Department of Automation, University of Science and Technology of China, Hefei, China
cla@mail.ustc.edu.cn, {xbtan,chensw}@ustc.edu.cn
[2] Institute of Artificial Intelligence, Hefei Comprehensive National Science Center, Hefei, China
pengchuang@mail.ustc.edu.cn
[3] Institute of Advanced Technology, University of Science and Technology of China, Hefei, China
mingyezhu@mail.ustc.edu.cn, zhxu86@ustc.edu.cn

Abstract. IoT devices classification from the network traffic have attract increasing attention due to the manage requirement of the growing IoT applications.

Current statistic feature based methods needs to sample most of the packets and requires much computation during the feature extracting. The features are easily affected by the network environment and user operations.

This paper proposes a network behavior analysis (NBA) based IoT devices classification scheme which takes the sequence of network session features as input and learns the behavior feature with LSTM for IoT devices classification. NBA bases on the network behavior analysis without parsing the packet of network traffic, thus can handle the traffic using encryption protocol. In addition, we built a testbed with IoT devices for evaluation.

The traffic generated in the testbed was captured for evaluation. The result of the experiment indicates that by incorporating destination and interval features, our method can accurately classify IoT and non-IoT devices and achieves the accuracy over 99%.

Keywords: Internet of Thing · Machine learning · Deep learning · Traffic classification

1 Introduction

The growing Internet of Things (IoT) devices in campuses and cities brings the need for knowing what IoT devices are connected and whether they are functioning normally for the administrator. Identifying IoT devices from the network

J. Lin and Q. Tang (Eds.): AC3 2022, LNICST 448, pp. 173–188, 2022.
https://doi.org/10.1007/978-3-031-17081-2_11

traffic is a reality method to address this problem. The traffic of IoT devices features mean rate, average packet size, sleep time, DNS interval etc. Such statistical characteristics can be used for Random Forest algorithm to classify IoT devices [1]. However, by using traffic camouflage technologies, malware may make the statistical features of its traffic look like those of normal IoT devices [2].

Because malware may split data into fragments of any size for transmission, such packet-length-based algorithms are also vulnerable to traffic disguise. IP addresses are difficult to conceal because of its importance in packet routing and forwarding. Web apps can be classified according to the destinations with which they communicate [3]. However network destinations may change over time and IoT devices from the same manufacturer may share the same set of destination.

The traffic generated by IoT devices comes from their network behaviors, such as DHCP, reporting logs, broadcasting device information, providing remote control services for users, etc. Different functions of IoT devices lead to different network behaviors. The traffic generated by different network behaviors of devices corresponds to different sessions, thus the sequence of sessions contains the network behavior information of devices. The network behavior of the device is not only which server to access, but also how to access the target server, in what order and frequency.

An IoT traffic categorization framework based on network behavior analysis was developed in this study. The framework introduces IoT devices' destinations to prevent traffic camouflage and overcomes the issue of changing IP addresses by grouping comparable destinations into IP pools. Our contribution can be summarised as follows:

– We designed an IoT traffic classification framework based on network behavior analysis. The framework analyses the sequence of session features and LSTM with attention mechanism was applied to extract network behavior features for IoT devices classification.
– We researched the network behavior of IoT devices and two effective features in the preliminary experiment. We introduces the behavior features into our framework to classify IoT devices. Our algorithm can apply to encrypted IoT traffic since it is based on network behavior analysis without parsing the content of packets.
– An IoT devices testbed was constructed. The network traffic generated in the testbed was collected for experiment and evaluation. We implemented the proposed IoT devices classification framework and evaluated it with the traffic collected from the testbed. Experiment result shows that our classifier can not only distinguish between IoT and non-IoT devices, but also uniquely classify IoT devices with over 99% accuracy.

2   Related Work

Traffic identification of IoT devices has attracted researchers' attention in recent years [4]. Work in [1] built an experimental testbed for IoT devices and collected the traffic generated by IoT devices. On this basis, they studied the statistical characteristics of these devices, such as mean rate, average packet size, sleep time, and DNS interval etc. After dividing the statistical characteristics into multiple bins, they applied random forest for device identification. In the next work [5] of the same team, more devices were added to their testbed and the distributions of remote port number, domain name and cipher suites were analysed. Then a two-stage classification algorithm based on random forest and Bayesian classifier was designed to classify IoT devices.

Work in [6] also applied machine learning algorithms to the identification of IoT devices based on statistical features. The difference is that PCA method is used to remove correlated features, and simpler machine learning algorithms are used, such as support vector machine, logistic regression and decision tree. Besides, some works [7,8] attempted to infer user activities from the network traffic of IoT devices.

In the broader field of traffic identificationthe DPI-based (Deep Packet Inspection) algorithms can reliably detect different types of traffic [9]. However, the DPI's application scenario has been limited by the growing adoption of the transport layer security (TLS) protocol [10], which is also applied to encrypt IoT traffic.

Following the development of deep learning technology in the areas of Computer Vision and Natural Language Processing (NLP), researchers began to study with applying it to classify encrypted traffic. Convolutional Neural Network (CNN) [11] was investigated for automatically extracting characteristics from encrypted traffic raw data [12–14]. Despite certain datasets' excellent accuracy, researchers revealed that CNN extracts features mostly from packet sizes rather than the encrypted load data itself [15]. CNN can also, in fact, perform efficiently with images derived from packet lengths and packet time stamps [16]. As a result, researchers were naturally considering extracting characteristics directly from the sequence of packet sizes, and the Long Short-Term Memory network (LSTM) [17], which was designed to extract features from sequence data and is extensively used in the field of NLP, is used to traffic categorization [18].

3   Network Behavior Analysis Based IoT Devices Classification

3.1   Motivation an Analysis

Although encryption of IoT traffic hinders the classification of IoT devices. the network behaviors of IoT devices such as log uploading, command receiving are reflected in the network behavior of which destination and how to access. This inspired us to identify IoT devices from the perspective of network behavior.

IP addresses themselves contain enough information for traffic classification [3]. However, there is a difficulty with using IP addresses as features. First, IP addresses may change over time as a result of load balancing or server migration. Classifiers based on IP addresses are likely to be overfitted and incapable of dealing with changing IP addresses. Second, various IoT devices can share common

Table 1. Preliminary experiment result on destination sequence of session in 30 min

ID	Devices	Precision	Recall	F1-score
0	Non-IoT	1.0000	0.9984	0.9992
1	Smart camera	0.9984	0.9996	0.9990
2	Temperature sensor	0.9556	0.8945	0.9240
3	Smart bulb	0.9695	0.9974	0.9832
4	Smart socket	0.1500	0.0327	0.0538
	Accuracy	0.9907		

destinations such as gateways, DNS servers, CDN servers and cloud servers. IoT devices of the same manufacturer may also share manufacturer-specific destinations.

Devices connected to specific IP addresses are expected to perform specified tasks. When a device connects to a different destination than it did previously but for the same purpose, the IP addresses before and after the modification are related and will have similar characteristics and tend to be clustered in the same IP pool. Consequently, the strategy for changing IP addresses is to divide IP addresses into clusters according to certain rules and then classify devices according to which cluster they access.

Table 2. Sessions of the DstIP of the Confused Devices

dstIP	Description	Sessions	
		Smart bulb	Smart socket
255.255.255.255	Broadcast	52	14
192.168.1.1	Gateway	3316	13
111.231.160.125	Tencet cloud	61	24
121.5.96.248	Founder bandwidth	6564	191
42.192.30.165	Yovole cloud	11	0
47.110.145.119	Alibaba cloud	3278	0

We carried up a preliminary experiment in which different devices were classified based on the destination sequence of sessions over 30 min. The result as shown in Table 1. demonstrates that this behavior characteristic can identify between non-IoT and IoT devices, as well as between devices of various brands, but that distinguishing between devices of the same manufacturer is challenging.

Table 2 shows the destination IPs of the devices. IoT devices connects to the broadcast destination to make themselves found by users, to the gateway to attain DHCP, DNS and NTP service, and to the destination of cloud service providers for their custom functions such as logging and remote controlling. It

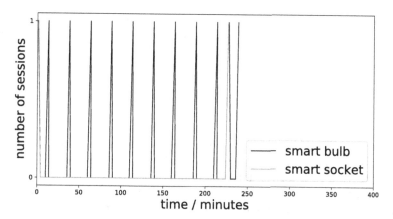

Fig. 1. Session behavior of confused devices

can be seen that the target IP of smart socket is identical to the destination of smart bulb, and the number of sessions of smart socket is much smaller than that of smart bulb, causing the deep learning model to mistake smart socket traffic for smart bulb traffic.

The difference in the number of sessions reveals the temporal behavior difference of the two devices. As shown in Fig. 1, there is a huge difference between the two devices in the frequency of establishing new sessions. In the preliminary experiment the smart socket's target address sequence can be as short as one or two sessions in a short period of time, making it difficult for the model to use the sequence's behavior information and forcing it to rely solely on the information contained in the IP address, directing the result to the smart bulb.

Although different devices may share common destinations, the network behavior of devices varies depending on their functionality and hardware, which may reflect on the order and temporal behavior pattern of destinations. Therefore, not only the combination of IP pool, but the order of IP pools and session interval that devices access, was considered.

3.2   Overview

Because the network behavior of devices is reflected in sessions, our framework is designed to extract behavior information from the sequence of sessions to classify devices. To achieve this goal, this framework needs to extract the features containing behavior information from the raw traffic from the sessions, then extract the behavior features and classify devices with a classifier. The overall framework of network behavior analysis based IoT devices classification is shown in the Fig. 2. The framework is mainly composed of four parts: session feature extraction, session feature preprocess, sequence feature extraction and multilayer perceptron (MLP) [19] classifier.

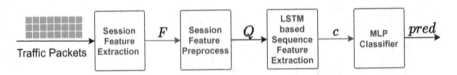

Fig. 2. System architecture of network behavior analysis

The session feature extraction module extracts session features F directly from the raw traffic data. Then F is processed by the session feature preprocess module into vectors Q for the following model fitting.

The LSTM based sequence feature extraction module generates the feature vector c of behavior, and the multilayer perceptron classifier can predict the IoT devices as $pred$ from the feature vector c.

3.3   Session Feature Extraction

The session feature extraction module is to extract the basic features for the following analysis as shown in Fig. 3.

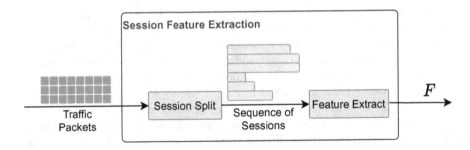

Fig. 3. Process of session feature extraction module

To begin with, the traffic is separated into sessions based on five tuples $(srcIP, srcPort, dstIP, dstPort, protocol)$, and the sessions are ordered by their begin time. Then the sequence of session features F can be abstracted as

$$F = [F_1, F_2, ..., F_n] \tag{1}$$

where the length n depends on the amount of sessions and the i-th session's feature F_i can be represented as:

$$F_i = [f_i^1, f_i^2, ..., f_i^m] \tag{2}$$

representing the combination of m features extracted from each session.

In our work the destination and the begin-time interval are chosen to feature the network behavior. They are easily to obtained that only the first packets of each session are needed. Sampling and processing of the full sessions can be avoided, which greatly reduces the difficulty for deploying on gateways in the future. Therefore in this case, F_i and $\boldsymbol{F}$ can also be represented as:

$$F_i = [\tau_j, d_j] \tag{3}$$

$$\boldsymbol{F} = [\boldsymbol{\tau}, \boldsymbol{d}] \tag{4}$$

where τ_j and d_j are the j-th session's begin-time interval and destination IP address respectively. Other session features such as volumes and average packet sizes can also be applied for further describe the network behavior.

3.4   Session Feature Preprocess

The function of this module is to preprocess the raw feature $\boldsymbol{F}$ into the sequence of numerical vectors Q for the following model training as shown in Fig. 4.

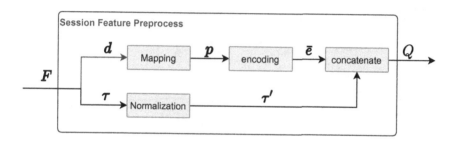

Fig. 4. Process of session feature preprocess module

For the numerical feature begin-time interval $\boldsymbol{\tau}$, normalization is applied and results in $\boldsymbol{\tau}'$. And for the destination IP addresses $\boldsymbol{d}$, we choose to map them into IP pools $\boldsymbol{p}$ and encode the IP pools into vectors $\bar{\boldsymbol{e}}$.

The destinations are clustered to the IP pools as:

$$p_i = Map(d_i) \tag{5}$$

$$\boldsymbol{p} = Map(\boldsymbol{d}) = [p_1, p_2, ..., p_n] \tag{6}$$

where d_i is the i-th destination, p_i is the i-th IP pool and the mapping function $M(\cdot)$ is determined by the result of IP clustering method such as [3] or the existing IP address database. The output of the IP clustering method determines the mapping function. IP address pools do not need to be labeled because the correlation between p_i will be learned during training.

Then p_i is encoded into vector $\boldsymbol{e}_i$:

$$\boldsymbol{e}_i = E(p_i) \tag{7}$$

$$\bar{e} = E(p) = [e_1, e_2, ..., e_n] \tag{8}$$

where encoder method $E(\cdot)$ can be one-hot or embedding. All the preprocessed session features are finally concatenated into a vector q_i before fed into the sequence feature extraction module:

$$q_i = Cat(e_i, \tau_i) \tag{9}$$

$$Q = [q_1, q_2, ..., q_n] \tag{10}$$

3.5   LSTM Based Sequence Feature Extraction

We designed an LSTM with attention mechanism-based sequence feature extraction model. Its structure is shown in the Fig. 5, which is mainly composed of an attention module and an LSTM module.

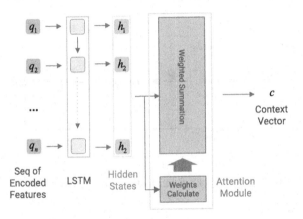

Fig. 5. LSTM based sequence feature extraction

As shown in the previous section, the input of the model is a sequence of encoded session features. The sequence of $[q_1, q_2, ..., q_n]$ is fed to an LSTM module, then the output for each step is:

$$[h_1, h_2, ..., h_n] = LSTM(Q) \tag{11}$$

where h_i is an m dimension vector that contains the information of $q_1, q_2, ..., q_i$. But q_i gives the most influence on h_i, so h_i is chosen to represent the feature of q_i.

To conclude the class of the sequence we need to calculate a vector to represent the features of the whole sequence, and that is the work of attention module. h_i is fed to the weight calculation module to determine the weight w_i, representing the importance of the i-th IP pool to feature the whole sequence. Then the context vector

$$c = \Sigma w_i h_i = [c_1, c_2, ..., c_m] \tag{12}$$

represents the sequence as the output of attention module and is encoded with the network behavior feature of the whole sequence.

The attention layer has two functions. First, it can help the LSTM layer to synthesize information between sequences within a long-time interval, and alleviate the lack of LSTM's ability to recognize long sequences. Second, it can show the focus of the model every time it extracts feature, increasing the interpretability of the network. In this article, attention can point out the sessions that the model focuses on when making predictions. We can use this to investigate whether the neural network has learned a reasonable model and prepare for future work.

3.6   Multilayer Perceptron Classifier

Multilayer perceptron classifier predicts the scores of devices from the context vector c. As shown in Fig. 6, The MLP is composed of multiple fully connected layers, and learns a non-linear function for classification:

$$f(\cdot) : R^m \rightarrow R^k \tag{13}$$

by training on a dataset where m is the dimension of for input and k is the dimension of output. Between the input and output layer, there can be one or more non-linear layers called hidden layers. Hidden layer consists of a set of neurons and each neuron in the hidden layer transforms the values from the previous layer with a weighted linear summation followed by a non-linear function. the output layer receives the values from the last hidden layer and transforms them into output values s, representing the score of IoT devices in our situation.

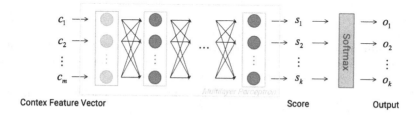

Fig. 6. Multilayer perceptron classifier

Finally the scores are normalized by the softmax function:

$$\sigma(s)_i = \frac{e^{s_i}}{\sum_{j=1}^{K} e^{s_j}} = o_i \tag{14}$$

to approximate the probability of IoT devices.

MLP is chosen to facilitate the training of neural network. After the LSTM model learned the ability to encode behavior features into context vector c during training, other classifiers such as Random Forest can also be applied to IoT devices classification.

4   Evaluation

4.1   IoT Testbed Construction and Traffic Collection

Our testbed constitutes a virtual gateway router, a virtual PC, an AP and four different IoT devices as in Table 3 and Fig. 7, all deployed on the CENI platform [20]. The virtual router with VSR1000_H3C-CMW710-E0618-X64-3 firmware installed serves as the gateway of the LAN. The WAN interface is linked to the public Internet and WLAN of the AP is connected to IoT devices. Besides, a LAN interface is connected to a Virtual Windows PC for controlling, monitoring, and traffic dumping via SSH. Additional package *tcpdump* is installed to dump the traffic of devices in the testbed. The IoT devices in the testbed include Tuya smart lightbulb, Tuya smart socket, Vemsee temperature sensor, and JOOAN wireless camera. Some other non-IoT devices connected to the testbed are smartphones and laptops.

Table 3. Devices in the Testbed

Device	Model	Firmware	Manufacturer	Description
Virtual router	–	VSR1000_H3C-CMW710	H3C	Gateway, traffic dumping
Virtual PC	–	Windows10 18362.1082	–	Saving captured traffic
Temperature sensor	DK-300C4-WS-WIFI	–	VMS	IoT device
Smart socket	YKYC-001	V1.1.1	Tuya	IoT device
Smart bulb	XDUO-S1	V1.1.7	Tuya	IoT device
WIFI Camera	JA-C10R	03.03.30.33	JOOAN	IoT device
Laptop	Xiaoxin Air 14ITL 2021	Windows10 18362.1082	Lenovo	Non-IoT device
Smart phone	GM1910	Hydrogen OS 10.0.10.GM21	OnePlus	Non-IoT device

The traffic in the testbed was captured via the *tcpdump* tool on the router, then it was delivered to the virtual PC through the SSH tunnel and eventually restored by the *dumpcap* tool of Wireshark.

The collecting of traffic lasted from May 26th, 2021 to September 15th, 2021. During this period, over 20000 flows and 500,000 packages are collected.

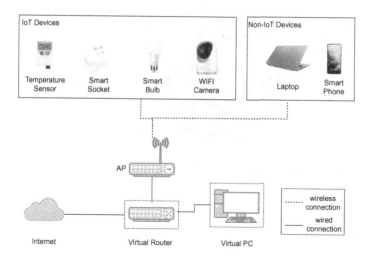

Fig. 7. IoT environment testbed

4.2 Experimental Settings

The algorithm of CCIT [1] is implemented for comparison because CCIT is one of the most classical methods in the field of IoT devices classification. CCIT extracts the sleep time, active volume, average packet size, mean rate, peak/mean rate, active time, No. of servers, No. of protocols, unique DNS request, DNS interval and NTP interval as characteristic then apply Random Forest algorithm as classifier. CCIT deals with the same task of our method and is reported to reach over 95% accuracy.

Our neural network model was implemented using pytorch. To map the IP address into pools the public IP address attribution database [21] was applied. It should be emphasized that although the IP address database can provide the geographic location of each IP address, it was only used to cluster the IP addresses without introducing their geographic location information. We used embedding layer to encode the IP pools into 3-dimension vectors because the embedding layer can learn the correlation of the pools and reflect such correlation into the distance in the feature space. The implemented model was trained on the CENI [20] platform with virtual machine of GeForce GTX 1080.

Because the number of sessions generated by different devices varies greatly as in Fig. 8, we copy multiple copies of the subset of devices with smaller number of instances during training to balance the data, so that the amount of data instances of each device is roughly the same. This is not data amplification, but a way to change the weight of the devices. During verification, we also calculate the evaluation criterions with the expanded dataset to reduce the impact of the results of devices with large amount of instances on the overall results. Our framework is denoted as NBA in the following description.

We evaluated the performance of classifying specific devices of the methods base on the precision, recall and F1-score. We also use the accuracy (the ratio of

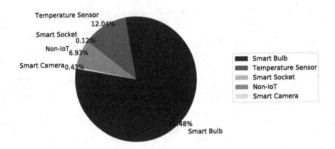

Fig. 8. Distribution of different devices in the dataset

all the correctly predicted instances and all the instances) to measure the overall performance. the definitions of the criterions are as follows:

$$precision = \frac{TP}{TP + FP} \qquad (15)$$

$$recall = \frac{TP}{TP + FN} \qquad (16)$$

$$F1 = \frac{precision \cdot recall}{precision + recall} \qquad (17)$$

where TP, FP, TN, and FN are instances of true positive, false positive, true negative, and false negative respectively. The performance of models was evaluated by the average of each criteria in the 5-fold cross validation. Due to the long time for IoT devices to generate sessions, the most time-consuming step in our method comes from data caption rather than data processing and result inference. Therefore, we only use the classification criteria to measure our proposed algorithm.

4.3 Experimental Result and Analysis

The evaluation results are shown in Table 3. The result of preliminary experiment is also included for comparison and indicated as Pre.

Table 4. Experiment results on precision, recall and F1-score

ID	Devices	CCIT			Pre			NBA(dst)			NBA(dst+interval)		
		Prec	Rec	F1	Prec	Rec	F1	Prec	Rec	F1	Prec	Rec	F1
0	Non-IoT	0.9838	0.9750	0.9793	**1.0000**	0.9984	0.9992	0.9999	0.9990	0.9995	0.9998	**1.0000**	0.9999
1	Smart camera	0.9703	0.9894	0.9798	0.9984	0.9996	0.9990	**0.9993**	0.9999	**0.9996**	0.9988	**1.0000**	0.9994
2	Temperature sensor	0.9817	0.9831	0.9824	0.9556	0.8945	0.9240	0.9998	**1.0000**	0.9999	**1.0000**	**1.0000**	**1.0000**
3	Smart bulb	**0.9958**	0.9942	**0.9950**	0.9695	**0.9974**	0.9832	0.8031	0.9755	0.8804	0.9865	0.9973	0.9918
4	Smart socket	0.9909	**0.9871**	0.9889	0.1500	0.0327	0.0538	0.9713	0.7706	0.8581	**0.9987**	0.9868	**0.9926**
	Accuracy	0.9836			0.9907			0.9476			**0.9967**		

Classification of IoT Devices and Non-IoT Devices. NBA with only destination as features is capable of accurately classifying IoT and non-IoT devices with precision and recall more than 0.99. This is due to the significant differences in IP accessing behavior between IoT and non-IoT devices. Non-IoT devices, such as laptops and smartphones, always connect to a variety of servers, depending on the Web apps on the platform. Such difference reflects in the sequence of the destination and can easily captured by the LSTM module. CCIT can also classify IoT devices and Non-IoT devices in precision over 0.98, but it also gets confused in some cases due to the overlapping of some features of IoT devices and Non-IoT devices. For example, the mean rate of IoT devices is usually lower than that of Non-IoT devices, but it can also reverse when Non-IoT devices are not active and IoT devices are active. When users remotely monitor through the smart camera, the camera can generate traffic in pretty high mean rate.

Classification of IoT Devices from Different Manufacturers. Among the IoT devices of the dataset only the smart socket and smart bulb are manufactured by the same company, while the rest are made by separate companies. Because servers from different manufacturers are often installed at separate locations, the results of preliminary experiments shown in Table 4 indicate that IP addresses can effectively differentiate IoT devices from different manufacturers. The results for CCIT reveal that statistical features change significantly for various IoT devices, although not as much as the address. The sequence of IP addresses is acquired in the preliminary experiment based on a predefined length of time, which results in the short sequence length of some data instances for equipment with less traffic, resulting in poor classifier performance. NBA with destination secures data sequence length by acquiring a fixed length sequence, which results in a data instance that requires more device traffic but increases the classifier's performance greatly. NBA with destinations and session intervals combines the benefits of CCIT and IP address, thus it has the ability in differentiating between IoT devices from various manufacturers with almost 100% precision and recall, better than CCIT.

Classification of IoT Devices from Same Manufacturer. The recognition ability of the classifier for various IoT devices from the same manufacturer can be reflected in the results for smart bulb and smart socket. Previous investigations as shown in the result of smart socket and smart bulb in Table 1 and Table 4 have demonstrated that it is hard to discern various devices by IP address alone since the server deployment addresses of the same manufacturer are identical. The NBA with destination has helped to solve this problem. Because the behavior of various devices visiting each target address is different in order, even though the target servers are the same, this performance is improved when the data sequence length is guaranteed, but not as good as CCIT. That is because this element has no effect on CCIT. We have to point out that when the session-begin-time interval is considered, the result of smart bulb is satisfactory with an 0.9918 F1 score under the influence of the smart socket from its same manufacturer.

This demonstrates that statistical characteristics can differentiate various devices from the same manufacturer, and we will investigate combining such features into our frame in the future work.

Therefore we can conclude that the NBA with destination and session-begin-time interval supplemented the behavioral information in time, allowing it to perform at the CCIT's level, in the IoT devices from the same manufacturer, reflecting in the result of smart socket and smart bulb in Table 4.

4.4 Summary

The framework design of NBA is expansionary and modular. Its behavior features mainly come from the sequence of sessions, so all session features can be introduced. The extraction of behavior features can also be replaced by other models that can extract sequence information.

By introducing the behavioral characteristics of IP address and session time interval, the NBA achieves accurate recognition of IoT devices with an overall accuracy of over 99.9%, which is higher than CCIT.

Clustering IP addresses is an a priori information that the model incorporates. This priori information can aid the trained model in slowing down its failure because both unsupervised clustering methods and manually labeled IP address databases can be updated in real time.

5 Conclusion

In this study, we investigated the topic of IoT device classification from IoT traffic by developing a smart environment using IoT devices. Current statistic feature based methods may be confused by traffic camouflage technologies. We proposed network behavior analysis (NBA) framework based IoT devices classification algorithm and compared it with statistics-based methods in the evaluation. The NBA can learn the behavior characteristics from multiple session features. We investigated the destination features to solve the traffic camouflage and introduce session interval to distinguish different devices of the same manufacturer. The result shows that the NBA can distinguish IoT devices and Non-IoT devices in high precision and has great potential in combining with statistics features. Our framework can not only classify IoT devices with encrypted traffic, but also take few computing resources in the traffic extracting phase. Moreover, our framework can flexibly configure different features and classifier, therefore there is great potential to be studied.

Our future work will be expanded from the following aspects. First, we will add more IoT devices to the testbed, including multiple devices of same manufacturer to obtain more data to verify the our algorithms. Secondly, there is less work on IP address clustering at present, so we will explore better IP address clustering methods to strengthen the performance of our algorithm. Finally, we will consider applying more efficient deep learning model as the backbone to fit IoT traffic.

Acknowledgment. This work was supportedinpart by the National Key RDProgramof China under Grant 2020YFA0711400, inpart of Key Science and Technology Project of Anhui under Grant 202103a05020007, inpart by the Key RDProgramof Anhui Province in 2020 under Grant 202004a05020078, inpart by the China Environment for Network Innovations (CENI) under Grant 2016-000052-73-01-000515.

References

1. Sivanathan, A., et al.: Characterizing and classifying IoT traffic in smart cities and campuses. In: 2017 IEEE Conference on Computer Communications Workshops (INFOCOM WKSHPS), pp. 559–564 (2017)
2. Wang, N., Chen, Y., Xiao, Y., Hu, Y., Lou, W., Hou, T.: Manda: on adversarial example detection for network intrusion detection system. In: IEEE INFOCOM 2021 - IEEE Conference on Computer Communications, pp. 1–10 (2021)
3. van Ede, T., et al.: Flowprint: semi-supervised mobile-app fingerprinting on encrypted network traffic. In: Network and Distributed System Security Symposium (NDSS), vol. 27
4. Lopez-Martin, M., Carro, B., Sanchez-Esguevillas, A., Lloret, J.: Network traffic classifier with convolutional and recurrent neural networks for Internet of Things. IEEE Access **5**, 18042–18050 (2017)
5. Sivanathan, A., et al.: Classifying IoT devices in smart environments using network traffic characteristics. IEEE Trans. Mob. Comput. **18**(8), 1745–1759 (2019)
6. Bikmukhamedov, R.F., Nadeev, A.F.: Lightweight machine learning classifiers of IoT traffic flows. In: 2019 Systems of Signal Synchronization, Generating and Processing in Telecommunications (SYNCHROINFO), pp. 1–5 (2019)
7. Junges, P.M., François, J., Festor, O.: Passive inference of user actions through IoT gateway encrypted traffic analysis. In: 2019 IFIP/IEEE Symposium on Integrated Network and Service Management (IM), pp. 7–12 (2019)
8. Das, A.K., Pathak, P.H., Chuah, C.N., Mohapatra, P.: Uncovering privacy leakage in BLE network traffic of wearable fitness trackers. In: Proceedings of the 17th International Workshop on Mobile Computing Systems and Applications, HotMobile 2016, pp. 99–104, New York, NY, USA (2016). Association for Computing Machinery
9. Deri, L., Martinelli, M., Bujlow, T., Cardigliano, A.: nDPI: open-source high-speed deep packet inspection. In: 2014 International Wireless Communications and Mobile Computing Conference (IWCMC), pp. 617–622 (2014)
10. Liu, J., Fu, Y., Ming, J., Ren, Y., Sun, L., Xiong, H.: Effective and real-time in-app activity analysis in encrypted internet traffic streams. In: Proceedings of the 23rd ACM SIGKDD International Conference on Knowledge Discovery and Data Mining, KDD 2017, pp. 335–344, New York, NY, USA (2017). Association for Computing Machinery
11. Lecun, Y., Bottou, L., Bengio, Y., Haffner, P.: Gradient-based learning applied to document recognition. Proc. IEEE **86**(11), 2278–2324 (1998)
12. Lotfollahi, M., Jafari Siavoshani, M., Shirali Hossein Zade, R., Saberian, M.: Deep packet: a novel approach for encrypted traffic classification using deep learning. Soft. Comput. **24**(3), 1999–2012 (2019). https://doi.org/10.1007/s00500-019-04030-2
13. Wang, W., et al.: HAST-IDS: learning hierarchical spatial-temporal features using deep neural networks to improve intrusion detection. IEEE Access **6**, 1792–1806 (2018)

14. Wang, W., Zhu, M., Wang, J., Zeng, X., Yang, Z.: End-to-end encrypted traffic classification with one-dimensional convolution neural networks. In: 2017 IEEE International Conference on Intelligence and Security Informatics (ISI), pp. 43–48 (2017)
15. Tong, X., Tan, X., Chen, L., Yang, J., Zheng, Q.: BFSN: a novel method of encrypted traffic classification based on bidirectional flow sequence network. In: 2020 3rd International Conference on Hot Information-Centric Networking (HotICN), pp. 160–165 (2020)
16. Shapira, T., Shavitt, Y.: Flowpic: encrypted internet traffic classification is as easy as image recognition. In: IEEE INFOCOM 2019 - IEEE Conference on Computer Communications Workshops (INFOCOM WKSHPS), pp. 680–687 (2019)
17. Hochreiter, S., Schmidhuber, J.: Long short-term memory. Neural Comput. **9**(8), 1735–1780 (1997)
18. Liu, C., He, L., Xiong, G., Cao, Z., Li, Z.: FS-Net: a flow sequence network for encrypted traffic classification. In: IEEE INFOCOM 2019 - IEEE Conference on Computer Communications, pp. 1171–1179 (2019)
19. Ruck, D.W., Rogers, S.K., Kabrisky, M., Oxley, M.E., Suter, B.W.: The multilayer perceptron as an approximation to a Bayes optimal discriminant function. IEEE Trans. Neural Networks **1**(4), 296–298 (1990)
20. China environment for network innovations (CENI). http://ceni.ustc.edu.cn/
21. Zx ipv6 address query. http://ip.zxinc.org/

Semi-supervised False Data Injection Attacks Detection in Smart Grid

Yasheng Zhou[1] , Li Yang[1(✉)] , and Yang Cao[2]

[1] School of Computer Science and Technology, Xidian University, Xi'an 710071, China
zhousheng396@163.com
[2] Guizhou Vocational College of Electronic Science and Technology, Guian 550025, China

Abstract. False data injection attacks (FDIAs) detection in smart grid, requires adequate labeled training samples to train a detection model. Due to the strong subjectivity, relying on expert knowledge and time-consuming nature of power system sample annotation, this task is intrinsically a small sample learning problem. In this paper, we propose a novel semi-supervised detection algorithm for FDIAs detection. The semi-supervised label propagation algorithm can dynamically propagate the label from labeled samples to unlabeled samples, automatically assign class labels to the unlabeled samples dataset, and enlarge the labeled samples dataset. Jointly use a small number of manually labeled samples dataset and a large number of auto-labeled samples dataset to construct a classifier via semi-supervised learning. Comparing the proposed algorithm with supervised learning algorithms, the results suggest that, with the scheme of semi-supervised learning from large unlabeled dataset, the proposed algorithm can significantly improve the accuracy of false data injection attacks detection.

Keywords: False data injection attacks · Semi-supervised learning · Label propagation · Small sample learning

1 Introduction

In recent years, with the improvement of the intelligent level of the power grid, the amount of communication data has increased exponentially, and the attack on the power monitoring system has been in various forms and the attack surface has been further expanded [1]. The integrity destruction and precise tampering of the measurement data of the supervisory control and data acquisition (SCADA) system can effectively affect the normal operation of the system and the final decision of the on-site personnel. Among the attacks on the power grid, the false data injection attack is a typical attack method that damages the integrity of the power grid information by tampering with the power measurement data [2]. It uses the loopholes in the state estimation of the power monitoring system to inject carefully designed false data into the data collection terminal, bypassing the bad data detection module in the state estimation, causing the dispatcher to misjudge the current power grid state, which can pose a great threat to the stability of the power system [3].

© ICST Institute for Computer Sciences, Social Informatics and Telecommunications Engineering 2022
Published by Springer Nature Switzerland AG 2022. All Rights Reserved
J. Lin and Q. Tang (Eds.): AC3 2022, LNICST 448, pp. 189–200, 2022.
https://doi.org/10.1007/978-3-031-17081-2_12

The identification of false data is to distinguish false data from normal data [4], which is essentially a classification problem [5]. With the continuous development of artificial intelligence technology, machine learning algorithms are more and more widely used to solve such problems due to their efficient modeling and learning capabilities. Liu et al. first proposed the concept of false data injection attacks in the power grid, and implemented the false data injection attack in the DC environment when part of the power system topology information and all the topology information are known, respectively [6]. Yu et al. proposed blind data injection attack, that is, when the system topology information is not clear and the Jacobian matrix is not considered, the principle component analysis method is used to implement false data injection attack [7]. Luo et al. proposed a method for detecting and isolating false data based on unknown input observers for residual characteristics [8]. Wang et al. used three traditional machine learning methods: state perceptron method, K-Nearest Neighbor (KNN) method, and Support Vector Machine (SVM) method to detect false data injection attack [9]. Liu et al. proposed information fuzzy reasoning algorithm to detect exceptional event by fusing physical information [10].

Although, machine learning algorithms have achieved many successful applications in grid false data injection attack detection and anomaly detection [11, 12]. However, most of the machine learning algorithms used in FDIAs detection are mainly based on supervised learning, in which only labeled samples can be used for model training and unlabeled samples cannot be used. The model performance depends on the quantity and quality of labeled samples when using supervised learning algorithms. Hence training a classification model by using supervised learning technique requires a large number of labeled samples. On the one hand, the types of labeled samples need to be able to cover the complete actual situation, and the number of labeled samples should be large enough to ensure that the sample features learned by the model can be strengthened. On the other hand, the labeled samples should be authoritative and accurate. However, in the actual operation process of the SCADA system, it is extremely difficult to obtain a large number of accurately labeled samples. The labeled power samples rely on the knowledge of power experts, and the artificially constructed labeled samples are highly subjective, with the result that it is time-consuming and laborious to construct a large number of labeled samples dataset by manual labeling. Therefore, there are usually only a very small number of labeled samples and a large number of unlabeled samples can be used in FDIAs detection in the power grid, which leads to low accuracy of most existing detection methods, and makes FDIAs detection to be intrinsically a small sample learning problem.

To address this issue, semi-supervised learning technique, which is capable of simultaneously using labelled and unlabeled training samples, should be used to construct the detection model. This paper proposes a novel semi-supervised-based false data injection attack detection (SS_FDIA) algorithm for FDIAs detection. We adopt the label propagation algorithm based on semi-supervised learning technique to automatically assign a reasonable class label to the large number of unlabeled samples dataset, when only a small number of labeled samples are used. Then we jointly use both a small number of manually labeled samples dataset and a large number of auto-labeled samples dataset to co-train a semi-supervised classifier. Finally, we evaluate the proposed SS_FDIA algorithm against the two state-of-the-art supervised learning methods: the decision tree (DT) method and the random forest (RF) method in the same false data injection attacks dataset.

2 False Data Injection Attacks

In the actual operating environment of power system, the sources of bad data include not only data abnormalities caused by power equipment trouble, but also false data maliciously constructed by attackers. Attackers can upload false data by attacking terminal device or implementing man-in-the-middle attacks on communication links. For attackers, it is very essential to design the optimal false data vector and construct the false data that can bypass the bad data detection module of power system based on the existing attack resources and system topology knowledge against the identification method of the state estimation module.

In power system, the relationship between the measurement value and the true state value is defined as:

$$z = Hx + v \tag{1}$$

where $z = (z_1, z_2, \cdots, z_m)^T$ is the m-dimensional measurement vector, $x = (x_1, x_2, \cdots, x_n)^T$ is the n-dimensional true state vector, H is a $m \times n$ Jacobian matrix, and v is noise. False data injection attacks are implemented by modifying the measurement vector, which constructs a malicious measurement vector a, shown as follows:

$$z_a = z + a \tag{2}$$

if z_a can pass the bad data detection module of power system, it indicates that the false data injection attack is successful. When the attacker knows the Jacobian matrix H, if the maliciously constructed vector a in Eq. (2) is a linear combination of the column vectors of the Jacobian matrix H, shown as follows:

$$a = Hc \tag{3}$$

where $c = (c_1, c_2, \cdots, c_n)^T$ is an any non-zero n-dimensional vector, the measurement vector z_a after which is injected the malicious measurement vector a can bypass the residual-based bad data detection module of the power system. Since the malicious measurement vector a has an infinite number of solutions, it is possible to construct successful false data and realize effective tampering of power monitoring data.

3 Method

3.1 Overview

The proposed SS_FDIA consists of four major steps, including (1) constructing samples dataset which contains a small number of labeled samples and a large number of unlabeled samples (2) baseline classifier construction (3) Unlabeled samples labeling based on label propagation, and (4) semi-supervised re-training of the classifier. The detailed diagram of proposed SS_FDIA algorithm for FDIAs detection is shown in Fig. 1.

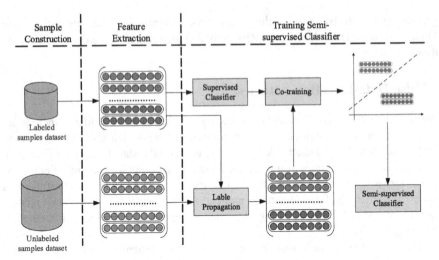

Fig. 1. Diagram of proposed SS_FDIA algorithm for FDIAs detection

3.2 Samples Dataset Construction

For false data injection attacks detection, we need simulate the grid environment. In this paper, we use IEEE-30 bus system for algorithm analysis, as shown in Fig. 2. We simulate the IEEE-30 bus system by using MatPower to construct the required samples dataset. It is generally acknowledged that there exists noises in the real power system and the measurement error of the SCADA system is normally distributed with the standard deviation σ about 0.5% to 2% of the normal measurement range. Therefore, in the experiments, the real value obtained in MatPower is randomly added with Gaussian noise error to construct the required dataset.

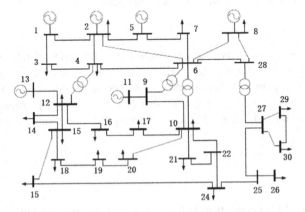

Fig. 2. IEEE-30 bus system

The samples dataset constructed for experiments are divided into normal samples and attacked samples. To construct normal samples, we take the measurement data on the IEEE-30 bus system at different times and randomly add Gaussian noise error to it, with the standard deviation σ within 1%. These samples are labeled as "normal". To construct attacked samples, we take vector $\{a|a = Hc, c \neq 0\}$ in Eq. (3) as attack vector to build attacked samples labeled as "attacked". In this study, the modulus of the vector $\|c\|$ is set to a small value, which exactly meet the formula $\|c\| \leq 0.001$ in the experiments. Therefore, these normal samples and attacked samples we constructed for study have close data distribution, which result in that false data injection attacks have higher concealment and are more difficult to detect.

3.3 Baseline Classifier Construction

We use a small number of labeled samples to train a supervised classifier. In this paper, we train a DT (Decision Tree) classifier and a RF (Random Forest, random forest) classifier as the baseline classifiers. The baseline classifiers trained by using small number of labeled samples have poor classification performance. Thus, in the next stage, we adopt the semi-supervised learning method to retrain these classifiers.

3.4 Label Propagation and Semi-Supervised Classifier

To expand the training labeled samples dataset, we adopt the label propagation algorithm to automatically propagate the category labels from the small number of labeled samples dataset to the large number of unlabeled samples dataset according to the similarity between each sample [13].

Let the samples dataset, which contains both labeled samples and unlabeled samples, be denoted by $X = \{x_1, x_2, \cdots, x_N\}$ and the corresponding labels set is denoted by $Y = \{y_1, y_2, \cdots, y_N\}$, where $x_i \in R^D$ represents the i-th sample's D-dimensional feature, and $y_i \in \{\lambda_1, \lambda_2\}$ represents the corresponding class label. Let the number of labeled samples be denoted by l and the number of unlabeled samples be denoted by u. Therefore, $N = l + u$. The rank of sample x_i relative to x is given by

$$\rho(x_i, x_j) = \left|\left\{x \in X | d(x_i, x) < d(x_i, x_j)\right\}\right| \tag{4}$$

where $d(x_i, x_j)$ represents the distance between x_i and x_j. Let $\tau_d(x_i)$ and τ_ρ be positive threshold values for item distances and ranks, respectively. The region of influence of sample x_i is defined as the set of samples simultaneously falling within distance $\tau_d(x_i)$ of x_i and rank τ_ρ of x_i, shown as follows

$$Infl(x_i) = \{x \in X | d(x_i, x) \leq \tau_d(x_i) \cap \rho(x_i, x) \leq \tau\} \tag{5}$$

sample x_i can influence sample x_j, if $x_j \in Infl(x_i)$ which means that x_j lies within the region of influence associated with x_i [14].

There are five major steps in the process of label propagation from labeled samples to unlabeled samples [15], as shown in Table 1.

(1) Initialize an influence graph G respect to the neighborhood relationships of items in X. Construct the influence graph $G(V_l \cup V_u, E)$ according to the sample set X,

Table 1. Label Propagation Algorithm.

Label Propagation algorithm
Input: Samples set X and the corresponding label set Y
Output: Score matrix S
1. $N \leftarrow |X| \; 1., t \leftarrow 2$
2.Construct an influence graph G respect to the neighborhoodrelationships of items in X;
3.Compute the $N \times N$ adjacency matrix A of G;
4.Compute the $N \times N$ propagation matrix P from A;
5.Initialize the $N \times t$ score matrix S;
6.**repeat**
7.$S' \leftarrow S$
8.$S \leftarrow PS'$
9.**until** $S \neq S'$

where V_l represents the small number of labeled samples dataset, and V_u represents the large number of unlabeled samples dataset. The edge set E is composed of two types of edges: strong edges that connect two mutually influenced samples and weak edges that connect two singly influenced samples.

(2) Compute the $N \times N$ adjacency matrix A of G. Entries of A can be computed by:

$$a_{i,j} = \begin{cases} \alpha \cdot \text{sim}(x_i, x_j), & \text{if } \langle j, i \rangle \text{ is a strong edge} \\ \text{sim}(x_i, x_j), & \text{if } \langle j, i \rangle \text{ is a weak edge} \\ 0, & \text{otherwise} \end{cases} \quad (6)$$

where $\alpha \geq 1$ is an amplifying factor that favors strong edges, and $\text{sim}(x_i, x_j)$ denotes the similarity value between two samples, shown as follows

$$\text{sim}(x_i, x_j) = 1 - \frac{d(x_i, x_j) - d_{min}}{d_{max} - d_{min}} \quad (7)$$

where d_{min} and d_{max} are the minimum and maximum pairwise distance between different samples in the graph, respectively.

(3) Compute the $N \times N$ propagation matrix P from A.Entries of P can be computed by

$$p_{i,j} = \begin{cases} a_{i,j}, & \text{if node } i \in V_l \\ \beta \cdot \frac{a_{i,j}}{\sum_{q=1}^{NT} a_{i,q}}, & \text{otherwise} \end{cases} \quad (8)$$

where $\beta \in (0, 1)$ is a damping factor used to penalize nodes that are far away from source nodes, and to accelerate the convergence.

(4) Initialize the $N \times t$ score matrix S.Entries of the $N \times t$ initial score matrix $S^{(0)}$ can be computed as

$$s_{i,j}^{(0)} = \begin{cases} 1, & \text{if } x_i \text{ is associated with } \lambda_j \\ 0, & \text{otherwise} \end{cases} \quad (9)$$

(5) Iteratively update score matrix S. $S^{(q)}$ is computed from the previous state $S^{(q-1)}$ according to the formula

$$S^{(q)} = PS^{(q-1)} \tag{10}$$

until the change of each element of S in two successive iterations is lower than the tolerance ε.

Once score matrix S converges, we assign each unlabeled sample a class label according to the score matrix S. Thus, we can jointly use both a small number of manually labeled samples dataset and a large number of auto-labeled samples dataset, to co-train a classifier in a semi-supervised learning way through label propagation method.

4 Results

4.1 Dataset

The entire samples dataset we construct includes 400 labeled samples (which can be divided into 200 normal samples and 200 attacked samples) and 380 unlabeled samples. For the sake of verifying the superiority of SS_FIDA algorithm in small sample learning problem, the 400 labeled samples are divided into a training dataset of 20 samples and a test dataset of 380 samples. The samples distribution is shown in Table 2.

Table 2. Samples distribution

Training dataset		Testing dataset
Labeled samples	Unlabeled samples	Labeled samples
20	380	380

4.2 Experimental Results

We performed the experiments 10 times and used the average classification accuracy as the evaluation criteria of the classification performance of each algorithm. We evaluated the proposed semi-supervised SS_FDIA algorithm against the two state-of-the-art supervised learning methods: DT (Decision Tree) method and RF (Random Forest) method. These classifiers were trained by using a training dataset of only 20 labeled samples and the classification performance were depicted in Fig. 3. The average classification accuracy of DT method is 76.71% and the accuracy of RF method is 81.26%. The average classification accuracy of SS_FDIA(DT) classifier, which is co-trained by jointly using SS_FDIA algorithm and DT method, is 88.68%. The average classification accuracy of SS_FDIA(RF) classifier, which is co-trained by jointly using SS_FDIA algorithm and RF method, is 99.0%.

It reveals that the proposed SS_FDIA algorithm outperforms the state-of-the-art DT method and RF method. The semi-supervised SS_FDIA algorithm learning from

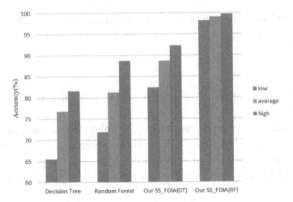

Fig. 3. Classification accuracy of different algorithms

unlabeled samples by using label propagation mechanism can substantially improve the classification accuracy. Compared with DT method and RF method, the classification accuracy of SS_FDIA algorithm is improved by 11.91% and 17.74%, respectively. It demonstrates that we can improve the performance of false data injection attacks detection by learning from unlabeled samples, though these samples may contain a lot of uncertainty.

5 Discussion

5.1 Amount of Unlabeled Samples

Generally, the accuracy of classifiers improves with the increase of labeled training samples. However, too many unlabeled training samples may deteriorate the classification performance in semi-supervised learning [16, 17]. Therefore, we performed FDIAs detection tasks to determine how many unlabeled samples should be used to facilitate training. Figure 4 shows the classification performance of SS_FDIA algorithm when using different numbers of unlabeled samples. The SS_FDIA(RF) classifier co-trained by the SS_FDIA algorithm and RF method achieves high classification accuracy when using 110 to 170 unlabeled samples and the classification accuracy can reach up to 99.74% when using 170 unlabeled samples. When using 190 ~ 310 unlabeled samples, the SS_FDIA(DT) classifier co-trained by the SS_FDIA algorithm and DT method achieves high classification accuracy and the classification accuracy can reach up to 92.63% when using 270 unlabeled samples. Later, when more unlabeled samples are used, the computational complexity will increase but the classification accuracy will not further improve.

Experimental results suggest that SS_FDIA can utilize unlabeled samples to improve the performance of the classification model to some extent to solve the small sample learning problem. As the number of unlabeled samples increases, the classification accuracy first increases, and after reaching a certain level, it will not continue to grow.

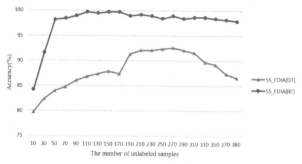

Fig. 4. Classification accuracy curve of the SS_FDIA algorithm when learning different numbers of unlabeled samples

5.2 Robustness of Parameters

In this paper, the proposed SS_FDIA algorithm can dynamically propagate the label information from 20 labeled samples dataset to large number of unlabeled samples dataset and automatically assign class labels to unlabeled samples in conformity with the similarity between each sample. The label propagation process involves two important parameters α and β, where $\alpha \geq 1$ and $\beta \in (0, 1)$. We ran experiments 10 times and calculated the average classification accuracy to investigate the impact of different parameter α and β on label propagation algorithm performance. The classification accuracy curve of parameter α and β are shown in Fig. 5 and Fig. 6. The label propagation algorithm achieves high classification accuracy when the value of α is between [2, 5] and the value of β is between [0.3, 0.7]. Therefore, in this study, we adopt the default parameters in the label propagation algorithm as $\alpha = 5$ and $\beta = 0.5$.

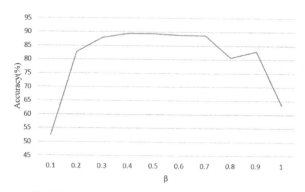

Fig. 5. Classification accuracy curve of parameter β

It reveals that SS_FDIA algorithm has strong robustness to parameters and strong generalization capability, which can achieve good experimental results with the parameters within a large range and easily converge to the optimal solution.

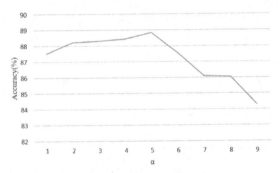

Fig. 6. Classification accuracy curve of parameter α

5.3 Computational Complexity

Table 3 shows the time cost of each stage of the random forest (RF) algorithm, decision tree (DT) algorithm and SS_FDIA algorithm. Applying the proposed SS_FDIA algorithm to FDIAs detection consists of two phrases: offline training and online testing. Since the SS_FDIA algorithm need to propagate class labels from the labeled samples to the unlabeled samples in the training phrase to automatically expand the labeled training samples dataset, and then use the labeled samples and unlabeled samples to retrain a semi-supervised classifier, the training phrase is quite time-consuming. Nevertheless, the SS_FDIA algorithm is very efficient in the testing phase, costing around 0.0006 s to detect each sample. It indicates that compared to traditional supervised learning methods, the proposed SS_FDIA algorithm can be better applied to real-time FDIAs detection in power system.

Table 3. Time complexity of different algorithms

Steps methods	Offline training				Testing each sample
	Feature Extraction	Training supervised classifier	Label propagation	Training semi-supervised classifier	
RF/DT	0.0001	0.00001	N/A	N/A	0.0005
SS_FDIA	0.0001	0.00001	92.8838	0.0087	0.0006

5.4 Amount of Labeled Samples

Table 4 gives the number of labeled training samples required by different algorithms: Wang [18], Lu [19], Xue [20] and proposed SS_FDIA algorithm. For false data injection attacks detection, the accuracy of the classification model depends on the number of labeled training samples. It is a very arduous task to train a high-performance classification model without large number of labeled training samples. Nevertheless, it's difficult to gather labeled attack samples in the real power grid and man-made samples are lack of objectivity. Hence, the results produced by most existing solutions are less accurate for FDIAs detection. Compared with other algorithms, the proposed SS_FDIA algorithm has achieved better classification performance when using a very small number (20) of labeled samples.

It reveals that the proposed SS_FDIA algorithm has a sense of superiority in solving the small sample learning problem for FDIAs detection in power system.

Table 4. Number of labeled training samples required by different algorithms.

Methods	Wang	Lu	Xue	Our SS_FDIA
Number of samples	30000	24192	3003	20

6 Conclusion

In this paper, we propose a novel FDIAs detection algorithm by using a large number of unlabeled samples in a semi-supervised way to alleviate the difficulties caused by the lack of high-quality adequate labeled samples, which can be ascribed to the time-consuming nature of attacked samples manual annotation. To expand the training samples dataset required by model learning, we apply semi-supervised label propagation method to automatically assign class labels for large unlabeled samples. Then, we jointly use a small number of manually labeled samples dataset and a large number of auto-labeled samples dataset to co-train a classifier via semi-supervised learning for FDIAs detection. Our results suggest that the proposed SS_FDIA algorithm can improve the accuracy of FDIAs detection by using large unlabeled training sample dataset in an appropriately designed semi-supervised learning way, which is of great significance for solving the small sample learning problem in FDIAs detection.

References

1. Zhu, H., Zhao, L., Qin, K., et al.: Active protection stratery of power monitoring network security based on big data analysis. Electr. Measur. Instrum. **57**(21), 133–139 (2020)
2. Zhang, Z., Deng, R., Cheng, P., et al.: On feasibility of coordinated time-delay and false data injection attacks on cyber-physical systems. IEEE Internet Things J. (2021)
3. Ahmed, M., Pathan, A.S.K.: False data injection attack (FDIA): an overview and new metrics for fair evaluation of its countermeasure. Complex Adapt. Syst. Model. **8**(1), 1–14 (2020)
4. Yin, X., Zhu, Y., Hu, J.: A subgrid-oriented privacy-preserving microservice framework based on deep neural network for false data injection attack detection in smart grids. IEEE Trans. Industr. Inf. **18**(3), 1957–1967 (2021)
5. Cao, J., Wang, D., Qu, Z., et al.: A novel false data injection attack detection model of the cyber-physical power system. IEEE Access **8**, 95109–95125 (2020)
6. Liu, Y., Ning, P., Reiter, M.K.: False data injection attacks against state estimation in electric power grids. ACM Trans. Inf. Syst. Secur. (TISSEC) **14**(1), 1–33 (2011)

7. Yu, Z.H., Chin, W.L.: Blind false data injection attack using PCA approximation method in smart grid. IEEE Trans. Smart Grid **6**(3), 1219–1226 (2015)
8. Luo, X., Wang, X., Pan, X., et al.: Detection and isolation of false data injection attack for smart grids via unknown input observers. Gener. Transm. Distrib. IET **13**(8), 1277–1286 (2019)
9. Wang, B., Zhao, Y., Zhang, S., et al.: Study of monitoring false data injection attacks based on machine-learning in electric systems. J. Electron. Inf. Sci. **2**(2), 122–128 (2017)
10. Liu, Y., Fang, Y., Sun, H., et al.: Cyber-physical fuzzy inference based attack detection method in smart grid. China Sci. Paper **11**(14), 1619–1625 (2016)
11. Zheng, S., Liang, Q., Peng, X., et al.: Research on abnormal power consumption behavior identification based on fuzzy clustering. Electr. Measur. Instrum. **57**(19), 40–44 (2020)
12. Zhou, Z., Chen, Q., Ma, B., et al.: An improved YOLO target detection method with its application in cable device abnormal condition recognition. Electr. Measur. Instrum. **57**(02), 14–20 (2020)
13. Hong, D., Naoto, Y., Jocelyn, C., et al.: Learning to propagate labels on graphs: An iterative multitask regression framework for semi-supervised hyperspectral dimensionality reduction. ISPRS J. Photogrammetry Remote Sens.: Official Publ. Int. Soc. Photogrammetry Remote Sens. (ISPRS) **158**, 35–49 (2019)
14. Li, N., Xia, Y.: Affective image classification via semi-supervised learning from web images. Multimedia Tools Appl. **77**(23), 30633–30650 (2018). https://doi.org/10.1007/s11042-018-6131-1
15. Houle, M.E., Oria, V., Satoh, S., et al.: Annotation propagation in image databases using similarity graphs. ACM Trans. Multimedia Comput. Commun. Appl. **10**(1), 1–21 (2013)
16. Dai, D., Van Gool, L.: Ensemble projection for semi-supervised image classification. IEEE Int. Conf. Comput. Vis. (ICCV) **2013**, 2072–2079 (2013)
17. Li, Y.F., Zhou, Z.H.: Towards making unlabeled data never hurt. IEEE Trans. Pattern Anal. Mach. Intell. **37**(1), 175–188 (2015)
18. Wang, G.: Research on detection method of power system false data injection attack based on machine learning. Northeast Electric Power University (2019)
19. Lu, J.: Research on false data attack detection of smart grid based on machine learning. North China Electric Power University (2019)
20. Xue, D.: Detecting false data injection attacks in smart grid. Chongqing University of Posts and Telecommunications (2019)

Security Application

A Novel Logistics Scheme Based on Zero-Trust Model

Haobo Wang, Wei Ou$^{(\boxtimes)}$, and Wenbao Han

School of Cyberspace Security, Hainan University, Haikou 570228, China
{20085400210068,ouwei,994338}@hainanu.edu.cn

Abstract. Big data and cloud computing have turned the old logistics sector into an intelligent and digital one, enhancing supply chain efficiency and enabling real-time information sharing. While digitization improves quality, reduces prices, and boosts efficiency in logistics, it also introduces new security risks. A combination of traditional security protection systems, network security borders collapsing and increased risks from both sides. An investigation into how to preserve logistic privacy and information security is critical given present system flaws such as data security, arbitrary data access rights allocation, disappearance of security limits, and absence of privacy protection. We developed a zero-trust logistics scheme based on commercial encryption, employing the SDP architecture to establish a zero-trust security system, and precisely managing network boundary access behavior. The system's underlying blockchain concept uses the domestic alliance chain FISCO BCOS to ensure transaction data traceability and party identification. Results show that this technique effectively protects user privacy, secures data storage, and allows autonomous operation of the logistics system. The solution places identity at the center, creates a new security border, protects user privacy, and aids in the digital transformation of logistics organizations.

Keywords: Logistics · Zero-trust · Commercial cryptography · SDP · Dynamic trust evaluation · Cross-chain

1 Introduction

The use of IoT, AI, big data, and cloud computing has increased in recent years. It boosted communication efficiency by allowing real-time information exchange. The security of logistics private information is further impacted by digitization [18, 24]. A logistics system hack causes financial losses, personal safety issues, and public and social security issues. Various incidents impacting logistics and personal data security have occurred in China recently. Data leaks have improved public awareness of logistics data security flaws. Issues of personal data security. This system does not provide a secure environment for transmitting personal data. Uninterrupted transmission of this data compromises user security. Data storage privacy protection. A WMS stores typical logistical data. It's also tough to verify third-party reliability and avoid data theft. Among the challenges are data traceability and trustworthiness. Inappropriate data access. When

J. Lin and Q. Tang (Eds.): AC3 2022, LNICST 448, pp. 203–215, 2022.
https://doi.org/10.1007/978-3-031-17081-2_13

a character acquires redundant information, privacy data may be leaked. Internal shippers' workers leaked customer privacy information. Theft of these data puts users and society at danger. Boundaries vanish. Industrial digitization has increased network complexity and security barriers are falling. To adapt traditional network security solutions to modern business networks is difficult. The logistics business has reported external staff stealing data on-site. Inadequate privacy protection. Shipping companies including SF Express, Shentong, and Zhongtong can track packages via the web page's courier number. An attacker need not even log in to attack the platform. We propose and build a zero-trust logistics service platform based on domestic cryptography to prevent customer privacy leaks. The latest information technology safeguards logistics data during transmission and storage. No-trust logistics security, full transaction recording, user privacy protection, and improved logistics experience. Read on for more details. The second part examined the technological background. 3rd segment outlines plan Performance is the final component. Security is examined in Sect. 5. 6. Conclusions and further research Contributions of this study include:

(1)   Through SM2, SM3, and other commercial cryptographic algorithms, user data security is ensured. Controllable security has also been implemented in existing technology and architecture.
(2)   Create a zero-trust security system, use SDP architecture, create a new network security boundary, use multi-factor authentication, and continuously evaluate participant credit rating. Furthermore, the security of business systems is ensured by finer granularity in border protection, communication transmission, authentication, and data confidentiality.
(3)   The decentralization, tamper-proof, and traceability of blockchain technology allows the storage of all transaction data in the logistics process. Our approach secures the origin of logistical transaction information and non-repudiation of all parties involved, protecting user privacy and boosting logistic credibility. Improved data flow through cross-domain management.

2   Background

(1)   As a result of this, the potential default link between network location and trust has been broken. Zero-trust security is "never trust, always validate" to optimize trusted resource access and enterprise IT security. Personnel or clients are not automatically trusted. Any attempt to access the network and its resources should be confirmed before permission [1–3, 6, 9, 19, 23]. Zero-trust principles include untrusted participation, minimal privilege, dynamic access management, and ongoing security protection. Existing network security solutions can benefit from zero-trust security principles. Components of the system's basic logic and data sources that are zero-trust (Fig. 1). In this design, participant objects and resource access are managed. Zero-trust relies on the control and data planes [11, 17]. Access requests are computed by the control plane's policy engine. The policy manager decides the outcomes. If the entry is allowed, the policy manager notifies the data plane's policy execution point. A fresh source of trust is evaluated if the participants or their

behavior change. An authorization policy update is made based on the evaluation results. The policy execution point is instructed to protect resources.

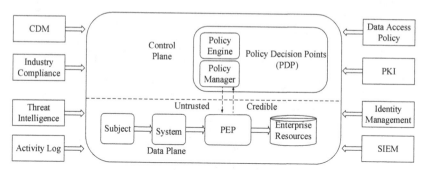

Fig. 1. Zero-trust logic architecture

(2) Enterprise Financial Alliance (EFA) is a chain of domestic enterprises led by FISCO BCOS. It can be used in many distributed business contexts. With the help of the State Encryption Bureau [4, 7, 12, 13], the golden chain alliance has developed commercial cryptography encryption and decryption, signature, signature verification, hash algorithm, and domestic SSL communication protocol [10, 15, 20, 21]. We have therefore decided to employ FISCO BCOS as the blockchain's underlying architecture.

(3) Officially recognized by the State Cryptographic Bureau. A set of national commercial cipher algorithm specifications has been prepared by the State Commercial Cipher Administration Office. Data is encoded in hexadecimal. SM2, SM3, and SM4 are covered. The SM4 block cryptography technique is used to encrypt and decrypt data in China [5, 8, 22]. This approach uses 128-bit group and key lengths for encryption and crucial extension. There are 32 iterative operations every game in SM4. SM4 is safer than 3DES since it uses AES's key size. It includes elliptic curve public-key cryptography techniques published by the DCA in 2010. SM2 replaces the well-known RSA algorithm in our commercial cryptography system. Only the SM3 algorithm can be used for digital signature and verification, random number generation, and message authentication code generation. The source code is available. More than 264-bit messages use padding and iterative compression to generate 256-bit hashes. It simply uses AND, OR, and NOT. Iteration, message expansion, and compression are included. The SM3 algorithm compresses data like SHA-256. The NSA compares it to SHA-256 for security and efficiency.

3 Scheme

3.1 Overall Process

Zero-trust logistics based on commercial cryptography. To access and use the business, users only need to use their browser. Deployment, maintenance, and upgrade are also simplified. Only the server needs to be upgraded. Refreshing previously visited pages is all it takes. Our architecture is divided into four layers: user business, data processing and interface, blockchain network, and basic support. Every employee in the logistics chain is regularly vetted (Fig. 2).

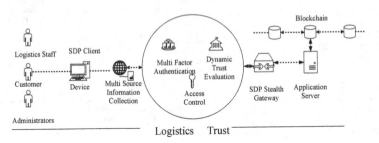

Fig. 2. Work flow

SDP clients placed on the device allow users (customers, logistical personnel, administrators) to access the SDP control scheme. User identification, system environment, dynamic user behavior, and other information are collected before the SDP control scheme can authenticate users with many factors. Ongoing multi-factor security inspection and authentication of data collected by users in various roles (user identity, system environment, dynamic user behavior). In order to assess a user's trust level, the dynamic trust evaluation method will resolve, evaluate, and make choices on many factors. Furthermore, trust assessment is ongoing throughout the access process. Access control scheme modifies user rights dynamically after trust evaluation in logistics scenario. For example, the invisible gateway's IP address and permission list are returned to the SDP client. SDP clients request the SDP Stealth Gateway using real-time authorization information. In response, the SDP Stealth Gateway either approves or denies user access. In order to grant lawful access, SDP Stealth Gateway establishes encrypted connections with clients. A specific data type will be recorded on the blockchain after each order is completed. Moreover, the blockchain stores logistical data.

3.2 Module

Identity Authentication and Management. MFA is the first layer. A dynamic user's behavior is included in this authentication. User login and business requirements must be checked first. This needs the SDP client to collect multi-source information such as dynamic user behavior and physical system data. In order to use data from several sources, the user must first authenticate. Difficult roles call for ID check. This information is sent to the SDP control scheme for system authentication. Our method catches both the network address and the OS version. Versions of OS can help analyze security. Login location information can detect odd changes and alert users. Authentication controls dynamic behavior such as login time and IP address. It also ensures that the user registers on with the correct tab. Multi-factor authentication demands flexibility. It affects system security. A user's odd dynamic behavior reduces confidence. Incorrect password logins, unexpected exits, and business demands that exceed their roles' privileges are examples of this data. SDP sends it. And so on for future certification. Multi-factor authentication findings are used to assess participants' emotional trust. Included is a decision-making model SDP control delivers access parsing requests to the client. That is trusted engine friendly. This allows the next trust evaluation to watch individuals and resources. The Trust Assessment Scheme dynamically evaluates each user based on received data and access requests. Each machine assesses internal factors based on its own criteria. Each engine then transmits the trust rating to the decision module. That's the first step. Score is 100. Not finding the requisite certification or anomalous risk reduces the dynamic score. It then aggregates the quantitative evaluations from each trust engine. The choice module has determination criteria for various logistic participant users.

Software Defined Perimeter. This implementation makes the service invisible to unauthorized users. This protocol guards against untrusted packets by requiring identity authentication. Our method hides the network via identity authentication. Data packets including the requester's IP address and port number Defining a Default-Drop firewall policy protects protected services. To learn about ports, the firewall should reject all TCP and UDP traffic.

Data Cross-Domain Management. The network then sends it cross-domain queries. The routing node accepts requests from sub-chains A and B. After passing the verification, the routing node forwards the request to the cross-domain message queue. If the inspection fails and an error message is returned, the transaction is canceled. Requests from subchain A to B are sent to the message queue, where the relay contract listens and queries for the request data. The request is forwarded to the subchain's cross-domain agreement. By voting on transactions, a route node verifies them across domains. Once the relay chain receives cross-domain information from sub-chain B, it performs simple payment verification. After successful validation, forwarded to cross-domain initiator A. Routers in cross-domain initiator sub-chain A monitor the relay chain for cross-domain confirmation messages. Secured cross-domain transactions can be used. The cross-domain contract verifies the confirmation transaction and receipt information, approves it, and returns it. Transaction Followed by syncing subchain data and waiting for cross-domain information to be validated. Also, a cross-domain deposit is made to assure authentic cross-domain transactions. Il indique l'achèvement de la transaction cross-domain.

4 Experiment

This section systematically tests the proposed scheme's performance and the blockchains' performance by chaining logistic transaction information.

4.1 Experimental Environment

The application server configuration used in our pilot scenario is shown in Table 1. Also, the test tool LoadRunner, whose client configuration is shown in Table 2, is used. We will then elaborate on our experimental process.

Table 1. Application server configuration information

Configuration items	Performance test environment
CPU	Intel i5–9500 3.00 GHz
MEM	8.00 GB
SSD	256G
Operating system and version number	Ubuntu 20.04
Database system and version number	Mysql 8.0.22

Table 2. LR client configuration information table

Configuration items	Performance test environment
CPU	Intel i7-8750H 2.20 GHz
MEM	8.00 GB
SSD	512G
Operating system and version number	Windows 10 enterprise
Database system and version number	8.0.22

4.2 System Test

We tested the project using LoadRunner and analyzed the test results to optimize the system's performance. LoadRunner is a load test tool that predicts system behavior and performance. Identify and find system performance bottlenecks by simulating how virtual users implement concurrent load and real-time performance monitoring. It applies to various architecture, supports a wide range of protocols and technologies, and provides a unique solution for testing. The requirements of this test verify that 2000 user logins are completed within 30 min, then basic logistics operations such as sending, designated couriers, cargo handover are carried out, and finally exit. System performance indicators are shown in Table 3.

Results

Summary of Results: After LoadRunner collects the scene test results, it first displays an overview of Fig. 3. The summary lists "Statistics Summary," "Transaction Summary," and "HTTP Responses Summary." List the test results with brief information.

Statistical Summary Information: After scenario execution, this part displays concurrency data, total throughput, average throughput per second, and completed requests. Our overall throughput for this test run is 842,037,409 bytes, and our average throughput per second is 451,979 bytes. There were 211,974 requests, with an average of 113.781 per second. Transaction Summary: This section gives the average response time and a pass rate of the related actions after the scene is executed, as shown in Fig. 4. This graph shows the average response time and business success rate for each step.

Table 3. Performance indicators

Test items	Target value
Average transaction response time	≤3 s
TPS	≥200
Error rate	=0%
CPU utilization	<70%
Memory utilization	<75%
Physical disk utilization	<70%
Network throughput	<60%

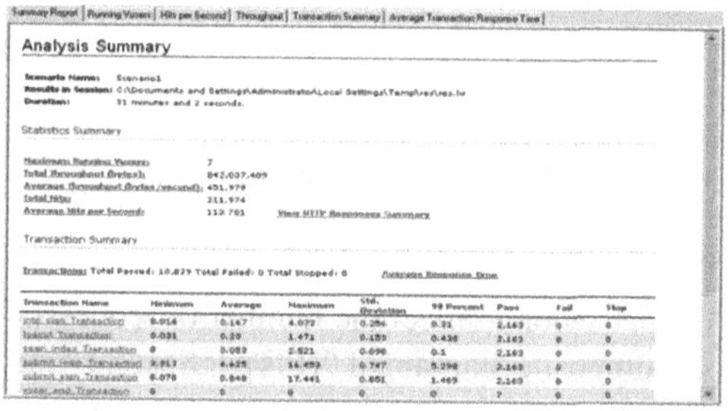

Fig. 3. Summary of performance test results

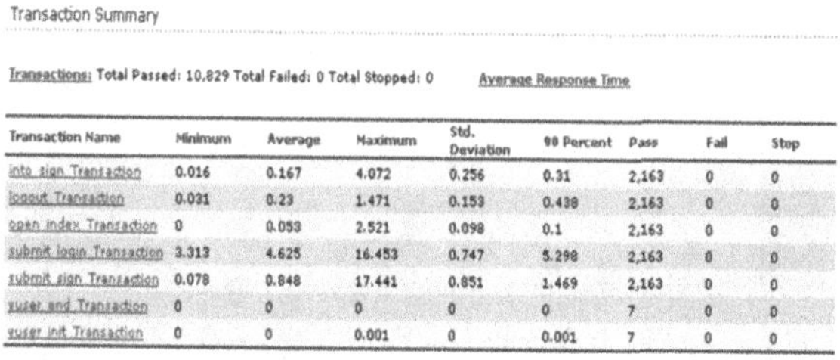
Transaction Summary

Transactions: Total Passed: 10,829 Total Failed: 0 Total Stopped: 0 Average Response Time

Transaction Name	Minimum	Average	Maximum	Std. Deviation	90 Percent	Pass	Fail	Stop
into_sign_Transaction	0.016	0.167	4.072	0.256	0.31	2,163	0	0
logout_Transaction	0.031	0.23	1.471	0.153	0.438	2,163	0	0
open_index_Transaction	0	0.053	2.521	0.098	0.1	2,163	0	0
submit_login_Transaction	3.313	4.625	16.453	0.747	5.298	2,163	0	0
submit_sign_Transaction	0.078	0.848	17.441	0.851	1.469	2,163	0	0
vuser_end_Transaction	0	0	0	0	0	7	0	0
vuser_init_Transaction	0	0	0.001	0	0.001	7	0	0

Fig. 4. Transaction summary

HTTP Response Summary: It can be seen from Fig. 5 that in this scenario test, Load-Runner simulated a total of 211974 requests (consistent with the "Total Hits" in the "Statistics Summary"). Among them, "HTTP 200" has 209,811 times, and "HTTP 404" has 2,163 times. Most of the requests sent out during this process could respond correctly, but some failed, but the test results were not affected.

Concurrency Number Analysis: Running Vusers shows the execution of concurrency during scene execution. They offer the status of the Vuser, the number of Vusers that completed the script, and collection statistics. Figure 6 shows how Vusers are running during the performance test. From the diagram, we can see that the trend of Vusers is

210   H. Wang et al.

HTTP Responses Summary

HTTP Responses	Total	Per second
HTTP_200	209,811	112.62
HTTP_404	2,163	1.161

Fig. 5. Summary of HTTP response

consistent with the settings in the execution plan, indicating that Vusers is running as expected without running errors.

Fig. 6. Number of concurrent runs

Clicks Per Second: Hits per second reflect the number of requests clients submit to the server. Figure 7 shows a composite diagram of "Hits per Second" and "Average Throughput (bytes/second)." The graph shows that the curves of both graphics are standard and identical, indicating that the server can accept requests from clients promptly and return results.

Fig. 7. Hits per second combined with throughput per second

Business Success Rate: As shown in Fig. 8 below, all Actions are green, meaning they are passed. At the same time, except for the two transactions vuser_init and vuser_end, the number of other transactions passed is 2163, which means that the total completed in 30 min 2163 business operations were performed. Based on these, it can be judged that the success rate of this test business is 100%.

System Resources: The system resource graph displays the machine's CPU, memory, network, disk, and other resource utilization during the scene's execution. This test monitors the test server's CPU, RAM, and processor queue length. Figure 9 shows the specific data: The graphic shows rather smooth curves for CPU utilization, available physical memory, and CPU queue length. The three averages are 53.582 percent, 2383.456 m,

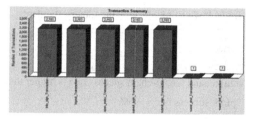

Fig. 8. Business status statistics

and 8.45. While the test server has 8192 MB of physical memory, the memory utilization is (70.91%).

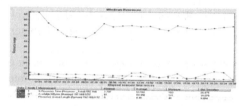

Fig. 9. System resource monitoring results of the test server

4.3 Blockchain Test

We use Hyperledger Caliper 2.0 to test and assess the project's blockchain module's performance. The process is given below. Caliper is a blockchain performance tester. PWSG) is a Hyperledger initiative set up to define performance measures (TPS, delay, resource utilization, etc.). Caliper is also designed to leverage this group of performance indicators. Integrates with blockchain systems while obscuring underlying data. Caliper creates a visual performance test report using user-defined test techniques. Caliper can readily manage the project's pressure measuring demands. An overview of major blockchain performance evaluation studies conducted both at home and abroad is presented (Table 4).

Results. By deploying a smart contract and starting a monitoring object, the Master process may keep an eye on the back-end blockchain system's resource consumption. The Master process runs tests according to the configuration file, generates tasks according to the defined load, and assigns them to the client terminal process. Finally, each client's performance information will be stored for later examination. We generated reports based on the statistics of all Client processes for each test round.

4.4 Security Test

To test our method's security, we mimic DDoS and replay assaults. Experiments show that our method secures data while being sent and defends against attacks. To test the

Table 4. Existing blockchain industry standards

Rule items	Standard
Pressure test	Transaction receipts per second are basically the same as the up-chain volume, and the up-chain success rate is higher than 95%
Performance index	Uplink success rate > 95%
	TPS > 200
	Average delay time < 0.5 s
	Delay < 1000 ms

module, we use Nmap port scanning, WireShark package scanning, and LOIC to simulate a DDoS attack on the server. We want to see if the SDP control platform can utilize network stealth to hide ports and if clients can access Web services using Fwknop authentication.

Results are as follows: Use the LOIC tool to attack DDoS on the client; enter the server IP address 172.16.1.1 as the attack mode; attack port 80; attack rate up to the maximum; and use WireShark to capture the package. On the client side, use Nmap to scan the port. The 80th port was filtered. WireShark authenticates SDP clients and analyzes packages. On the control platform, the client transmits encrypted UDP authentication traffic to port 62201. This approach also assures that each UDP packet delivered is unique, making it difficult to duplicate an activity. On the client, we use Nmap to do a port scan to ensure that port 80 is open. Fwknop has developed four firewall rules to allow IP connections from Fwknop clients to port 80, according to the current firewall policy.

5 Analysis

5.1 Performance

System Performance. We use LoadRunner to mimic virtual user concurrent load and real-time performance monitoring to identify system bottlenecks. 2000 logistical services in 30 min. We devised seven system performance measures. Table 5 shows the latest test result record. Maximum concurrency is 237, total throughput is 842,037,409. That's 451,979 byte/s. The total requests are 211,974, averaging 113.781 per second. So the system can handle daily concurrencies and concurrency amount. These data show that the Web server's hardware resources must be increased.

Blockchain Performance. On behalf of the Hyperledger Performance and Extensibility Working Group (PWSG), we deployed Hyperledger Cailper to benchmark block chain performance. We set up smart contracts to monitor items in the backend blockchain system. Every client's performance was tested many times. Our system's blockchain satisfies industry standards, according to the results of our testing.

Table 5. Test results

Test items	Target value	Actual value	Is satisfied
Average transaction response time	≤3 s	2.298	Y
Business SuccessRate	100%	100%	Y
TPS	≥200	217	Y
Total number of businesses	2000 (30 min)	2163	Y
CPU usage	<75%	53.582%	Y
Memory usage	<70%	70.91%	Y
Physical disk utilization	<70%	63.32%	Y
Network throughput	<60%	57.92%	Y

5.2 Security

Authentication data is encrypted in one UDP packet using AES. In addition, SHA-256's HMAC encryption protects data from replay attacks. Also, all data will be transferred across a TLS connection channel created by the client and server. Multi-factor authentication verifies a user's identity by using both static and dynamic factors. Single-factor authentication is improved by using multi-source data (user identity, device environment, dynamic behavior). Defined clients can only connect dynamically to the stealth security gateway if the authentication policy is published. Separating access control and data channels prevents network attacks. They also guard against DDoS. During logistics, the user's credit score is added to the blockchain. A geocentric organization is no longer required to participate in blockchain networks. Multiple private keys perform data validation and access control using cryptography. It guards against manipulation and loss.

6 Conclusion

The primary body is a commercial cryptographic method, and the center is identification, which addresses the frequent information security challenges in China's logistics industry. It restructures the blockchain node network to match the logistics industry's physical network layout. An unique, integrated, and complete blockchain-based logistics service scheme, the zero-trust logistics service scheme. The logistics platform's data security and privacy are ensured by commercial encryption, zero-trust security architecture, blockchain technology, and other emerging technologies. It improves information, digitization, and intelligence in the logistics business while providing high-quality services to diverse users. Our plan has the following advantages according to our tests: Built with the SDP architecture, this scheme verifies users are who they claim to be and monitors their activities. A two-way encrypted tunnel protects users' privacy by limiting access to enterprise application servers to authorized users. We do commercial cryptography transformation using the domestic alliance chain FISCO BCOS as the bottom framework. Every server node records and backs up every transaction in the logistics process. Centralization, traceability, and tamper prevention provide data storage security, transaction origin and validity of all parties are realized, and parcel disputes are successfully addressed utilizing blockchain characteristics. Interdomain management also improves data flow. An SDP architecture based on zero-trust security is proposed, with the local federation chain FISCO BCOS as the foundation. On this program, we will study how blockchain service platforms can be used to improve security in the logistics industry.

In the future, we will research and improve the current functions, strengthen the stability of each component connection, strengthen system security protection, optimize SDP architecture and related algorithms, and optimize blockchain performance and stability.

References

1. Mohan, C.: State of public and private blockchains: myths and reality. In: Proceedings of the 2019 International Conference on Management of Data, pp. 404–411 (2019)
2. Collier, Z.A., Sarkis, J.: The zero trust supply chain: managing supply chain risk in the absence of trust. Int. J. Prod. Res. **59**, 3430–3445 (2021)
3. Gao, Q., Zhang, J., Ma, J., Yang, C., Guo, J., Miao, Y.: LIP-PA: a logistics information privacy protection scheme with position and attribute-based access control on mobile devices. Wirel. Commun. Mob. Comput. **2018**, 1–14 (2018)
4. Issaoui, Y., Khiat, A., Bahnasse, A., Ouajji, H.: Smart logistics: study of the application of blockchain technology. Procedia Comput. Sci. **160**, 266–271 (2019)
5. Keluo, Z.: Research on privacy data protection and access rights management for logistics user. Southeast University (2018)
6. Papakonstantinou, N., Van Bossuyt, D.L., Linnosmaa, J., Hale, B., O'Halloran, B.: A zero trust hybrid security and safety risk analysis method. J. Comput. Inf. Sci. Eng **21**(5), 1–10 (2021)
7. Perboli, G., Musso, S., Rosano, M.: Blockchain in logistics and supply chain: a lean approach for designing real-world use cases. IEEE Access **6**, 62018–62028 (2018)
8. Qi, G.: Research and optimization of blockchain system for supply chain tracking. Xi'an University of Electronic Science and Technology (2019)
9. Qigui, Z., Hai, H., Youjie, W.: Research on software-defined boundary security model based on zero trust. Inf. Technol. Informatiz. 92–94 (2020)
10. Shengshi, Z.: The design and optimization of SoC based on the encrypted technology of national cryptography. Guangdong University of Technology (2019)
11. Silang, W., Xuan, F., Youbao, C., Yi, C.: Application research of zero trust architecture. J. Inf. Secur. Res. **6**, 966–971 (2020)
12. Tijan, E., Aksentijević, S., Ivanić, K., et al.: Blockchain technology implementation in logistics. Sustainability **11**, 1185 (2019)
13. Wang, Y., Wang, C., Luo, X., Zhang, K., Li, H.: A blockchain-based IoT data management system for secure and scalable data sharing. In: Liu, J.K., Huang, X. (eds.) NSS 2019. LNCS, vol. 11928, pp. 167–184. Springer, Cham (2019). https://doi.org/10.1007/978-3-030-36938-5_10
14. Wubin, P., Guoqiang, R.: Software defined perimeter SDP: an overview of concepts, techniques, and application. Res. Digit. Commun. World 192–195 (2021)
15. Xin, Z.: A flexible HW/SW co-design system based on SM2/3/4 for encryption/decryption and signature/verification. Guangdong University of Technology (2018)

16. Xinyue, Y., Gang, S., Yawei, Z.: Research on software-defined-perimeter network stealth technology based on zero trust. Commun. Technol. **54**, 1229–1234 (2021)
17. Xuan, L., Tianyu, M.: Research and application thinking of zero-trust architecture China nuclear. Power **13**, 582–586 (2020)
18. Yi, F.: Research and implementation of intelligent logistics system based on blockchain. University of Electronic Science and Technology (2019)
19. Yifei, Q., Yingtao, Z., Xiaodong, Z.: Zero trust transformation research. Inf. Secur. Commun. Priv. 84–91 (2021)
20. Yu, M.: Research on Chinese domestic cipher algorithms in mobile network payment. Harbin University of Science and Technology (2018)
21. Yuhang, X.: Design and implementation of instant messaging system base on commercial cryptography algorithm. Guangxi Normal University (2020)
22. Zeyan, T.: Research and application of threshold-based mobile security key distribution mechanism. Southwest University of Science and Technology (2019)
23. Zezhou, Z.: Zero-trust security architecture in the new IT environment. Secur. Informatiz. 50–51 (2021)
24. Ziyue, W.: Research and optimization of blockchain system for supply chain tracing. Beijing Jiaotong University (2019)
25. Zongxiao, X., Kunxiang, D., Jie, Z.: Introduction of domestic commercial cipher algorithms and related standards. China Qual. Stand. Rev. 12–14+23 (2020)

ALFLAT: Chinese NER Using ALBERT, Flat-Lattice Transformer, Word Segmentation and Entity Dictionary

Haifeng Lv[1,3]([⊠]) and Yong Ding[2]

[1] School of Data Science and Software Engineering, Wuzhou University, Wuzhou, China
421538806@qq.com
[2] Guangxi Key Laboratory of Cryptography and Information Security, School of Computer Science and Information Security, Guilin University of Electronic Technology, Guilin, China
[3] Guangxi Key Laboratory of Machine Vision and Intelligent Control, Wuzhou University, Wuzhou, China

Abstract. Recently, the character-word lattice structure has been proved to be effective for Chinese named entity recognition (NER) by incorporating the word information. However, one hand, since the lattice structure is dynamic and complex, although some existing lattice-based models are effectively utilize the parallel computation of GPUs, they do not fully utilize word segmentation boundary tags that as features are helpful for NER task. On the other hand, the character-word vector needs to be trained, and the user-defined entity dictionary cannot be effectively used. In this paper, we propose ALFLAT: based on a flat-lattice Transformer to incorporate ALBERT pre-trained model, word segmentation information and user-defined entity dictionary for Chinese NER. ALFLAT converts the lattice structure into a flat structure consisting of spans, integrate word segmentation embedding with the output of flat-lattice Transformer model, then modifies the emission scores according to the user-defined entity dictionary, finally utilize Viterbi decoding of the CRF layer to obtain the correct entity results. Each span corresponds to a character or latent word and its position in the original lattice. With the power of ALBERT pre-trained model, Transformer and position encoding, ALFLAT can fully leverage the lattice, word segmentation and user-defined entity dictionary information. Experiments on MSRA dataset show ALFLAT outperforms other lexicon-based models in performance and efficiency.

Keywords: NER · ALBERT · Lattice transformer · CRF · Word segmentation

1 Introduction

Named entity recognition (NER) plays an indispensable role in many downstream natural language processing (NLP) tasks [1, 2]. Compared with English NER [3–6], Chinese NER is more difficult since it usually involves word segmentation.

Recently, the lattice structure has been proved to have a great benefit to utilize the word information and avoid the error propagation of word segmentation [7, 8]. We can

J. Lin and Q. Tang (Eds.): AC3 2022, LNICST 448, pp. 216–227, 2022.
https://doi.org/10.1007/978-3-031-17081-2_14

match a sentence with a lexicon to obtain the latent words in it, and then we get a lattice like in Fig. 1(a). The lattice is a directed acyclic graph, where each node is a character or a latent word. The lattice includes a sequence of characters and potential words in the sentence. They are not ordered sequentially, and the word's first character and last character determine its position. Some words in lattice may be important for

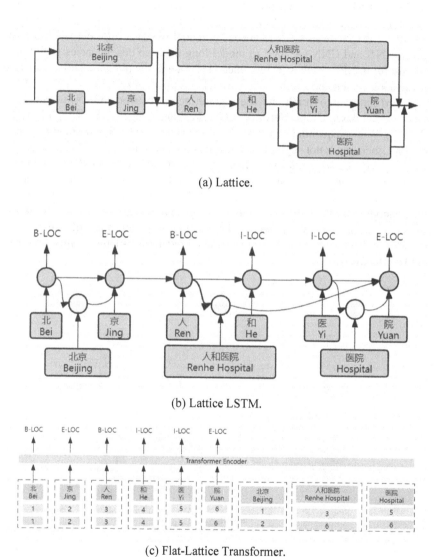

(a) Lattice.

(b) Lattice LSTM.

(c) Flat-Lattice Transformer.

Fig. 1. While lattice LSTM indicates lattice structure by dynamically adjusting its structure, FLAT only needs to leverage the span position encoding. In (c) ■, ■, ■, denotes tokens, heads and tails, respectively.

NER. For example, in Fig. 1(a), "人和医院(Renhe Hospital)" can be used to distinguish between the geographic entity "北京(Beijing)" and the organization entity "北京人(Beijing People)".

There are three lines of methods to leverage the lattice. (1) First line is to design a model to be compatible with lattice input, such as lattice LSTM [7] and LR-CNN [9]. In lattice LSTM, an extra word cell is employed to encode the potential words, and attention mechanism is used to fuse variable-number nodes at each position, as in Fig. 1(b). LR-CNN uses CNN to encode potential words at different window sizes. However, RNN and CNN are hard to model long-distance dependencies [10], which may be useful in NER, such as coreference [11]. Due to the dynamic lattice structure, these methods cannot fully utilize the parallel computation of GPU. (2) Second line is to convert lattice into graph and use a graph neural network (GNN) to encode it, such as Lexicon-based Graph Network (LGN) [12] and Collaborative Graph Network (CGN) [13]. While sequential structure is still important for NER and graph is general counterpart, their gap is not negligible. These methods need to use LSTM as the bottom encoder to carry the sequential inductive bias, which makes the model complicated. (3)Third line is to converts the lattice structure into a flat structure consisting of spans to encode it, such as Flat Lattice Transformer [14]. In Flat Lattice Transformer, an ingenious position encoding for the lattice-structure is designed to reconstruct a lattice from a set of tokens, as in Fig. 1(c). While word segmentation information is still important for NER, the character-word vector needs to be trained and the user-defined entity dictionary cannot be effectively used.

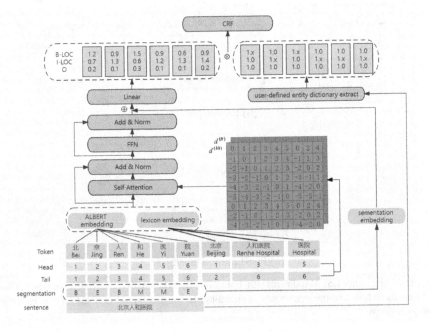

Fig. 2. The overall architecture of ALFLAT.

In this paper, we propose ALFLAT: based on a flat-lattice Transformer to incorporate ALBERT [15] pre-trained model, word segmentation information and user-defined entity dictionary for Chinese NER as shown in Fig. 2. Transformer [10] adopts fully-connected self-attention to model the long-distance dependencies in a sequence. To keep the position information, Transformer introduces the position representation for each token in the sequence. Inspired by the idea of position representation, we use an ingenious position encoding for the lattice-structure to reconstruct a lattice from a set of tokens, then we can directly use ALBERT pre-trained model and Transformer to fully model the lattice input. The self-attention mechanism of Transformer enables characters to directly interact with any potential word, including self-matched words. After obtaining the context representation of each token, we integrate word segmentation embedding with the context representation, and use a linear fully connected layer to obtain the emission matrix scores of each tag corresponding to the token, modify the emission matrix scores according to the user-defined entity dictionary, finally utilize Viterbi [16] decoding of CRF [17] to obtain the correct entities. Experimental results show our model outperforms other lexicon-based methods on the performance.

2 Background

In this section, we briefly introduce the Transformer architecture. Focusing on the NER task, we only discuss the Transformer encoder. It is composed of self-attention and feed forward network (FFN) layers. Each sublayer is followed by residual connection and layer normalization. FFN is a position-wise multi-layer Perceptron with nonlinear transformation. Transformer performs self-attention over the sequence by H heads of attention individually and then concatenates the result of H heads. For simplicity, we ignore the head index in the following formula. The result of per head is calculated as:

$$\text{Att}(\mathbf{A},\mathbf{V}) = \text{softmax}(\mathbf{A})\mathbf{V} \tag{1}$$

$$\mathbf{A}_{ij} = \left(\frac{Q_i K_j^{\mathsf{T}}}{\sqrt{d_{head}}} \right) \tag{2}$$

$$[Q,K,V] = E_x[\mathbf{W}_q, \mathbf{W}_k, \mathbf{W}_v] \tag{3}$$

where E is the token embedding lookup table or the output of last Transformer layer. $\mathbf{W}_q, \mathbf{W}_k, \mathbf{W}_v \in \mathbb{R}^{d_{\text{model}} \times d_{head}}$ are learnable parameters, and $d_{\text{model}} = H \times d_{head}$, d_{head} is the dimension of each head. The vanilla Transformer also uses absolute position encoding to capture the sequential information. Inspired by [18], we think commutativity of the vector inner dot will cause the loss of directionality in self-attention. Therefore, we consider the relative position of lattice also significant for NER.

3 Model

3.1 Converting Lattice into Flat Structure

After getting a lattice from characters with a lexicon, we can flatten it into flat counterpart. The flat-lattice can be defined as a set of spans, and a span corresponds to a token, a head and a tail, like in Fig. 1(c), proposed by [14]. The token is a character or word. The head and tail denote the position index of the token's first and last characters in the original sentence, and they indicate the position of the token in the lattice. For the character, its head and tail are the same. There is a simple algorithm to recover flat-lattice into its original structure. We can first take the token which has the same head and tail, to construct the character sequence. Then we use other tokens (words) with their heads and tails to build skip-paths. Since our transformation is recoverable, we assume flat-lattice can maintain the original structure of lattice.

3.2 Relative Position Encoding of Spans

The flat-lattice structure consists of spans with different lengths. To encode the interactions among spans, we use the relative position encoding of spans [14]. For two spans x_i and x_j in the lattice, there are three kinds of relations between them: intersection, inclusion and separation, determined by their heads and tails. Instead of directly encoding these three kinds of relations, we use a dense vector to model their relations. It is calculated by continuous transformation of the head and tail information. Thus, we think it can not only represent the relation between two tokens, but also indicate more detailed information, such as the distance between a character and a word. Let $head[i]$ and $tail[i]$ denote the head and tail position of span x_i. we only use two kinds of relative distances can be used to indicate the relation between x_i and x_j. They can be calculated as:

$$d_{ij}^{(hh)} = head[i] - head[j] \tag{4}$$

$$d_{ij}^{(tt)} = tail[i] - tail[j] \tag{5}$$

where $d_{ij}^{(hh)}$ denotes the distance between head of x_i and x_j, and $d_{ij}^{(tt)}$ denotes the distance between tail of x_i and x_j. The final relative position encoding of spans is a simple non-linear transformation of the two distances:

$$R_{ij} = ReLU(W_r(\mathrm{p}_{d_{ij}^{(hh)}} \oplus \mathrm{p}_{d_{ij}^{(tt)}})) \tag{6}$$

where W_r is a learnable parameter, $\oplus$ denotes the concatenation operator, and p_d is calculated as in [10],

$$\mathrm{p}_d^{(2\kappa)} = \sin\left(d/10000^{2\kappa/d \bmod el}\right) \tag{7}$$

$$\mathrm{p}_d^{(2\kappa+1)} = \cos\left(d/10000^{2\kappa/d \bmod el}\right) \tag{8}$$

where d is $d_{ij}^{(hh)}$, $d_{ij}^{(tt)}$ and κ denotes the index of dimension of position encoding. Then we use a variant of self-attention [19] to leverage the relative span position encoding as follows:

$$\begin{aligned} A_{i,j}^* &= W_q^T E_{x_i}^T E_{x_j} W_{k,E} + W_q^T E_{x_i}^T R_{ij} W_{k,R} \\ &+ u^T E_{x_j} W_{k,E} + v^T R_{ij} W_{k,R} \end{aligned} \tag{9}$$

where $W_q, W_{\kappa,R}, W_{\kappa,E} \in \mathbb{R}^{d \bmod el \times d_{head}}$ and $u, v \in \mathbb{R}^{d_{head}}$ are learnable parameters. Then we replace A with A^* in Eq. (1). The following calculation is the same with vanilla Transformer.

3.3 Chinese Word Segmentation

Word segmentation is helpful for generating features for an NER task. Chinese word segmentation can be regarded as a character sequence labeling task, where each character in the sentence is assigned a segment label from left to right, including {B, M, E, S}, to indicate the segmentation [8]. B, M, E represent the character is the beginning, middle or end of a multi-character word, respectively. S represents that the current character is a single character word. Figure 3 gives an intuitive explaination.

Fig. 3. Chinese word segmentation as a sequence labeling task.

In our paper, we use jieba chinese word segmentation tool [20] to assign segmentation label for each character. Given a sentence with length n: $\{w_1, w_2, ..., w_n\}$ and its corresponding segmentation labels: $\{t_1, t_2, ..., t_n\}$, each segmentation label is initialized as a d dimensional embedding. It has been shown in [21] that word embedding plays a vital role to improve sequence tagging performance. We initialize randomly the embedding which has 4 vocabulary size and each word corresponds to a d-dimensional embedding vector. To use this embedding, the segmentation labels of the given sentence were transform into embeddings. This transformation is done by lookup table operation. This embeddings were modified during its training. After the lookup table operation, we obtained a matrix $X \in \mathbb{R}^{n \times d}$, where the $i'th$ row is the segmentation label embedding of t_i.

Next, we integrate segmentation embeddings with the output of flat-lattice transformer module, which is defined as:

$$H' = H \oplus X \tag{10}$$

where H denotes the output of the flat-lattice transformer module, $\oplus$ denotes the concatenation operation.

Then the output of concatenation operation was fed to a fully connected linear model, which projects each token's encoded representation to the tag space.

3.4 Modify the Emission Matrix Scores

This module aims to extract all named entities from the input original sentence accord to the user-defined entity dictionary, including the entity name and the corresponding entity type. For example, given a sentence with n length:$\{w_1, w_2, ..., w_n\}$,we extract the entity labels:$\{a_1, a_2, ..., a_n\}$ according to the user-defined entity dictionary. Then we initialize a matrix $B \in \mathbb{R}^{n \times K}$ with element 1, where K is the number of name entities tags, and appropriately modify the matrix B, let $B_{ij} = 1.x$, where $i \in \{1, ..., n\}$, j denotes the index of label a_i, which a_i is not label 'O'. The modification of emission matrix scores process can be define as:

$$P' = P \otimes B \tag{11}$$

where $\otimes$ denotes the multiplication operation, P denotes the output of the fully connected linear model, named as emission matrix scores $p \in \mathbb{R}^{n \times K}$. This module serves as an auxiliary method to improve the effect of entity recognition, and is only used in evaluation process.

3.5 Conditional Random Fields

If the emission matrix scores learned by ALFLAT will deviate from the actual, then we need to introduce CRF to optimize it. It happens that CRF can constrain between tags and tags. There is a dependency between them, and the use of CRF can reduce errors. For an input sequence of n tokens, we integrate segmentation embeddings with the output of flat-lattice transformer model, outputs an encoded token sequence with hidden dimension d $_{mod\,el}$. The fully connected layer linear model projects each token's encoded representation to the tag space, i.e. $\mathbb{R}^{d\,mod\,el} \mapsto \mathbb{R}^K$, where K is the number of name entity tags. The emission matrix scores $p \in \mathbb{R}^{n \times K}$ of the linear model are then modified according to the user-defined entity dictionary. Finally, the new emission matrix scores $p' \in \mathbb{R}^{n \times K}$ fed to the CRF layer, whose parameters are a matrix of tag transitions $A \in \mathbb{R}^{K \times K}$. The matrix A is such that $A_{i,j}$ represents the score of transitioning from tag i to tag j. As described by [22], for an input sequence $X = (x_1,...,x_n)$ and a sequence of tag predictions $y = (y_1,...,y_n)$, $y_i \in \{1, ..., K\}$, the score of the sequence is defined as

$$s(X, y) = \sum_{i=0}^{n} A_{y_i,y_{i+1}} + \sum_{i=1}^{n} p_{i,y_i} \tag{12}$$

where y_0 and y_{n+1} are start and end tags. A softmax over all possible tag sequences yields a probability for the sequence y:

$$p(y|X) = \frac{e^{s(X,y)}}{\sum_{y' \in Y_X} e^{s(X,y')}} \tag{13}$$

During training, we maximize the log-probability of the correct tag sequence:

$$\log(p(y|X)) = s(X, y) - \log\left(\sum_{y' \in Y_X} e^{s(X,y')}\right) \tag{14}$$

where Y_X are all possible tag sequences. The summation in Eq. 14 is computed using dynamic programming. During evaluation, we predict the output sequence that obtains the maximum score given by:

$$y^* = \arg\max_{y' \in Y_X} s(X, y')$$

(15)

This can be computed using the Viterbi decoding [16].

4 Experiments

4.1 Experimental Setup

In order to evaluate our model, we used **MSRA** [23] Chinese NER dataset and show statistics of the dataset in Table 1. We take TENER [18], BiLSTM-CRF as baseline models, and use the same train, test, dev split as Gui [12]. The embeddings and lexicons are the same as Zhang and Yang [7]. We select the hyper-parameters are the same as Li [14], which based on the development experiment of MSRA. The Table 2 lists the hyper-parameters obtained from the development experiment of MSRA. In particular, we use only one layer Transformer encoder for our model.

Table 1. Statistics of MSRA dataset. 'Train' is the size of training set. 'Char$_{avg}$', 'Word$_{avg}$', 'Entity$_{avg}$' are the average number of chars, words matched by lexicon and entities in an instance.

Name	Size
Train	46675
Char$_{avg}$	45.87
Word$_{avg}$	22.38
Entity$_{avg}$	1.58

In terms of evaluation metrics, we not only use the common F1 score, but also use two metrics proposed by Li [14], including **Span F** and **Type Acc.**

4.2 Overall Performance

As shown in Table 3, our model outperforms baseline models and other lexicon-based models on MSRA Chinese NER dataset. Our model outperforms TENER [18] by 3.54 in average F1 score. For lattice LSTM, our model has an average F1 improvement of 3.27 over it. For FLAT [14], our model has an average F1 improvement of 2.33 over it. We also compare ALFLAT with BERT + FLAT tagger on MSAR dataset, our model also outperforms it by 0.34 in average F1 score.

Table 2. Hyper-parameters for ALFLAT model.

Name	Value
lr	1e-3
-decay	0.05
optimizer	SGD
-momentum	0.9
d_{model}	160
head	8
FFN size	480
Embed dropout	0.5
Output dropout	0.3
warmup	10(epoch)

Table 3. MSRA dataset results (F1). BiLSTM results are from Zhang and Yang [7]. 'YJ' denotes the lexicon released by Zhang and Yang [7]. 'FLAT + BERT' results are from Li [14]. The result of other models are from their original paper. ALFLAT uses ALBERT embedding. We finetune ALBERT in our model during training. The ALBERT in the experiment is 'albert_base_zh' released by albert [25]. We use it by the AlbertModel embedding in transformers [26].

Model	Lexicon	F1 score
BiLSTM	-	91.84
TENER	-	92.89
Lattice LSTM	YJ	93.16
FLAT	YJ	94.10
FLAT + BERT	YJ	96.09
ALFLAT	YJ	**96.43**

4.3 How ALFLAT Use ALBERT Instead of BERT

ALBERT architecture has significantly fewer parameters than a traditional BERT architecture. ALBERT incorporates two parameter reduction techniques that lift the major obstacles in scaling pre-trained models. Both two techniques significantly reduce the number of parameters for BERT without seriously hurting performance, thus improving parameter-efficiency. An ALBERT configuration similar to BERT-large has 18x fewer parameters and can be trained about 1.7x faster. The parameter reduction techniques also act as a form of regularization that stabilizes the training and helps with generalization.

4.4 How ALFLAT Brings Improvement

Table 4 shows the **Span F** and the **Type Acc** of four models on the evaluation set of MSRA. We can find: 1) ALFLAT outperforms FLAT in two metrics significantly. 2) The improvement on **Span F** brought by ALFLAT is more significant than that on **Type Acc**. These show: 1) The position encoding helps ALFLAT locate entities more accurately. 2) The pre-trained word embedding makes ALFLAT more powerful in entity recognition [24].

Table 4. Two metrics of models. FLAT results are from Li [14]. The result of other models are from their original paper. Except that the superscript * means the result is not provided in the original paper, and we get the result by running the public source code.

Model	Span F	Type Acc
TENER	93.17	99.29
FLAT	94.58	99.52
FLAT + BERT	96.26*	99.38*
ALFLAT	**96.64**	**99.56**

5 Conclusion

In this paper, we introduce a new Chinese NER method according to use a flat-lattice Transformer to incorporate ALBERT pre-trained model, user-defined entity dictionary, word segmentation information. The core of our model is using a set of spans of lattice structure, the specific position encoding, word segmentation and modifying the emission matrix scores according to user-defined entity dictionary. Experimental results show our model outperforms other lexicon based models in the performance. We leave adjusting our model to different kinds of lattice or graph as our future work.

Funding. The author(s) disclosed receipt of the following financial support for the research, authorship, and/or publication of this article: This article is supported in part by the National Key R&D Program of China under project (2020YFB1006003), the National Natural Science Foundation of China under project (62172119), the Guangxi Natural Science Foundation under grant (2019GXNSFGA245004), and the Major Key Project of PCL under grants (PCL2022A03, PCL2021A02, PCL2021A09).

References

1. Chen, Y., Xu, L., Liu, K., Zeng, D., Zhao, J.: Event extraction via dynamic multipooling convolutional neural networks. In: Proceedings of the 53rd Annual Meeting of the Association for Computational Linguistics and the 7th International Joint Conference on Natural Language Processing, Beijing, China, pp. 167–176. Association for Computational Linguistics (2015)

2. Diefenbach, D., Lopez, V., Singh, K., Maret, P.: Core techniques of question answering systems over knowledge bases: a survey. Knowl. Inf. Syst. **55**(3), 529–569 (2017). https://doi.org/10.1007/s10115-017-1100-y

3. Lample, G., Ballesteros, M., Subramanian, S., Kawakami, K., Dyer, C.: Neural architectures for named entity recognition. In: Proceedings of the 2016 Conference of the North American Chapter of the Association for Computational Linguistics: Human Language Technologies, San Diego, California, pp. 260–270. Association for Computational Linguistics (2016)

4. Yang, J., Zhang, Y., Dong, F.: Neural reranking for named entity recognition. arXiv preprint arXiv:1707.05127 (2017)

5. Liu, L., et al.: Empower sequence labeling with task-aware neural language model. In: Proceedings of the AAAI Conference on Artificial Intelligence, vol. 32, no. 1 (2018)

6. Sun, T., Shao, Y., Li, X., Liu, P., Yan, H., Qiu, X., Huang, X.: Learning sparse sharing architectures for multiple tasks. In: Proceedings of the AAAI Conference on Artificial Intelligence, vol. 34, no. 5, pp. 8936–8943 (2020)

7. Zhang, Y., Yang, J.: Chinese NER using lattice LSTM. arXiv preprint arXiv:1805.02023 (2018)

8. Zhao, H., Huang, C.-N., Li, M.: An improved Chinese word segmentation system with conditional random field. In: Proceedings of the Fifth SIGHAN Workshop on Chinese Language Processing, Sydney, pp. 162–165 (2006)

9. Gui, T., Ma, R., Zhang, Q., Zhao, L., Jiang, Y.-G., Huang, X.: CNN-based Chinese NER with lexicon rethinking. In: Proceedings of the 28th International Joint Conference on Artificial Intelligence, IJCAI 2019, pp. 4982–4988. AAAI Press (2019)

10. Vaswani, A., et al.: Attention is all you need. In: Guyon, I., et al. (eds.) Advances in Neural Information Processing Systems, vol. 30, pp. 5998–6008. Curran Associates, Inc. (2017)

11. Stanislawek, T., Wróblewska, A., Wójcicka, A., Ziembicki, D., Biecek, P.: Named entity recognition - is there a glass ceiling? In: Proceedings of the 23rd Conference on Computational Natural Language Learning (CoNLL), Hong Kong, China, pp. 624–633. Association for Computational Linguistics (2019)

12. Gui, T., Zou, Y., Zhang, Q., Peng, M., Fu, J., Wei, Z., Huang, X.: A lexicon-based graph neural network for Chinese NER. In: Proceedings of the 2019 Conference on Empirical Methods in Natural Language Processing and the 9th International Joint Conference on Natural Language Processing (EMNLP-IJCNLP), Hong Kong, China, pp. 1039–1049. Association for Computational Linguistics (2019)

13. Sui, D., Chen, Y., Liu, K., Zhao, J., Liu, S.: Leverage lexical knowledge for Chinese named entity recognition via collaborative graph network. In: Proceedings of the 2019 Conference on Empirical Methods in Natural Language Processing and the 9th International Joint Conference on Natural Language Processing (EMNLPIJCNLP), Hong Kong, China, pp. 3821–3831. Association for Computational Linguistics (2019)

14. Li, X., et al. FLAT: Chinese NER using flat-lattice transformer. arXiv preprint arXiv:2004.11795 (2020)

15. Lan, Z., et al. ALBERT: a lite BERT for self-supervised learning of language representations. arXiv preprint arXiv:1909.11942 (2019)

16. Viterbi, A.J., et al.: A pragmatic approach to trellis-coded modulation. IEEE Commun. Mag. **27**(7), 11–19 (1989)

17. Lafferty, J., McCallum, A., Pereira, F.C.N.: Conditional random fields: probabilistic models for segmenting and labeling sequence data (2001)

18. Yan, H., et al.: TENER: adapting transformer encoder for named entity recognition. arXiv preprint arXiv:1911.04474 (2019)

19. Dai, Z., et al.: Transformer-xl: attentive language models beyond a fixed-length context. arXiv preprint arXiv:1901.02860 (2019)

20. Sun, J.: Jieba Chinese word segmentation tool (2012)
21. Collobert, R., Weston, J., Bottou, L., Karlen, M., Kavukcuoglu, K., Kuksa, P.: Natural language processing (almost) from scratch. J. Mach. Learn. Res. **12**(1), 2493–2537 (2011)
22. Lample, G., Ballesteros, M., Subramanian, S., Kawakami, K., Dyer, C.: Neural architectures for named entity recognition. Computing Research Repository arXiv:1603.01360 (2016)
23. Levow, G.-A.: The third international Chinese language processing bakeoff: Word segmentation and named entity recognition. In: Proceedings of the Fifth SIGHAN Workshop on Chinese Language Processing, Sydney, Australia, pp. 108–117. Association for Computational Linguistics (2006)
24. Agarwal, O., Yang, Y., Wallace, B., Nenkova, A.: Interpretability analysis for named entity recognition to understand system predictions and how they can improve. Comput. Linguist. **47**(1), 117–140 (2021)
25. ALBERT Homepage. https://github.com/google-research/albert
26. TRANSFORMERS Homepage. https://github.com/huggingface/transformers

Author Index

Printed in the United States
by Baker & Taylor Publisher Services